PAST FORGETTING

My Love Affair with Dwight D. Eisenhower

by Kay Summersby Morgan

Simon and Schuster
New York

Why will the foolish tears
Tremble across the years?

—from *Bittersweet*
by Noël Coward

From the Publisher

KAY SUMMERSBY MORGAN wrote this book under a death sentence. In late 1973, her doctors gave her six months to live, but Kay stretched it into more than a year—and lived every day until the very last with her customary gaiety and relish. "There's no point in dwelling on it," she would say.

She kept on working. Her last job was as fashion consultant for the film *The Stepford Wives*. On weekends she drove her beat-up secondhand Volkswagen to the Hamptons, where she played bridge and an occasional few holes of golf with old friends. And she wrote. She wrote this book because she wanted the truth to be known.

"I was always extremely discreet," she said. "But now the General is dead. And I am dying. Once I am dead, then I would like this book to speak for me. I would like the world to know the truth of the Eisenhower affair."

Two weeks before Kay died, she moved from New York City to a tiny cottage in Southampton. "I don't want to die in the city," she said, and mustered her strength to make the move and to set out her autographed pictures of Dwight D. Eisenhower, Prime Minister Winston Churchill and President Franklin D. Roosevelt—all men who had appreciated Kay's special gallantry and integrity.

She spent two January weeks delighting in the winter-fresh

salt air of Long Island. It reminded her, she told friends, of the salt breezes of the Atlantic that blew across the meadows surrounding Innis Beg, her family's square old stone house in County Cork. The day came when she had to go to the hospital. The following day, she died.

Kay's ashes have been scattered over the Irish acres where she was born and grew up. But her book remains, and we are proud to present it. We salute her as a loving and courageous woman; "an officer and a lady"—to twist the phrase in a way that we suspect would have made her laugh and say, "Oh, that's gorgeous!" Kathleen Helen McCarthy-Morrogh Summersby Morgan always made people feel good about themselves.

1

MORE than half my life I have felt like the girl in the hair-coloring advertisement, the one that asks the question, "Does she . . . or doesn't she?" In my case, they were not speculating about my hair color.

It used to distress me enormously, but as time went by, emotional scar tissue formed over the raw nerve ends, and eventually "Did she . . . or didn't she?" became a curiously old-fashioned speculation. If, through some time warp, I were to be in my early thirties again, serving as driver, secretary and confidante to the stalwart and utterly charming Supreme Commander of the Allied Forces in Europe, General Dwight David Eisenhower, no one would wonder "Did they . . . ?" Today people would simply assume that we did—and given modern mores, forget the whole thing.

But that was not the way it was. It took years and years, decades, for people to forget. And just when I thought the whole issue had disappeared from people's minds, it was raised again—this time with a vengeance that ripped open that emotional scar tissue—in *Plain Speaking: An Oral Biography of Harry S. Truman* by Merle Miller. Late in the autumn of 1973, even before the book was officially published, the few paragraphs in it about General Eisenhower and me made the front pages of newspapers all over the world.

It was absolutely unbelievable. The General had been dead for four years. And I had not seen him—except from a determinedly anonymous distance—for more than a quarter of a century. It was ancient history. Or so I had thought. But the world did not agree. As Lloyd Shearer wrote in *Parade* magazine, "Journalists began an intensive search for Kay Summersby. But Kay Summersby could be found nowhere."

There was a reason for that. I had been on the operating table when the story broke. But journalists are a persistent breed. An Englishman finally tracked me down. He had looked up the old newspaper clippings and called a friend of mine who had been mentioned in one of them.

"Mrs. P——?" he had asked. "I'm calling from London. Weren't you present when Kay married Reginald Morgan?"

She was quite unsuspecting. "I certainly was," she replied. "They were married right here in my apartment."

"I'm an old friend of Kay's," he said, "and I've been trying to get in touch with her. Can you tell me where she is?"

This was a lie. I had never heard of him, but there was no way for her to know that. She told him, "Kay's in New York Hospital. She has had some surgery."

So there I was, barely out of the recovery room, with an intravenous solution dripping through a tube into my arm and another tube threaded through my nostril, and the hospital switchboard was calling to say that it had an overseas call for me. Did I feel up to taking it? I did not, but I took it anyway, positive that it was my brother, Seamus, calling me from Johannesburg, eight thousand miles away. Instead, it was this man.

"I'm calling from London," he said. "What about all this?"

Only someone who has had major surgery can understand the state I was in. The effects of the anesthetic had not worn off completely, and I was drained, just terribly fatigued by the shock of surgery. Talking was an immense effort.

"What about all what?" I asked feebly.

"About you and Ike," he said. "Is it true or isn't it?"

I did not know what he was talking about. I thought he was just one more person raking up that old did-they-or-didn't-they speculation. I have had my share of middle-of-the-night calls from drunkards wanting to settle a bet and sick-sick people spilling vituperation into the telephone, but pursuing me into the hospital to ask about my relationship with General Eisenhower was just about the worst.

"No comment," I said. And hung up. But he had his story. "Kay Summersby Morgan, convalescing from surgery in New York City, refused to comment on report she and Ike planned to marry."

The mischief had been done. Now the world knew where I was. Telephone calls and wires came into the hospital from all over the globe. I quickly learned what had prompted that call, of course, and one of my dearest friends brought me a copy of the book—complete with a bookmark flagging the pages with President Truman's revelations about General Eisenhower.

It was no secret that Harry S. Truman did not care for Dwight D. Eisenhower, but I had liked President Truman when he and his Secretary of State James Byrnes visited General Eisenhower's headquarters in Frankfurt at the time of the Potsdam Conference in 1945. The Big Three had had serious matters to discuss at Potsdam, including America's new weapon, the atomic bomb. (When I had heard Ike discussing the military and political implications of the Bomb with his top staff members several weeks before its existence was revealed, I remember thinking, Oh, oh! It's time to leave the room. This is something I don't want to know about.)

Toward the end of the conference, Truman came to Frankfurt to inspect the 84th Infantry Division (there were a lot of men from Missouri in it), and after driving through the dusty German countryside on that hot July day and talking to scores of American soldiers, he came back to headquarters. As he walked in, he said to General Eisenhower that it reminded him of the Pentagon it was so big, and Eisenhower told him it used to be

the hub of the huge I. G. Farben industrial complex. After the
President and the General had concluded their talk, Ike called
me in and introduced me to the President. I thought him extremely friendly and straightforwardly natural. A very appealing
man.

My office diary, in which I often jotted down personal notes
as well as the General's appointments, contains this entry for
that day:

> *E. leaves office early to meet the President . . . Unex-
> pectedly Ike brings the President and Secretary of State
> Byrnes into the office at 2:30. Ike talked to the President
> about my wanting to become an American citizen.*

That had truly been a red-letter day for me, and about three
months later, as a result of that conversation, I flew to Washington to take out my first papers for American citizenship.

Now, twenty-eight years later, I sat cranked up to a half-sitting
position in my hospital bed reading and rereading a story that I
could hardly believe. President Truman had told his biographer,
Merle Miller, that "right after the war was over, he [Eisen-
hower] wrote a letter to General Marshall saying that he wanted
to come back to the United States and divorce Mrs. Eisenhower
so that he could marry this Englishwoman."

His request was brutally denied. Even outspoken President
Truman seems to have been shocked at the harshness of the de-
nial.

"Marshall wrote him back a letter," said the President, "the
like of which I never did see. He said that if he . . . if Eisenhower even came close to doing such a thing, he'd not only bust
him out of the Army, he'd see to it that never for the rest of his
life would he be able to draw a peaceful breath . . . and that if
he ever again even mentioned a thing like that, he'd see to it
that the rest of his life was a living hell."

President Truman then said, "One of the last things I did as

President, I got those letters from his file in the Pentagon and I destroyed them."

I would have liked to stay quietly in my spartan hospital cot, well away from the world, and have time to think about those long-ago days with Ike. These few paragraphs had shaken me. I needed to get my emotions in order.

But that kind of peace was unattainable. Even though the hospital no longer put calls through to me, it was impossible to escape the reporters. They were incredibly persistent. I returned from my first walk down the hall—ten paces to the bathroom and ten paces back on the arm of a nurse—to find an attractive girl sitting at the foot of my bed. I thought she must be the daughter of one of my friends who had grown so that I did not recognize her. She was a reporter from *The Philadelphia Inquirer*. She had walked into my hospital room and plunked herself down. I was indignant.

"How can you come in here like this?" I asked. "I have had serious surgery and I am not feeling at all well." As a matter of fact, this was the day that the full report had come back from pathology, and yes, it was cancer. Liver cancer. And no, there was no hope. I had understood what my doctor had told me, and I was upset, but I had not really absorbed what it meant. It was literally weeks before I registered the finality of what he had told me. But even so, I was unable to cope with my own feelings that day, let alone cope with a reporter.

"I'm sure your editor would not approve of what you are doing," I said.

She just sat there.

"Will you please leave? Or do I have to call for someone to remove you?" I asked.

At that she got up. "You won't say anything?" she asked.

I wouldn't. I didn't. Not even good-bye. I simply turned my face away. I was shaking with weakness and frustration. My feet were cold, and I had beads of perspiration on my forehead.

There were dozens of others who invaded the hospital. "No

comment," I would say, and they would go away. The nurses teased me about it. "Unseal your lips," one used to tell me; "it's time for your medication." As soon as I could muster the strength, I fled the hospital, despite the nervous protests of my doctor, to stay with friends who promised tranquil anonymity.

For the record, I swear that I had no idea that the General had written such a letter to General Marshall. Absolutely no idea at all. Not at the time that he was supposed to have written it. And not later.

I was interested to read that Major General Harry Vaughan, who had been President Truman's aide in the White House, told reporters that there had been rumors about those letters as early as 1952. "Before the Republican National Convention," he said, "Senator Robert Taft of Ohio and Eisenhower were jockeying for position to get the Presidential nomination. The Taft boys heard about Ike's letters to Marshall and wanted to get copies. Truman heard about that. He ordered the Pentagon to send him the letters. He didn't want the Taft gang spreading them all over the country. But I don't think he destroyed them. I think he sent them to General Marshall with a covering note that said, 'These belong in your personal files. I don't think they should be used for dirty politics.'"

I had heard none of those 1952 rumors.

I *had* been given a hint later on that some such letters existed, but I had not believed it. A few years ago—it must have been four or five years ago—David Susskind called and said, "Kay, I want you on the program."

"Oh, lovely!" I said. "What do you want me to talk about?"

"The letter, of course," David said.

"What letter?" I asked, truly mystified. "I don't have an inkling of what you're talking about."

And he said, "Oh, come on, Kay. You know what I'm talking about. The Eisenhower letter. The letter Ike wrote telling Marshall that he wanted to divorce Mamie and marry you."

For a moment I was stunned, and then I thought, Oh, that's

nonsense. David's just trying to dredge up something sensational for his program.

"David," I said, "I never heard of any such thing. Somebody's been feeding you a story. It's no good my going on your program. I have nothing to say."

And that was that. I forgot all about it. I never heard another word about the letters until I was in the hospital in 1973—more than twenty years after the rumors presumably started. I myself have no way of knowing whether or not Ike really wrote such a letter. But I have great faith in Harry Truman's integrity. I do not believe that he would have said such a thing if it were not true. Nor would Harry Vaughan have said what he said if the letters did not exist.

I confess that I hope with all my heart that Ike did write to General Marshall. I believe that he did. And it is my belief that has given me the strength and the courage to write this book.

The public reaction to the disclosure of these letters startled me. Who would ever have believed that one Irishwoman's (I was born in County Cork and am not an "Englishwoman" as President Truman described me) relationship with an American general, a relationship that began more than thirty-five years ago and was abruptly terminated three years later, could still be of interest to anyone at all? I suppose the whole thing stayed alive because Ike was not only a war hero and a two-term President of the United States, he was above all a man who had captured the heart of America. The heart of the world. And my heart, too.

So for those who are interested, here is the story of a general and his Irish driver. I feel free to talk about it now. The General is dead. I am dying. When I wrote *Eisenhower Was My Boss* in 1948, I omitted many things, changed some details, glossed over others to disguise as best I could the intimacy that had grown between General Eisenhower and me. It was better that way. And when Captain Harry C. Butcher, USNR, wrote his book, *My Three Years with Eisenhower*, he did the same thing for the same reason. Butch mentioned me only in passing, often simply referring to me as "the driver." We were both intent on keeping the General's private life private. In those days anything that could have been construed as a shadow on the General's character would have been seized upon as a political weapon. But times have changed. I do not believe that anyone today will construe our relationship as shameful. It certainly can cast no shadow on the General's character. I believe that truth makes for better history than evasions. And someday—perhaps—my truth will serve as a small, clarifying footnote to history.

The story I am about to tell happened a long time ago. I ask the reader to be lenient. My sources are my memory, my old blue leather diary—and my heart. If an occasional time sequence is twisted or a fact misplaced, it is only because of the tricks that memory plays as one grows older. The conversations in this book ring true to my ear and my heart, but it must be understood that they have been reconstructed from my memories. The events that I am writing about meant so much to me, however, and I have lived them over to myself during so many long nights, that I think my story is as close to reality as if it were only last night that I said my unsuspecting good-bye to the General, to Ike, to the man I loved.

2

You never know when something important is going to happen, and when it does, you often don't realize that it did until long after. That is the way it was when I met General Eisenhower. He was Major General Eisenhower then, and he had two stars—and they did not impress me one bit.

I was a member of Britain's Motor Transport Corps. This was *the* volunteer corps that the debutantes and post debutantes flocked to when war was declared. I knew many of them. We had gone to the same dances, watched polo at Hurlingham together, spent long weekends in Scotland together, but there was a difference between them and me. Most of them were wealthy. I was not.

I had recently separated from my husband Gordon Summersby, a young publisher, and was earning my living modeling for Worth of Paris. Worth represented the cream of the couture and dressed—with superb materials and elegantly understated style—generations of the solid rich from debutante to dowager. There was a Winterhalter painting in the salon of a beautiful young woman who had sat for her portrait, half a century before, wearing a Worth ball gown. It was quite usual for me to go to one of the great balls in London in a new Worth design lent to me for the evening (it was good advertising, and the directress of the salon would often arrange to borrow jewelry for me to wear) and see one of the girls who would later join the Motor Transport Corps fox-trotting by in a gown that I had modeled for her approval earlier in the season. We would tell each other how absolutely marvelous we looked.

But Worth gowns were now a thing of the past. I had left the salon on September 4, 1939, the day after Prime Minister Neville Chamberlain told us we were at war with Germany. "It is the evil things that we shall be fighting against," he had said. He was right. They were evil things. To actually be at war was a thudding shock, even though we had all sensed it must come. The world changed overnight. My sister Evie had joined the Motor Transport Corps a few weeks earlier, and I decided to follow her example.

I was assigned to Post Number One, an old schoolhouse in the East End, near London's great maze of docks. Our Cockney neighbors there used to jeer at the "society girls playing war." Who could blame them? Many of them were heartbreakingly poor, and there we were with our smart uniforms, our Mayfair chatter and very little to do. There was an eerie few months of quiet after war was declared. Some called it a phony war. Then Norway and Denmark became captive nations, and the Nazis blitzed their way through Holland and through Belgium, forcing our troops to the very edge of the Continent, the beaches at Dunkirk.

There was a nightmare week in early June 1940 when a makeshift rescue armada had set out from English ports and brought back several hundred thousand soldiers from Dunkirk. It was a kind of miracle. The Germans bombed the helpless troops on the beaches. They bombed the destroyers and troop carriers and ferryboats scurrying back to England with their precious loads of husbands and fathers and brothers and sons. They even strafed the little cockleshell pleasure boats that had valiantly bobbed their way across the Channel to do their bit. Just a few days later, Paris fell. It was no phony war.

But all that was still in the future. The first order of business in the Corps was to get oneself properly outfitted. Our uniforms were very smart, almost exactly like the British Army officers' uniforms, except that we wore skirts. They had the same Sam Browne belt and everything. We bought them at an Army supply store, and they cost the earth—something like fifty pounds, a staggering sum of money in those days. It was for me, anyway, since the Corps was a voluntary outfit, which meant we weren't paid twopence. Eventually they did pay us. Two pounds ten a week it was, and barely enough to keep us in tea and stockings (on the black market—without ration coupons—a pair of silk stockings cost nearly eight shillings).

Of course, when the time came that the women of the Motor Transport Corps were doing their part in the Battle of Britain, uniforms could not have mattered less. At the height of the Blitz, when German bombers were making nightly sorties, my "uniform" consisted of an old pair of corduroy pants, an Army shirt and a sweater that belonged to my brother Seamus. I topped this with a tin hat, slung my gas mask (where I kept my lipstick and compact) over my shoulder and was ready for duty. So much for uniforms. When the bombs were dropping and I was driving my MTC ambulance around the dock area in the East End, no one made us stand inspection.

The Battle of Britain had started early in September of 1940—it was a year almost to the day after I had joined up—with a daylight bombing raid. The Germans sent a thousand planes over London and blanketed the city with bombs. The worst damage was in our area. Hundreds of people were killed that day, and thousands wounded.

After that, most of the raids were by night. There was a nasty little traitor—we called him Lord Haw-Haw—who broadcast from Germany. He would come on the radio and chant, "There's going to *be* a *bomb*ing. There's going to *be* a *bomb*ing," in the same cadence in which a child might chant "I'm going to *tell* your *moth*er. You're going to *get* a *spank*ing." And he was always right. Some nights it was as if London were being shaken the way one shakes out a rug. It trembled and reeled from end to end. I remember one night in particular—it was just after Christmas—when the Germans dropped tens of thousands of incendiary bombs. It seemed as if all London were burning. The sky was red, with vast gusts of black smoke streaming across it like clouds in hell. Even the December-cold water of the Thames was warm as it spurted out of the fire fighters' hoses. It was the most terrifying night of my life. I will never forget one of the men in my ambulance crew saying over and over, "Hitler didn't ought to do this. He didn't ought to *do* it."

Despite the horror, life went on. Our MTC ambulances picked up the dead and dying. The Cockneys, now our staunch supporters, trudged off to the "chube," as they called the London subway, every night with their children, their blankets, their playing cards and their thermoses of tea to wait out the bombing hours hundreds of feet underground. Londoners looked terrible. No one had enough sleep. Many people had lost their homes. Rationing promised everyone fair shares, but it was fair shares of starchy foods for the most part. We all craved meat and butter and fresh fruit. Our clothes became shabbier each day from diving into trenches or flinging ourselves flat when the sirens' banshee screams sounded warning. But everyone kept going. There was no panic. We queued for food, for newspapers, for cigarettes, for buses. We grumbled. We were scared. We were tired. And bored. But no one ever thought of giving in to Hitler.

For me, it was a time of personal turmoil as well. Gordon and I had decided to take the next step after separation. Divorce. It was not easy. My whole world seemed to be disintegrating.

The Blitz stopped suddenly in May 1941. It was an uneasy pause, rather like waiting for the second boot to drop. There was nothing for my Motor Transport Corps unit to do once the bombings stopped. All of us were sitting around, bored and gossiping. Then I met an American colonel at a cocktail party who became very attentive when I told him that we were out of our

minds with boredom. "Hmm," he said, "you give me an idea." I
can't even remember that colonel's name now, but I have always
been grateful to him. Within a week, the American Embassy
had requested the Motor Transport Corps to lend it a couple of
drivers who knew their way around London.

The Americans were not yet in the war, but their embassy
was full of Special Observers who kept forgetting they were in
civilian clothes and would salute each other all the time. Groups
of American brass were constantly being shepherded around
England and Scotland. Some went to see airfields; others inspected coastal defenses; others filled their days—and nights—
conferring with British military and government leaders. The
embassy needed drivers to get these visitors where they wanted
to go—and on time. This was not an easy job.

London, indeed the whole of England, was under the tightest
security. There were no street signs, no highway route markers,
nothing. Nothing that could possibly aid or enlighten a German
parachutist. (A German invasion was a very real fear at that
time.) At night, there was a total blackout. Any cars that were
on the roads were allowed only the merest pinpoint of light from
their headlamps. Add the infamous London fogs to this and it
was easy to see why the Americans never got to an evening engagement on time. They did very little better in the daylight.
The American Army drivers, who did not know London at all,
were constantly getting lost. And the blood pressures of their
high-ranking military passengers climbed to dangerous highs.

I was delighted to be chosen as one of the drivers. I had
known a few Americans before, but now at Number 20 Grosvenor Square, I was surrounded by them. In the days before
Pearl Harbor, I think I knew every American officer in London.
I liked their informality and their warmth and their energy. My
social life became all-American, and soon it focused on one
American in particular. Captain Richard Arnold. He was a
West Pointer. Very handsome. And, I was told, a brilliant engineer.

Dick was one of the "commuters." He would be in London for three days, then fly to Washington for five, then back for two weeks or two days. I never knew when he would arrive or when he would have to leave. But we both knew that something special was going on between us. After a few months, Dick came back from Washington and told me that he had asked his wife for a divorce and that she had agreed. "When I'm free, Kay," he asked, "would you—" I did not even wait for him to finish before accepting his proposal.

Our engagement did not change things much. We still had to steal an hour here, an evening there. It did not matter. We knew we were going to get married—sometime. Sometime when we were free. Sometime when the war permitted. Sometime. Somehow. And in the meantime, we just had to muddle along the best we could.

Then the American tempo changed. Pearl Harbor was the precipitant. The United States was finally at war. There was an air of near-frantic urgency. One spring day our Motor Transport group—there were now several of us driving for the Americans—was alerted that a very important group of American generals was expected. I made up my mind that by sheer right of seniority I would drive the top man. Any Army man will understand how I felt. It was a matter of rank by association.

As it turned out, however, I got just about the lowest-ranking man—a two-star general—and I almost got off on the wrong foot with him. I was late. On the other hand, if I had not been late in the beginning, I would probably never have got to know General Eisenhower.

It happened this way. The day the assignments were made, I had nothing to do, so I trotted off to the hairdresser, who took forever. When I got back to Grosvenor Square, the other girls had skimmed the cream of the lot. The second lieutenant in charge of handing out assignments to the motor pool said apologetically, "Kay, you don't mind, I hope. This Eisenhower? He's the only one left." He knew I wanted a crack at the top general, not a two-star nonentity. I made a face and said, "Okay."

After that it was days before the generals arrived. Their plane had been weathered in at Prestwick. Forty-eight hours later, they decided to come down from Scotland by train. That was late, too. But finally, one bright May morning, they were here, closeted with Ambassador John Winant at Grosvenor Square. Our instructions were to await instructions. The cars were lined up in a khaki-colored parade out front. We waited and waited. The lunch hour passed. I became so hungry I could not bear it. So hungry I risked ducking out for a sandwich.

When I came sauntering back, I was appalled to see the other embassy cars driving away, leaving one lone khaki Packard by the curb. There were two American officers standing beside it. I cast ladylike dignity aside and ran as if my life depended on it. Skidding to a stop and trying to salute at the same time, I asked if one of them was General Eisenhower. One was. The short one.

"I'm your driver, sir," I panted. "Here's your car, sir." I opened the door and stood at attention as General Eisenhower and General Mark Clark settled themselves in the back seat.

"We'd like to go to Claridge's, please," Eisenhower told me. I could have screamed. All that for a two-block drive.

Later that afternoon, one of the Americans at headquarters asked, "How did you like Ike?"

"Ike?"

"General Eisenhower," he said.

I shrugged my shoulders. "He's all right. I only saw him for a few minutes."

"There are a lot of rumors about him," he said. "They say he's going to be in charge of the whole shooting match."

I knew better than that. My father had been an Army man. Two-star generals are never in charge of anything important. Fortunately, I kept my mouth shut.

3

Now I was to learn what a working day really meant. The next morning I met my two generals in front of Claridge's on the dot of nine and delivered them back there some sixteen hours later. As I held the door, Eisenhower turned to me and said, "We'll expect you at nine, Miss Summersby."

The following days were more of the same. It was obvious that there were great projects afoot. I remember one day very well. It was common knowledge that Field Marshal Sir Bernard Law Montgomery, that character with the beret and the swagger stick, was—to put it mildly—a thorn in Eisenhower's side throughout the war. There was friction between the two of them from the very first moment they met.

I had driven Clark and Eisenhower to a base outside London to observe Monty in action. He was just a lieutenant general then, with a reputation for being very able. On the way back to London late in the afternoon, the two American generals discussed their day and the military exercise Monty had conducted. I usually paid very little attention to backseat conversations, but Eisenhower's voice caught my attention. It had turned harsh. I heard something about "that son of a bitch" and started listening. He meant Monty. Within minutes of meeting chain smoker Eisenhower, nonsmoker Montgomery had stated crisply that he did not permit smoking in his headquarters. The

General had obediently stubbed out his cigarette, but he was furious—really steaming mad. And he was still mad. It was my first exposure to the Eisenhower temper. I sneaked a look in the rearview mirror. His face was flaming red, and the veins in his forehead looked like worms. The relationship between the two men never got any better; in fact, as the war progressed, Monty's self-righteousness and rigidity often had the General actually gasping in anger.

Situations that might make another man angry, however, often did not perturb the General at all. For instance, Eisenhower was tremendously impressed by the total security-consciousness of the English. One day when I was not quite sure which way to go, I stopped to ask directions from a group of soldiers.

"I've got General Clark and General Eisenhower in the car," I said, "and I'm not sure which fork to take for the base. Can you tell me?"

Not one of them would give me directions. "We don't know," they said. And that was that. They were quite right, of course. In those days no one had ever heard of General Eisenhower. All they saw was a military car with a woman driver. And at that time there were all kinds of stories going around about audacious German spies and infiltrators. This changed later when England was crammed full of American soldiers asking how to get here or there. Then the English reverted to their naturally courteous ways and would give directions in the most minute detail. (One American GI told me that what he remembers best about the English penchant for detailed directions was that "After five minutes of telling you to bear left at the second meadow and right at the third pub, they'd end up saying, 'You cawn't miss it.' That always gave me a kick," he said.) But in 1942 these soldiers were not going to tell anyone anything. I was furious, but Eisenhower was not upset in the least. "Goddamnit," he said to General Clark, "that's the spirit."

Another day I drove the two generals to Dover, site of those famous white cliffs, where they inspected the defenses that had been thrown up against a German invasion. Afterwards both men stood for a long time peering through high-powered glasses at the Continent, only a few miles across the English Channel—and distant as the moon.

"In 1928," Eisenhower said, "I made a tour of the battlefields of the last war, and I remember standing over there one afternoon looking at these white cliffs over here." He was in a reminiscent mood and told a number of stories about French villagers he had met during that trip.

"I'd certainly like to look some of them up again," he told Clark, "when we get over there." *Over there!* It sounded like a dream. I truly did not believe I would ever again sit in a sidewalk cafe on the Champs-Élysées or go riding in the Bois de Boulogne.

As we started back to London, I mentioned that the London–Dover highway was known as Bomb Alley. It had got the name during the Blitz when the Germans jettisoned their leftover bombs along this stretch as they lumbered back to the Continent pursued by the RAF in their Spitfires and Hurricanes. General Eisenhower asked me what I had done during the Blitz.

"Me? Oh, I drove," I said. "I drove an ambulance in the East End."

That started the questions. Eisenhower wanted to know about the part women had played in the Battle of Britain. I told him that my sister and almost all the women I knew were in uniform. And that my mother and many of her contemporaries had served as incendiary-bomb spotters. Incendiary bombs were about a foot long. They would drop on the street or the roof. All you would hear was a thud or a bump. After a certain amount of time, the incendiary would ignite and there would be a big blaze. Mummy's job was to pick them up as soon as they were dropped and take them to a depot where they could be dealt with. It was really quite dangerous work. Eisenhower was a persistent interviewer. By the time he finished, he knew everything I knew about women's roles in the defense of Britain.

As the days went by, the two American generals lost their bounce. Their faces were drawn, their eyes bloodshot from lack of sleep. It seemed to be a real effort for them to get out of the car and stride briskly into yet another conference. I was beginning to droop myself. One day they announced happily that they were going to take the afternoon off.

"The war can get along without us for a few hours," Eisenhower said. "Now, where is a good place to have lunch, Kay? You should know. Some place where they won't feed us cabbage."

It took me a moment to gather my wits. All the other Americans called me Kay, but Clark and Eisenhower had always been very correct and called me Miss Summersby. I was thrown by the new informality.

I knew what the General meant when he vetoed cabbage so firmly. One afternoon I had overheard him mutter to General Clark that "this must be the fartingest war in history." I had stared right ahead and never let on that I had caught this particular remark. Almost every base they visited served them boiled cabbage or brussels sprouts, and the result often kept the generals rolling down the car windows.

"The Connaught," I said finally. "That's a very good place. You'll have an excellent meal there."

"The Connaught it is, then," said General Eisenhower, and off we went to Mount Street. I let them out and started to get back into the car.

"Come on, Kay," said Eisenhower. "You'll join us, won't you?"

Never had such a thing happened to me. Generals don't ask their drivers to lunch with them. But it appeared that American generals did. At least some American generals. I accepted with pleasure, and the three of us walked into the Edwardianly elegant Connaught under the scandalized eyes of the doorman, who believed people should know their places—and this applied to American generals as well as to their drivers.

It was the first time that I had ever looked General Eisenhower in the face for more than a fleeting moment as I said, "Good morning, General" or held the door for him. Now I had a good look across the table. Brilliant blue eyes. Sandy hair—but not very much of it. A fair, ruddy complexion. A nice face—not conventionally handsome, but strong and, I thought, very American. Certainly very appealing. And I succumbed immediately to that grin that was to become so famous.

He and General Clark were happy truants at that lunch, and they entertained me with all kinds of stories from their Army past. We laughed and had a glorious time. The lunch was superb. I can remember it as if it were last week. General Eisenhower ordered a bottle of white wine. We had poached salmon and green salad. Salad, believe it or not, was even more of a luxury than salmon in London those days. For dessert there were little strawberry tarts that were so beautiful that one hesitated to break into them with a fork. We devoured them in two bites and asked for seconds. There were no seconds. That was the only blot on the day.

For that hour or two, the war did not seem to exist. We were in another world. But it is the laughter that still rings in my memory. A long time afterward—we were in Versailles, I think—Ike asked me, "Do you remember that first time we went out together? That lunch at the Connaught? I'll never forget it," he said. "I had never laughed so much in my life."

It was that kind of day.

After lunch, General Eisenhower said, "Kay, how about taking us sight-seeing? We'd like to see a little something of England besides the military installations."

"Yes, sir," I said happily, and suggested that we drive up-country toward Oxford. "It's awfully pretty there," I told them.

"Whatever you say. You're in command this afternoon. Isn't that right, Wayne?" And General Clark nodded agreeably.

So off we went. Both men were fascinated by the picturesque little villages. They asked me to stop in one—West Wycombe, I think it was—so they could have a closer look at the quaint shops and thatched cottages with flowers at the windows.

"How old would you say that house is?" General Eisenhower would ask.

"Three hundred years old, perhaps," I would hazard, and he would shake his head. We had a wonderful time wandering about aimlessly and staring like tourists. It was almost June, and England was at its best—all green and gold and perfumed with roses.

Eventually we piled back into the car. It was warm, and I was parched. Without thinking how outrageous I was being, I pulled up in Beaconsfield and said, "You absolutely must visit an English pub." Obviously just as warm and thirsty as I was, the two of them were out of the car before I could run around and open the door for them. (It may seem strange that on such an occasion I would hold the door, but it must be remembered that this was wartime and we were in uniform. Door holding, saluting and such were all part of that way of life. Although General Eisenhower still insisted on some of the peacetime courtesies, such as letting a woman precede him through the door, he accepted the rest as part of very necessary military discipline.)

It was a gin-and-tonic kind of day. As we sat there and sipped our drinks, the late-spring afternoon slipped into evening. The nightingales were singing. It was high time for the three truants to get back to London.

The next morning we were back in our routine, but when I picked up my generals at Claridge's, I was pleased to see that some of their bounce was back and their faces no longer so drawn. In a few days, their mission was over. My last assignment was to drive them to the airport. One can always count on English weather. That day it was so bad that their departure was postponed for twenty-four hours.

On impulse I called Claridge's. If I'd stopped to think, I

would never have done it, but I had come to feel so comfortable with these two Americans that it seemed natural.

"General, this is Kay," I said. "I wondered, since you can't leave today, if you would like to do some more sight-seeing. I'd love to show you around." Suddenly I was horrified at my brashness and held on to the receiver expecting a curt military "No, thanks."

"Just the thing," he said, sounding pleased. "We're at loose ends."

That day I showed them all the traditional sights—and others not so traditional, such as Threadneedle Street, which is the home of the Bank of England, and Fleet Street, the heart of the London journalistic world. I also showed them the Guildhall, but none of us was psychic enough to sense that this ancient building would one day be the scene of one of Eisenhower's greatest triumphs.

I showed them the Tower of London and even drove by Bryanston Court, where Mrs. Simpson had lived when the Prince of Wales was courting her. Eisenhower shook his head. "A shame," he said. "The King lost sight of duty." I remember thinking that this General Eisenhower was not a man who would ever lose sight of duty. I told them that it was in a house on Grosvenor Square that Mrs. Simpson was first introduced to the Prince of Wales. "That house used to stand right where your headquarters is," I told them. "They tore it down when they built 20 Grosvenor." Eisenhower was really very much interested. Turning to General Clark, he said, "You know, I met the Duke of Windsor last year. He was visiting the States with his wife and touching all the bases in Washington, including the War Department. I was there in the War Room when he came in. Everyone was kowtowing and pointing at maps, but I realized that he was being told nothing whatsoever. They didn't trust him. This man who had once been King. It was shocking how the man had gone down."

As I drove about, they kept up a running comment on the

way whole blocks of buildings had been leveled in one spot while on the other side of the street only one building might have been demolished. I told them how one morning during the Blitz when I had just got off duty, I had decided to drop in on my mother at Warwick Court for breakfast. As I turned the corner, I stopped. Half of her house was torn away. My knees began to shake. I had never felt so weak in my life. Then I started running toward the house. My mother was safe, thank God; she had gone to the shelter.

"Would you like to see where I was stationed then?" I asked. Without waiting for their answer, I turned the big Packard toward the East End, and soon we were driving down the streets where a year ago I had been piloting an ambulance through bombs and fires and collapsing buildings. We walked around the blasted warehouses and skeletons of tenements that still remained. "Some call it Hitler's slum-clearance project," I said.

Eisenhower shook his head. "You must have been frightened during the bombings," he said.

"General, it was like hell must be," I blurted out. "There would be all those buildings on fire. I would be driving and then we'd hear a bomb. I never knew what to do—stop, go back or go on. I always elected to press on. And my crew always backed me. 'That's right, lady,' they would say. 'Press on. That's best.' The men would bring the bodies out. Usually they were burned. All black and twisted. Sometimes there was no body. Just bits and pieces. They had these big canvas bags to put them in. The smell was so bad that we would wear gauze masks.

"The very worst thing," I remembered, "was to have the ambulance crammed full of bodies, so many bodies that we ran out of shrouds and there would be these arms and legs sticking out with tags tied to them—and then there would be no place to leave them. I would drive from mortuary to mortuary only to be told, 'No room' and have to drive off again. I remember one night when the bombing was particularly brutal. I finally found a mortuary with room for more bodies. I sat at the wheel, as I always did while the crew unloaded. One of the attendants came out and said, 'Better come in. It's bad out tonight.'

"It was an old warehouse. There were two double beds off to one side, and a sort of bomb shelter had been built around them. We all sat there on those beds. The five men in the ambulance crew. The three mortuary men. Me. And all the bodies stacked high in their shrouds just a few feet away. They passed a bottle of whisky around and we all took a swig—right from the bottle. It was just what I needed. It burned that taste of dead flesh out of my mouth. That horrible taste! It was in the very air we breathed. And . . ."

I stopped. I was embarrassed to have made such a dramatic fool of myself running on like that.

There was silence. General Clark looked acutely uncomfortable, and that embarrassed me even more. "Poor Kay," he said.

"Poor people. Poor London," Eisenhower added. Then he patted me on the back as if I were a child with hiccups. "You were very brave," he said.

The next morning I drove them to Northolt Airport. They were really off this time. General Clark shook my hand and thanked me for driving them about. General Eisenhower shook my hand too, then reached back into the car and brought out a box.

"This is from both of us, Kay," he said.

"Chocolates!" In rationed England, sweets were a magnificent present. I broke into such a smile that they both laughed.

"If I'm ever back this way," General Eisenhower said, "I hope you will drive for me again."

"I'd like that, sir," I replied. And I meant it. I liked that man they called Ike. But I never expected to drive for him or even see him again.

4

It was a letdown, going back to the motor pool after the generals had left, but within a few days I was driving another two-star general—Carl Spaatz, familiarly known as Tooey, who was in charge of the Eighth Air Force. He had been suffering—and not quietly—from his American sergeant driver's unfamiliarity with London.

"Ike says you're tops," he told me the first morning I reported. I was startled and flattered to think that these generals had found time to discuss my merits as a driver.

General Spaatz had been in London all through the Blitz. It was well known that he had never taken shelter. Instead, he would station himself on a rooftop and make notes on the bombings. He was a serious man, serious to the point of grimness, and certainly the hardest-working man in the whole U.S. Army Air Force.

Despite his rather dour personality, there was a party in his suite at Claridge's practically every night. The Air Force had the reputation of being the glamorous service, and his staff worked hard at maintaining that reputation. His aides entertained all the top English theater people as well as the Hollywood stars who passed through London to entertain the troops. Liquor and food were dispensed on a lavish scale.

When General Spaatz and I would walk in at the end of a

long day spent at Bushey Park, the Air Force headquarters outside London, it was like entering a crowded cocktail lounge—lots of people, lots of smoke, lots of chatter, lots of flirtations—but the General would not even break his stride as he made his way through the living room nodding briskly right and left, I tagging along behind him carrying his briefcase. He would go straight to his study and close the door. Then the fatigue of the day was allowed to show. His shoulders slumped; his ramrod spine seemed to crumple, and he would sit in his big chair at the desk silently staring into space.

At the beginning I felt uncomfortable, not knowing quite what he expected from me, but I soon got into the habit of bringing along a book, and I would read while the General either stared into space or sighed and attacked the paperwork that had piled up. Some nights he would sit there for half an hour and then he'd say, "Time to be off. How long will it take us to get to Hornchurch?" or some such destination.

"Oh, twenty minutes," I might say.

"You'll have to do better than that," he would instruct me. "You've got exactly fifteen minutes to get me there."

"Yes, sir." And I would rush down to bring the car around.

Far more demanding than Eisenhower had been, General Spaatz always made me estimate the time it would take me to reach where he was going—and then would shave a few minutes off my estimate. I began to feel more like a fighter pilot than a driver as I careened through London, my gas pedal constantly pressed to the floor, thanking God for the absence of civilian traffic.

Then there were nights when the General made a command decision to relax. Sometimes he and his staff would settle in for an all-night poker game. They all loved to play cards with the boss—he usually lost. Other nights, he would bring out his guitar. I used to adore those evenings. The American officers were like boys—sitting around, their heads thrown back, singing rackety old songs they had learned at West Point. One of their favorites that they would absolutely bellow out was "I want to be, I want to be, /I want to be away on furlough . . . ," sung to the tune of "Dixie." They also loved the sentimental old songs from the last war like "There's a long, long trail awinding/Into the land of my dreams" and "Pack up your troubles in your old kit bag/And smile, smile, smile." Another favorite was "Over There." There weren't many songs from the present war that caught their fancy the way the old ones did except for "Lili Marleen." I used to join in occasionally, and I would help with the drinks and answer the telephone and feel as much at home as if it were one of the after-the-hunt parties we used to have at home in Ireland.

I settled down happily into Air Force life. When I heard that General Eisenhower had been appointed Commander of the European Theater and was back in London, I did not give it a second thought. I had enjoyed driving him, but I liked General Spaatz, too. One evening, just about a month after I started driving for him—it was rather late but still bright, since we were on double summer time—I pulled up in front of Claridge's and General Spaatz jumped into the car.

"Hendon Airport," he said. "And don't spare the horses."

There was an impressive array of brass at Hendon. This must be someone extra special, I thought. The plane taxied up. The door opened. The brass stood at attention. And General Eisenhower came down the stairs.

After he had greeted the brass, Eisenhower came over to me. "Kay, where have you been?" he said. "I've been looking all over London for you."

He looked at Spaatz. "Tooey, you've been hiding her in the Air Force," he accused.

"Now, don't you take Kay away from me," Spaatz growled. "She's the only driver who knows her way around."

"We'll see," Eisenhower said. He turned to me again. "Kay, I brought some fruit back from the States for you, but it won't keep forever."

"Fruit!" I exclaimed. "I'd love some! Could I come get it tomorrow?"

General Spaatz laughed and said, "Stop trying to bribe my driver."

When I walked into General Eisenhower's headquarters on Grosvenor Square the next day, I discovered that he really had been looking for me. One of his aides said, "Kay Summersby! Where have you been? I've been turning London upside down trying to get in touch with you. Didn't you get my note?"

Indeed I had, but I had thrown it away. There had been a note tucked under the windshield wiper of General Spaatz's car asking me to stop by 20 Grosvenor and see a Colonel Lee. But I did not know any Colonel Lee and I was not about to stop by anyone's office unless General Spaatz told me to. I had not the slightest idea that this Lee was one of General Eisenhower's aides. The General made time to see me immediately, and on his desk was a box of fruit: oranges and grapefruit—rarer than emeralds in England. I was truly deeply touched that the General had remembered me and impressed by the thoughtfulness of the gift.

"I can't thank you enough, General," I said. "I just can't tell you what a treat these will be."

"I don't want any thanks," he said. "All I want to know is if you are willing to come back and drive for me. For good this time." And he smiled.

I didn't know what to say. I liked Tooey Spaatz, but it would be silly to turn down the opportunity to drive for the top commander, so I murmured something stupid about I would like to if it was all right with General Spaatz.

Within two days, I was back driving General Eisenhower.

5

Eisenhower was back for the long pull toward victory. His responsibilities as the commanding general were truly crushing, and he set about organizing his life in the most efficient manner to accomplish his mission. This included establishing a family for himself.

More than most men in public life, Eisenhower relished the comforts of home and hearth. His work and his home were the two great poles of his life during the war, and despite the fact that he was tremendously sought after by London hostesses, he became almost as much of a recluse as Greta Garbo. Not that he particularly wanted to be alone; in fact, he usually detested being alone; but he was impatient with anything that took his time or energy away from the war. He had very little sympathy with what he called "all that la-di-da"—the airs and pretensions of London's social upper crust. I remember him getting into the car after one reception grumbling, "I don't think my blood pressure can take it if one more silly woman calls me 'My deeaaah general.' I'm nobody's goddamned 'deeaah general,' and I'm not fighting this war over teacups."

In ordinary circumstances, General Eisenhower was probably more gregarious than most people, but these were not ordinary times. Shortly after he arrived in London, he established a policy of refusing all invitations that were not directly connected with his work. Three incidents had prompted the decision.

The first was Ambassador John Winant's Fourth of July reception, where Eisenhower shook so many hands in the course of the afternoon that the next morning his right hand was terribly swollen, all puffy and black and blue. He complained that even his fingernails hurt, and he was literally not able to initial memos with his right hand.

The second was a luncheon with King Haakon of Norway. I had been instructed to pick up the General shortly after two. I was there right on time, but it was hours before the General appeared—in a fury of exasperation. Protocol prohibits anyone from leaving a social gathering before royalty, and King Haakon had been having such a royal good time that it was practically teatime before he left.

The only kind of protocol Eisenhower had any patience with was Army protocol, and he often complained about that. Some of the English customs and traditional courtesies might have been expressly designed to enrage him. One morning after he had attended a formal dinner party given by Ambassador Winant, there was a call from the Ambassador asking if the General could spare him a few minutes.

I was in the outer office when the Ambassador walked in. Winant was quite handsome, a very courteous, gentle and very, very shy man. That day he was twisting his hands together as if he were some great schoolboy about to get caned. When he left the General's office five minutes later, he looked even more distressed. I heard about what had happened behind the closed doors later that day when I was driving the General back to the hotel. Eisenhower told the story with a mixture of righteous indignation and impish little-boy glee.

The Ambassador had come to the point immediately. "General," he had said rather uncomfortably, "in this country it is the custom not to smoke at a dinner party until after the toast to the King." The General, who was never without a cigarette, had automatically lit up the moment he sat down at the dinner table. "Now, how could I have known that?" Eisenhower asked. "Of all the goddamned silly customs!" To a chain smoker like the General, this not only seemed silly, it was intolerable. "I told Winant that I was sorry," he said, "and that I'd certainly never offend in that way again. I also told him that last night was the last time I will ever attend a formal dinner in London."

It was not, of course, but it did mark the end of purely social dinner parties. Invitations to luncheons, dinners, dances, drinks, weekends in the country continued to pour in—and were all declined. Lady Astor insisted that the General come to dinner and meet George Bernard Shaw. Lady Cunard dangled Noël Coward as social bait. The General sent his regrets. Any social event that was not directly associated with his job—like his weekly lunch and dinner with Prime Minister Winston Churchill—was out.

He knew what he needed, and it was not a glittering social life; it was a home and a family and all the warmth and laughter and sympathy that a family generates. He had put together his immediate wartime family in Washington. It was a tight little group: Butch and Tex and Mickey.

Butch—Harry Butcher—was the sparkler. Eisenhower had known him for years. Their families were so close that Mrs. Eisenhower and Mrs. Butcher were sharing an apartment in Washington and Butch had moved into the General's hotel suite in London. Butch was utterly charming, very handsome, with a captivating smile and a million friends. A former vice-president of the Columbia Broadcasting System, he handled public relations for Ike. And, more important, he helped the General keep his sanity. Time and again, I heard Eisenhower tell people, "There are days when I just want to curl up in the corner like a sick dog, but Butch won't let me. That's why I need him. To keep me from going crazy." He really loved Butch. Butch was comfortable, merry, trusted—and someone from home. He had grown up in a small town in Iowa not all that far in miles or outlook from the small town in Kansas where Eisenhower grew up. Both of them loved to play bridge and golf, and they had a lot of friends in common. I always thought of Butch as playing the role of a favorite younger brother—full of admiration, but with enough brash confidence to speak up when he disagreed with the General.

Tex—Colonel Ernest Lee from Texas—was the other aide and a very different character. He resembled a worried bloodhound and was incredibly efficient. Tex was the one who ran the office and saw to it that everything worked. He could untangle red tape faster than the Army could tangle it. He never relaxed and was uneasy if he had to be away from the headquarters office routine for even a day. Eisenhower's seven-day week suited him to the bottom of his shiny Army boots. Some people thought Tex was cold, but the truth was that he was very shy, despite the fact that he had been a salesman before the war. He was extremely reticent and quiet—except (and this was a big except) for his voice. He had a big, booming voice that used to drive us crazy. Tex was never as close to the General as Butch, but still, he was part of the family—something like a brother-in-law who was never on quite the same wavelength as anyone else.

Then there was Mickey—Sergeant Michael McKeogh, who was Eisenhower's orderly, and living proof that the saying about no man's being a hero to his valet is incorrect. Mickey polished the General's shoes, shined his brass, ironed his shoestrings, changed his razor blades, squeezed the paste onto his toothbrush, helped him dress and undress, packed for him, unpacked for him, worried about him—and felt privileged to do it.

His hero worship sometimes struck the rest of us as funny. I remember one morning in Algiers when the General came downstairs all buffed and pressed and brushed and polished, and Mickey looked at him and sighed, "He's better looking than Gary Cooper." The General burst out laughing, and the rest of us joined in. Mickey could not understand what was so funny.

As I list Mickey's duties, I have to smile when I think of his helping Eisenhower dress and undress. During the General's first trip to London, the orderly who had been temporarily assigned to him confided in a burst of democratic exasperation that he was even expected to help Eisenhower on with his underpants in the morning. I went into peals of laughter at the thought of that nice, unassuming American being helped on with his underwear. I could not believe it. Later I learned it was true. The General had learned to enjoy being waited on hand and foot when he served under General Douglas MacArthur in the Philippines, where servants were plentiful. "When I came back from Manila," he told me once, "General Marshall asked if I had learned how to put my pants on again now that I was back in the States. I told him I'd never lost the knack. It was tying my shoelaces that bothered me."

Mickey was no mere pants holder. He could never do enough for the Boss. He saw to it that his bedside table was well supplied with chocolate bars, chewing gum and cigarettes, and he made it his business to see that the General had a steady supply of new Westerns, his favorite—and almost only—reading matter apart from official papers.

Mickey also wrote a weekly report to Mrs. Eisenhower. There were times when this self-imposed assignment of his made Butch and me a little nervous.

The last thing that I had expected when I left General Spaatz to return to General Eisenhower was to become a member of his little family, but as each day went by I found myself being included more and more until I felt like one of the charter members. It could not have come about more naturally. When I was not driving the General, I had very little to do, so I would pitch in and answer the telephones and help with the mail and make appointments for him. I probably spent more time with General Eisenhower than anyone else did. I would pick him up early in the morning, drive him here and there, work at this and that at the office and get him back to his hotel whenever he decided to call it a day.

The General was fiercely protective of us and made it clear that Butch, Tex and I were responsible to him and him alone. "That goes for you especially, Kay," he said meaningfully. He knew that some officers at headquarters often asked me to run errands and do this or that. He would have none of this. We were his staff, his personal staff, and no one was to take advantage of us.

The more I did for the General, the more we had to talk about and the better we got to know each other. At one point, he said, "Kay, I've heard so much about your mother. I'd really like to meet her. Why don't you ask her to have dinner with us some evening?"

It was like the time he and General Clark had invited me to lunch at the Connaught. Unprecedented. My mother to dine with the General! "Oh, I'm sure she'd love to, General. Thank you," I said.

We had a wonderful evening. Eisenhower wanted to know about every member of the family, and my mother was more than willing to tell him. She told him about my sister Evie and her husband; about our youngest sister, Sheila, who died. (Poor baby, she died at seven from the same rotten disease that is killing me. I wonder if it is hereditary.) And she told him about my brother, Seamus, an engineer, who was fighting with Wingate.

"Shaymus?" the General said. "That's an odd name. It's what we call detectives."

"It's not odd at all, General," my mother said indignantly. "It is the Irish of James. We spell it S-E-A-M-U-S."

"If it's S, why does it sound like S-H?" he asked.

"Oh, that's the Irish of it," she laughed. "In Ireland, everything is S-H. It's like Innis Beg. We say Innish."

"And what's Innis Beg the Irish for?"

"That's our home," I interrupted eagerly. "Innis Beg means Little Isle. Our house is all by itself on an island in a river that flows into the Atlantic. It's a beautiful place."

At the end of the evening, the General took my mother's hand in both of his. "This won't be the last evening we'll be spending together," he told her. "I want to hear more of your stories of Ireland." Mummy was captivated by him. "A very intelligent man," she said, "and so warm and charming. I liked him, Kathleen," she told me. After that dinner, I truly felt as if I were a member of the family, or the General a member of mine.

6

THE General hated hotel living, and Claridge's was too rich for his taste. His sitting room in that home away from home for potentates and multimillionaires was decorated in black and gold like some Hollywood set, and although I always felt that Fred Astaire might come tap-tap-tapping along at any minute, the General disagreed. "It looks like a goddamned fancy funeral parlor to me," he stated. The bedroom made him even more uncomfortable. "Whorehouse pink" was the way he described the color scheme. "Makes me feel as if I'm living in sin," he complained.

He moved to the Dorchester—still elegant and luxurious, but somewhat noisier, somewhat shinier; somewhat, in fact, American. He felt a bit more at home here, especially after Butch moved in with him, but the four walls kept closing in on him.

"I'm a captive," he complained. "I can't even go for a walk without starting a parade." Unknown a few weeks ago, he found that his name and face had become familiar to Londoners. Every morning when he stepped out of the elevator at the side entrance of the hotel and crossed the sidewalk to the car, there were people staring—even at seven in the morning. This had never happened to him before, and he did not like it. The General even came to resent room service as an intrusion, with the result that Butch added cooking to his other duties. In the morning, Butch brewed coffee on a little spirit stove. It was never strong enough for the General. "I use two tablespoons of coffee for every cup," Butch told me, "and then Ike says, 'How do you expect me to drink this dishwater?'" When the General had no official dinner scheduled, Butch would make soup by adding boiling water to a little packet of powder. This, together with bread and butter and chocolate bars, was supper, a meal I often shared if I had to drive the Boss to an evening appointment.

General Eisenhower actually spent very little time at the Dorchester. Six or seven hours' sleep was all he allowed himself—and often he got less. Ten to twelve hours out of every twenty-four were spent at Grosvenor Square. His days were filled with meetings. Meetings to resolve the political conflicts that arose between the British and the Americans. Meetings to resolve the personality conflicts. Meetings to work out the details for the operation called Torch aimed at the liberation of North Africa. (Although it is not within the realm of this book, or indeed within the scope of my abilities, to reconstruct the campaigns and intrigues of the Second World War, it is a fact that after what seemed like insurmountable—and unending—political problems, it had been agreed that the first order of Allied business was to liberate North Africa, and all the General's energies were directed toward preparing the invasion—an enormous task made even more agonizing by the difficulties of setting up a workable and unified Allied command. The General's book *Crusade in Europe* tells about all this far better than I could ever hope to.) And there were countless meetings with the Prime Minister for war-gaming sessions in which the P.M. and the General went over and over all possible eventualities like two chess players with the world at stake. Usually these sessions would be held after dinner at 10 Downing Street or in the bombproof underground shelter off St. James's Park where the P.M. spent a lot of time, but on weekends they would be at Chequers, the P.M.'s country residence. The General detested going there, because—even in full summer—it was cold. He called it a "damned icebox," and when he had to go there he always wore two suits of underwear. Part of Chequers was more than five hundred years old, and of course, there was no central heating. Quite often the P.M. and Mrs. Churchill would wear their coats to the dining table when Ike was there, but he did not feel that he should follow their example. Harry Hopkins, President Roosevelt's special emissary to the P.M., probably hated going to Chequers even more than the General did. Once when I drove the two of them out there, I heard Mr. Hopkins complain that there was only one bearable room in the house—the downstairs lavatory. Later on, Eisenhower told me a story about that. It seems that the P.M. wanted to talk to Mr. Hopkins, but nobody could find him. He was not in his bedroom. Not in the library, nor in the great gallery. Finally he was discovered in that little lavatory. He was wearing his overcoat, gloves, muffler and hat, perched on the toilet reading the newspaper.

The pressure never seemed to let up. There were times when the Boss would look up from his desk at 20 Grosvenor at four or five in the afternoon and say wearily, "Kay, get me out of here. I'm going stir crazy."

"Certainly, General," I'd say, and tear down to get the car. Then I would drive him about until the last glimmering of twilight. Sometimes Butch would come along and amuse him with bits of gossip he had picked up, but usually it was just the two of us. One of his favorite drives, when he had time, was the run to Windsor. "It's like a storybook," he said once, looking at the big gray stone castle sprawling above the town. He always liked to see the Eton schoolboys wandering about in their traditional top hats and never failed to say what he would have done if anyone had ever forced him to wear such a getup when he was a youngster. Once we drove to Beaconsfield, where we had spent a stolen couple of hours over gin and tonics just two months before. Now it was impossible for the General to drop into a pub. He would have been recognized immediately.

Sometimes as I was driving along, he would lean forward and say, "This looks pleasant here, Kay. Why don't you stop and we'll walk a bit." He really enjoyed those walks. Sometimes we would chat about this and that, but he usually stepped right out at a pace that kept me next to breathless, and we would march along in silence until the General would say, "Well, I guess we'd better be getting back."

Once in a while he would fall asleep in the back seat. I always knew his appointment schedule, so I would drive about, choosing the smoothest roads, until it was time for him to be back at the Dorchester. Then, shortly before we arrived, I would hit a few bumps so that he would be awake when I drew up to the door. He would shake his head, blink his eyes, pull at his tie and put his hat back on. "I must have dozed off," he would say.

There were not enough of these respites, however, to alleviate the General's very deep—and deepening—fatigue. His temper erupted at the least provocation, and he was a three-star bundle of nervous tension. (He had received that gratifying third star very shortly after returning to London.) Butch reported that there were many nights when Eisenhower just could not sleep and that he would get out of bed and sit by the window staring out into the dark for hours. He was losing weight, and the wrinkles on his face were suddenly much too deep for a man of fifty-two.

One night when I was driving him and Butch back to London after an inspection trip, the General said, "There ought to be some place where I could get away and have some peace. Some place in the country."

"Why not rent a place outside London?" Butch asked. "You could get some fresh air and exercise without feeling as if a spotlight were on you every second if you had a house of your own."

"Sounds good to me," the General said.

That was enough of a go-ahead for Butch, and one afternoon in August, he walked into headquarters looking like the cat who swallowed the canary. "I've got it!" he said. "Ike, I've found you a dream house."

He was right. Everything about Telegraph Cottage was right. It was in Kingston, a very pleasant suburb less than a half-hour drive from Grosvenor Square and only minutes from Bushey Park, then the U.S. Army Air Forces headquarters. Set in ten acres of woods and lawns amidst flowering shrubs, Telegraph Cottage was like an adorable Tudor dollhouse, with a slate roof and a chimney that almost always had a plume of woodsmoke curling up into the sky. It looked as if it belonged on a Christmas card.

And it was blessedly private. A winding driveway with a white pole across the entrance led up to the house, which was completely invisible from the road. I used to curse that pole when I drove the General home at night. I would have to stop the car, hop out and swing the pole aside, drive the car through and then hop out again to put that blasted pole back. During the day a one-armed gatekeeper—a veteran of the last war—was there to swing the pole aside, but at night it was my detested job. It seems strange when one thinks back on it in these violent times, but that white pole was all that was needed in England, even in wartime, to keep unwelcome visitors away.

Naturally, no one knew that the General was there. The fact that he had a hideaway outside London was top secret then. And with wartime security, it was easy to keep the secret. This made Telegraph Cottage a true oasis of privacy and calm. There was only one telephone, a direct line to headquarters, which was in the General's bedroom.

The cottage was so secret that very few people knew it existed and even fewer knew where it was. The first time Averell Harriman was there—for a very important dinner meeting with Robert Murphy, the head of the American underground network in North Africa—Butch picked up Mr. Harriman in London after dark and drove him to the cottage and then back to his hotel after the meeting. Mr. Harriman had been instructed to tell his daughter Kathy that he was going to inspect a factory that was turning out supersecret devices for airplanes. With blackout conditions what they were, it was certain that Mr. Harriman would never be able to pinpoint the cottage's location. Not that he was not trusted: it was simply that the existence of Telegraph Cottage and its whereabouts were confided on a need-to-know basis. Later on, things became somewhat more relaxed, but the cottage was never common knowledge.

The house had five tiny bedrooms and a really old-fashioned bathroom (when anyone pulled the chain, one would have thought it was the cataracts of the Nile, it was so noisy). Each bedroom had its own basin and pitcher and, yes, commode. There was no central heating, but between the fireplace in the living room and the big old stove in the kitchen, we were always very comfortable.

The little living room had French doors that opened out onto a small terrace, where we would sit with our drinks on the rare evenings when it was warm enough, but usually we were happy to be in front of the fire. The living room itself was furnished nicely if rather shabbily. There was just about room for two comfortable chairs by the fireplace and a quite uncomfortable sofa with a mahogany coffee table in front of it. In one corner there were a bookcase and a game table; in another corner, an old chest. One day Butch bought four pillows to make the sofa a bit kinder to the human anatomy, but then Eisenhower spotted the bill. "What's this?" he exclaimed. "Forty dollars for cushions! They must have solid-gold fringe!" He was quite angry, and Butch had to return them. If the truth must be told, the General did have a tendency to be just a little stingy.

The dining room had a round oak table that sat six comfortably, eight elbow to elbow, and there were evenings when we squeezed ten people around it. Against the wall was a sideboard that we turned into a bar.

And that was it. It was a very simple little house, but it could not have been cozier or happier. From the very first time we drove out there, the General felt at home and so did the rest of us. It is hard to explain just how important the hours we spent there were. It was not a weekend house in any sense of the term, since Eisenhower worked a seven-day week and so did the rest of us. But it did represent an escape, and whenever we could escape we did. As time went by, the General spent three or four nights a week there.

One evening, early on, when I drove the General out to Kingston to spend the night, he said, "Kay, you'd better wait and have a bite before you go back to London." I was only too pleased to accept. By the time I got back to my little flat in Kensington Close, I knew I would be too tired to even boil water for tea.

"Mickey!" the Boss shouted. "We're starving and we're cold and we're tired. Light the fire and rustle us up something to eat." Mickey was in his element at Telegraph Cottage. He and the two soldiers, John Moaney and John Hunt, who did the cleaning, cooking and serving saw to it that everything was spotless, that the kitchen and the little bar were always well supplied and a fire always laid in the fireplace. Usually a fire would be burning when we arrived, but this evening Eisenhower had decided to come out on the spur of the moment, with no advance notice. No matter. Mickey had everything under control in minutes.

The General went straight to his sideboard bar and made us each a Scotch and water. By the time the drinks were poured, Mickey had the fire blazing away and plates of salted peanuts—the General's favorite—set out on the little tables beside the armchairs. We sat sprawled by the fire. Two tired people, feeling absolutely relaxed and comfortable with each other. I loosened my tie, and Mickey helped the Boss off with his coat and into his old brown woolly cardigan. We sat and sipped and sighed in total relaxation. I don't exactly know how to describe this quality Eisenhower had, but he was a very comfortable man to be with. He was easy to talk to, and what is to my mind even more important, he was one of those people who know how to make a silence companionable. I don't think I have ever in my life felt so much at ease with any other human being or felt so much at home as I did at Telegraph Cottage.

In due course Mickey brought two trays so we could eat in front of the fire. I can't for the life of me remember what we ate, but I know that it was something warm and tasty. What with the drinks, the fire and the food, I was as cozy as a cat.

"You know something, Kay?" the General said. "We don't have enough fun in our lives. What should we do to make life a bit pleasanter? I know how hard it must be on you to work seven days a week. And don't think I don't realize that you rarely get to see Dick these days."

I was touched that the Boss had taken time to think of my personal problems when he had so many of his own. More important and burdensome problems. "Oh, Dick and I are managing," I said. "It's wartime, after all. We have to do what we have to do."

Actually Dick, although very busy and harassed himself, was somewhat unhappy about my new life. I never asked the General for a day off. It just would not have been right. Dick would complain, "Now that I'm permanently based in London, I don't see you as much as I did when I was only here a few days a month."

"What can I do?" I would ask. "The General drives himself even harder than he drives his staff. And he depends on me. I can't let him down. We have to wait. Someday our divorces will be final, and then things will be better." Life was very different in those days. I would no more have suggested that Dick move into my little flat in Kensington Close before we were married than I would have walked down Piccadilly naked.

But this was nothing I felt I should talk to the General about. Instead I addressed myself to his question. "I know what we could do for fun," I said. "Remember what a good time we had with General Gruenther?"

General Alfred Gruenther, who was an old friend of Eisenhower's and working with him on the planning for Torch, also happened to be one of the world's truly great bridge players. He and Butch had played General Eisenhower and me the previous week at the Dorchester, and it had been a hard-fought game. While we were playing cards, we had forgotten all about where we were and why. The game completely absorbed us. And afterwards the Boss had said, "Goddamnit, we should do this more often."

I have loved to play bridge ever since I was a child. My brother and sister and I used to sit around the schoolroom on the third floor at Innis Beg and play—auction bridge it was then—for hours at a time. We would shout at each other and fight and do a lot of cheating. Our games usually ended with our throwing our cards at each other and running out. We must have been little barbarians, but we had a lot of fun.

"Only one thing," I said to the General: "we shouldn't have any postmortems. Once my husband and I did not say one syllable to each other for three days after a postmortem."

"Okay, that's it. Bridge. And no postmortems," Eisenhower said. He really brightened up. I could tell he liked the idea. "We'll start tomorrow night."

That was the beginning of a nightly routine that lasted throughout the war wherever we were—in North Africa and in Italy, in France and in Germany. Whenever the Boss was free in the evening, we played bridge. And we played seriously, concentrating fiercely on our hands. There was no chatter at the card table. The General rarely spoke, and he discouraged newcomers who displayed a tendency toward conversation. When he had a good hand or a slam or something like that, he would chuckle and say, "Oh, that's great!" but that was the extent of it. He would smoke one cigarette after another, and Mickey would be in the background busy emptying ashtrays, filling the peanut dishes—and the glasses—and putting fresh logs on the fire.

We never lacked for a foursome. Butch liked to play, and he

would often bring along a friend for dinner and bridge. General Mark Clark, whom Eisenhower always called Wayne, was one of the steadies, and so was General T. J. Davis, an old friend of the General's. Once in a blue moon we would be very lucky and General Gruenther would take a hand. He was such a good player that people would call him up from all over the European Theater to ask advice or have him settle a dispute over some fine point.

Harry Hopkins usually took a hand when he was around. He was quite a good player, although he preferred gin rummy to bridge. I was always nervous when he played, because he was so thin. So thin that his clothes looked as if they had been thrown onto a skeleton. I would look at him and think, My goodness, that man is going to fall over if anyone breathes too hard. He was quite tall and seemed terribly frail, although he worked like a demon.

We always played for money—threepence a hundred points. The General refused to keep score or involve himself with the bookkeeping. "I'm pulling rank," he'd say with a grin. "I've got enough aides here to keep score for me." He insisted on the losers paying promptly. He was prompt himself. If he lost, someone, usually I, would figure out how much he owed and then he would reach into his pocket very slowly drawling out, "I just happen to have a little money here." It was always very little. The General's paycheck went directly to his wife, and he never had more than a few dollars of spending money. There were times when he would make his little announcement and reach into his pocket only to find he had no money at all. Mickey would have forgotten to give the General his pocket money when he dressed that morning—or the General would have spent his daily allowance on cigarettes and chocolate bars. Then he would bellow, "Mickey-ey-ey! Money-ey-ey!" even if Mickey was at his elbow, and Mickey would run upstairs and come back with a handful of small change so that the General could settle his bridge debt.

Bridge was not our only game. "The frosting on the cake," as Butch put it, was the fact that Telegraph Cottage was next to a golf course. A path led from the back of the house through the woods to a gate in a high wooden fence that marked the edge of the property. When we walked through the gate, we were at the thirteenth hole.

We got to know that thirteenth hole very well. If the General left headquarters early on a Saturday or Sunday, he would head straight for Telegraph Cottage and the thirteenth hole. Occasionally we would play three or four holes. I don't believe we ever visited the clubhouse, and I know that we never played the full eighteen holes. Many an evening we contented ourselves practicing chipping and putting. But the situation was absolutely made to order for the General. The course could not have been more private. Most of the golfers we saw were elderly ladies, playing through with placid determination.

And just off the path that wound between the house and the golf course, we discovered a little rustic bench hidden behind some shrubbery. Later on, when we wanted to be completely alone, we would sit there and talk, away from everybody and everything.

We set up a badminton net and dragooned visitors into playing fast, sweaty games. And the General, Butch and Tex or Mark Clark would toss a football around, playing a childish game with rules they changed every time they played. It was always two against one, and the odd man tried to intercept the ball as the other two threw it back and forth to each other while they ran around in circles.

Moaney and Hunt used to save tin cans for pistol practice. Butch, the General and I would take turns shooting cans off the top of a stake driven into the ground. Later we got a regular target and set it up on the lawn. When the General learned that I did not have a gun, he went rummaging through his trunk and came up with one for me to use.

A few days later, he called me into his office at Grosvenor

Square and said, "I've got something for you." He reached into the desk drawer and took out a small Beretta.

"I want you to get familiar with this," he said. "It's yours. When we're overseas, you never know what might happen. I'd prefer to see you dead rather than a prisoner of the Germans," he added grimly.

This was the first hint I had had that he was considering taking me overseas with him. I knew that once the planning for Torch was completed, he would be off to North Africa, and I supposed I would be back in the motor pool waiting for another assignment. He did not say any more about it, but from that time on I spent hours potting away at those old tin cans with my Beretta. Fortunately, I had done a lot of shooting when I was growing up, so it did not take long before I could ping away pretty accurately.

When the General really wanted to get his mind off things, he would ask Mickey to get out his drawing paraphernalia and would make sketch after sketch of Telegraph Cottage. He could never capture it to his satisfaction. He would rip the pages off his pad and tear them up, and one could just see his blood pressure mounting. It got so that when he called Mickey to get out his sketch pad and set up a chair for him on the lawn, we would all roll our eyes at each other and try to distract him by suggesting that we go for a walk or something. We never succeeded—and neither did the General. Later, when he was in the White House, I was always surprised by how much he had improved when I saw his paintings reproduced in a newspaper or magazine. But one thing can certainly be said for his early efforts: they did get his mind off the war.

After the first few evenings at Telegraph Cottage, Eisenhower decided that it was too much for me to drive back to London on the nights he decided to sleep over and then come back to pick him up in the morning, so he requisitioned a billet for me at Bushey Park, which was very close, so that I could get more sleep. This worked out very well. I would arrive at the cottage shortly before seven in the morning. Moaney and Hunt would be bustling around the kitchen getting breakfast. There would be bacon or a piece of ham and eggs. There was usually real butter, and there were always hot biscuits with lots of jam. We ate better—our supplies came from the Army mess—than almost anyone else in England; I am convinced of that. And there were gallons, or so it seemed, of blistering-hot black coffee. If the coffee was not as black as midnight and one degree short of boiling, the General would blow his top. Mickey would rush out to the kitchen and bring in a fresh pot that had obviously been boiling when he snatched it off the stove. "It's hot, General. Watch your tongue," he would say.

I remember one morning when Eisenhower had a breakfast guest, a high-ranking British officer, who was quite obviously taken aback by the bustling informality of this little household—and particularly by the idea of a batman's presuming to tell a general to watch out and not burn his tongue and by a woman driver's arriving for breakfast with a very unprofessional salute and a cry of "Eggs! Oh, General, that's smashing!" It was not what one would call your ordinary general's household. But it was just what this American general wanted, needed and got.

As soon as the General had had his final cup of coffee and gone upstairs for Mickey to help him on with his coat and give him a final brushing, we would be off to Grosvenor Square.

Wartime is much more concentrated than peacetime. It was only a matter of days until our little family felt as if we had been leading this kind of life together for years. In the middle of a vast world war, the commanding general had managed to establish a happy home in that precarious calm of the eye of the storm.

7

T HE General had been as good as his word, and my mother was often invited to the Dorchester and Telegraph Cottage. She and the General hit it off beautifully. They were both history buffs. My mother had been well educated—far better than I had been—in convents in France and Belgium where the nuns drilled their pupils in history and languages as well as needlework and etiquette, since these young ladies were expected to marry into important Catholic families, not to espouse land-poor cavalry officers as my mother had. She was insatiably curious about the American Civil War, and the General loved to refight the battles for her at the dinner table.

I have fond memories of the two of them, both smoking one cigarette after another over their coffee cups, engrossed in setting up battles between the Confederate and Union forces. The General used coins to represent soldiers, and Mickey often had to rush down to the lobby of the Dorchester and change a pound note to provide troops for my mother and the General.

The two of them became really good friends and used to chat and laugh together as if they had known each other for ages. In some ways they were remarkably alike. They had the same magnetic warmth and could establish almost instant rapport with people.

Mummy had separated from my father when I was sixteen or

seventeen and come with me and my sister Evie to London, where she found a post as office manager. In those days I hated my father and was sure I knew why Mummy had left him: he was angry, cantankerous, impossible to live with. He was the villain. I was convinced of it. But now, looking back, I imagine it was a bit more complicated a relationship.

My father had his gentle, loving side as well as his black Irish furies. He loved his land. Those hundreds of green Irish acres that had belonged to his father and his father's father before him meant the world to him. He loved his flowers. His gardens were famous in southern Ireland. There were always two or three gardeners trundling wheelbarrows of manure about, staking the rosebushes, clipping the shrubbery and all that.

He loved his son, Seamus, and took a stern pride in the fact that he had an heir—strong, handsome and intelligent. And Seamus loved Innis Beg as much as our father did.

And my father loved his beautiful, vivacious and opinionated English wife. Today I am sure of that. But there was a disparity in their ages and in their background. And they were both willful, stubborn souls. My father had spent much of his Army life in West Africa—"the white man's grave" they called it then—and when he came back home and married, I suspect that he was not prepared for his young bride's dismay when she was introduced to the lonely old house that he loved so much.

Southern Ireland could be bitterly cold and damp. I remember that all of us children always had chilblains in the winter—raw, red, itching knuckles and ankles. We thought nothing of it. Chilblains were a way of life, part of winter, as were our streaming eyes and runny noses. Those chillingly damp Irish winters, when the smoke from open fires swooped through the house and billowed down the halls, driven by the wet Atlantic winds gusting in from the west, were probably responsible for Mummy's getting the touch of tuberculosis that prompted my father to pack her off to visit one of her friends in Italy to get her health back in the Mediterranean sun. That long separation coupled with unrealized expectations and sullen frustrations on both sides may have triggered the final separation.

Whatever the reason or reasons, she finally left my father. Ostensibly she was simply giving Evie and me a season in London, but she never returned to Innis Beg to live. Mummy told me, "You can either be presented at Court or have a trip. I think it would be far more interesting for you to travel, but you have the choice." It did not take me a minute to make that choice. I would travel. Who wanted all that nonsense of curtsies and ostrich feathers when it was possible to see the world instead? Also, to tell the truth, the thought of curtsying to the austerely regal Queen Mary rather daunted me. I was still a raw country girl fresh from County Cork.

Mummy arranged for me to visit one of her old schoolmates in Helsinki. It was a marvelous experience. I traveled all over Finland, and I think I met every important person in the country at my hostess' dinner table—including Field Marshal Mannerheim, the famous statesman. I went to Oslo next, then to Brussels and Paris. I would stay with friends of Mummy's, and then other friends would come by and say, "Oh, you must come visit with us too." So every place I went, there were several families to take me around.

When I came back to London after six months, Mummy told me that I now had to learn how to earn my own living. "There will be no money for you girls when your father dies," she said. "The property will go to Seamus. I want you to be self-supporting so you won't have to marry to get a roof over your head."

So off I went to school. Not too eagerly. In the mornings I went to business school and learned how to type and write proper business letters. In the afternoon, I went to art school. But my social life soon turned into such an exciting whirl that I neglected my studies. Then I had a chance to work as an extra in a film that was being made at Elstree and stopped going to classes altogether. I was flirting with the idea of becoming an actress when I met Gordon Summersby.

It was love at first waltz. The party was in one of those wonderful old houses on St. James's Square with a wide staircase curving up to a ballroom that probably was not used more than twice a year, if that. I wonder if any London houses today still boast ballrooms. They were part of a far different day, a more romantic one. After Gordon and I were introduced, we danced almost every dance with each other, drank champagne, which we were not used to, and talked a lot of nonsense. Finally we drifted back down that beautiful staircase and walked out into the sunrise. We were married within months.

Marriage was a hectic round of partying. We went out almost every night and would spend weekends at this place and that in the country visiting friends who, like us, were mad about racing and everything to do with horses. All play and no work turned out to be a very dull way of life, and eventually Gordon and I drifted apart. I started working as a model at Worth, the first job that was offered to me. The pay was peanuts, but it seemed a lot to me, because I had never earned any money before. I enjoyed the glamour, and I was fascinated by the process of artistic creation. Fashion became a living, breathing art to me. To be able to observe the creation of a design from the first sketch to the final fitting—quite often on me—was a privilege I would have been willing to pay for.

I had told the General all this in bits and pieces as I drove him around and in the evenings we spent chatting at Telegraph Cottage. He often said that he felt as if he had known my family for years. When I told him that Seamus was in London on leave, he said, "Well, I've got to meet him. Why don't you ask your brother to come over for dinner tonight?"

"Oh, that would be lovely," I said, and when Seamus came by the office, I told him that General Eisenhower had invited us to have dinner with him that evening.

He looked at me disbelievingly. I can still see his face. "What's that you said?"

"You heard me," I laughed. "The General wants to meet you. I've told him all about you."

"I can just imagine," Seamus said.

We had a marvelous evening. It was completely informal. In the office and in public I was always careful to give the General every mark of formal respect. I never overstepped. I always saluted and was absolutely punctilious. But in private, that was different. I now saw him as a man and a friend, not just a general and a boss, and I had begun to call him Ike as the others did. That evening with Seamus was one of an absolutely at-home kind of fun for the three of us. It was ages since I had seen Seamus, and we started reminiscing about things we had done when we were children. It reached the point where we were clutching at our stomachs because we laughed so much. And the General laughed just as hard as Seamus and I did.

One of the funniest bits I remember was our telling the General about all the governesses—mostly young Englishwomen, although there was one elderly mademoiselle—that my mother managed to entice to Innis Beg. They never stayed long. And who could blame them? Seamus, of course, went off to school in Cork when he was eight or nine, but until then he was taught at home; and we girls were always taught at home, with the result that we did not learn much except how to ride and sail and dance and play bridge, all of which we taught ourselves or learned from our parents and their friends.

Seamus reminded me of the time we offered to show a new governess around in our pony cart. We were barely out of sight of the house when Seamus whipped the poor fat pony, who toddled off as fast as his stubby legs could carry him, which was not very fast. Seamus, after making sure that there was no one who could hear him, shouted, "Runaway! Runaway horse!" Evie and I joined in shrieking, "Help! Help! Runaway horse!" and the poor governess just sat there hanging on for dear life and looking scared to death. Finally the pony got tired of exerting

himself and ambled to a stop. The new governess hugged
Seamus and called him a brave young hero.

Seamus and I flung ourselves about the living room of the
General's suite at the Dorchester as we told him the story, inter-
rupting each other with freshly remembered details.

Then Seamus told the story of how I smashed my father's
shotgun. I had been nine or maybe ten at the time and, quite
disobediently, had taken one of my father's precious Purdeys
out of the enormous glass-fronted gun case in the hall to go
shooting. Scrambling over a gate, I dropped the shotgun—and
cracked the stock!

I was ready to run away from home. His Purdeys were more
precious than jewels to my father, certainly more precious than I
was, or so I was convinced. I was so frightened that I hid in the
stables. Seamus brought me a sandwich after supper, but I was
too terrified to eat.

"What shall I do?" I quavered. "He'll beat me until I'm
dead." I think I really believed that he would.

"You have to tell him," Seamus said. He considered for a moment and added, "You can't run away from home. You are not
old enough to take care of yourself."

"All right," I decided. "I'll tell him." I marched into the house
and knocked on the door of the library, where my father spent
his evenings. He was going over papers at his desk and was very
much surprised to see me. Surprised and obviously not pleased. I
told him what had happened.

He looked at me. I suppose that what he saw must have appalled him. A bedraggled girl child. We all looked like urchins.
Our day-in, day-out costumes had been devised by our mother
for freedom and practicality. They consisted of floppy brown
corduroy bloomers with tight elastic at the knee and sweaters
that my mother knitted of a particularly horrid porridge-colored
wool. I used to wear my bloomers pulled way up to the crotch,
where the elastic would cut into my legs with circulation-stop-
ping cruelty, or pulled way down so that they looked like

knickers, or so I hoped. With them we wore long woolen stockings that were more or less held up by suspenders that buckled around our waists—miserable contraptions that were always getting twisted.

There I was—dirty, guilty and sniveling—in this dismal outfit. Poor Father. It took me years to understand how bewildered he must have felt to have produced these strange, noisy, undisciplined offspring so late in life—especially after a career in the cavalry, where men were men and horses were horses and each performed properly or else. (He had been lieutenant colonel of the Royal Munster Fusiliers, an Irish regiment, now disbanded.)

He surprised me. He did not beat me. He did not even shout at me. "Go wash your face, Kathleen," he said, "and then come back."

I came back, dragging my sleeve over my face to dry it. "Come here," Father said. He put his arm around me and said, "You know that you should not have taken my gun. That was wrong. But you were right to tell me about it. That was brave. We'll hear no more about it."

When I listened to Seamus telling that old story, I had a feeling of sympathy and respect for my father. It suddenly dawned on me that perhaps he had loved me, but had not known how to express his feelings.

With all this talk about old times, Seamus and I were having a glorious reunion. And Ike was having fun too. He even told a story of his own about one of his uncles who had been a preacher on the prairie. His Uncle Abraham (I *think* that was his name) would stand on the seat of his wagon in the middle of a tiny village and shout, "This way to Heaven! This way to Heaven!" In no time at all, he had gathered fifteen or twenty people and launched into his sermon.

"I always thought there was a lesson in that," Ike said, "but I'm damned if I have ever been able to figure out what it is. I know the old man was mighty proud of himself the way he could raise an audience out of the dust, so to speak."

The next morning he told me that he had had a fine time. "Those stories you and Seamus told are almost as good as my Westerns," he said with a smile, knowing my scorn for his favorite reading matter.

But evenings like this became increasingly rare as the preparations for North Africa neared completion. We were constantly on the go, and whenever the General had an evening to himself, all he wanted was to retreat to Telegraph Cottage and relax. There were nights when he was so bone-tired that he would fall asleep by the fire. He always asked us to wake him up when he did, because afterwards he would have trouble getting to sleep at night. The tensions were building up, and he would lie awake for hours going over problem after problem. All of us tried to think of ways to distract him and get his mind off the war for at least a few hours, but it became increasingly difficult.

As it turned out, an addition to our little family proved to be far more effective in helping the General relax than anything Butch and Beetle (General Walter Bedell Smith, Ike's chief of staff) and I had been able to dream up. The new member of the family was a perfect gentleman who was to be my almost constant companion, forever faithful and loving. His name was Telek, and he was a coal-black Scottie who deserves a chapter all his own.

8

ONE lovely sunny October day when I was driving the General back from Cheltenham, our road lay among the rolling green hills of the Cotswolds with tiny villages of gray stone cottages and farmhouses surrounded by their barns and pens dotted here and there on the landscape. "One of these days I'm going to have a farm," Ike told me. "Cows, horses, maybe some sheep. A kitchen garden. Nothing too big. But I want to have a real home. I've never had one since I was a youngster, you know. I've always gone from Army post to Army post. Telegraph Cottage is more of a home than most of the places I've lived in."

"It's the homiest place I've ever known," I agreed. "When I walk into Telegraph Cottage, it's like coming home."

"That's the way I feel about it," Ike said. "All it needs is some youngsters running around playing ball and climbing trees."

"And a few dogs," I added, entering into the spirit of the thing. "I miss having a dog. We always had dogs around the house. My favorite was a Scottie, MacTavish. He was really adorable. Tavvy was so spunky you had to laugh."

"Kay, would you like a dog? Another Scottie?" Ike asked.

I braked the car sharply. "Would I like a dog? Oh, General, having a dog would be heaven!"

"Well," he grinned, "if you want one, we'll get one. I think I can manage that. I'd like to do something for you for working all these crazy hours and everything."

I had no idea of the proportions Operation Dog would assume. The moment the word got out that the Commander wanted a dog, you should have seen the scurrying. The first thing I knew, Butch asked, "Have you heard the latest? The Boss wants a dog for his birthday."

"Oh," I said very carefully. "He does, does he?"

"He certainly does. He wants a Scottie. I told him he should get a Dandie Dinmont. That's a great little dog. But no, he wants a Scottie."

"Well then," I said, "we certainly will have to get him a Scottie."

The whole headquarters staff was out combing London and the suburbs for the finest Scottie to be had. Beetle and I joined forces and found two Scotties that were close to perfect. Of course, our notions of perfection differed.

One dog was about a year old, very sweet but without much spirit. Beetle liked him because he was already housebroken. The other, my favorite, was just a puppy, a three-month-old ball of black fur. I loved him. We decided to let the General choose, and in we went to his office carrying the dogs in our arms. The older dog just sat there quietly, but the puppy was adorable. The first thing he did was make a puddle in the exact center of the rug; then he pranced around looking very proud of himself. "Come here, fella," the General said, and that little puppy went right over to him.

Ike looked at me. "What do you think? Do you like him?"

"Oh, General, I love him," I said.

He grinned. "This is the one, Beetle." As far as the world knew, this was the General's dog. "You understand, don't you?" he asked me concernedly. "There would be such a rumpus if it got out that I was getting a dog for my driver. God knows what people would say—or think."

"Oh, I understand perfectly," I assured him. And I did.

"That's good," he said, "because I'm the one who is going to name him."

"Oh? And what is his name?"

"Telek."

"Telek?"

"T-E-L-E-K," he spelled it out. "It's a combination of Telegraph Cottage and Kay," he said. "Two parts of my life that make me very happy."

The formal presentation was on October 14, the General's birthday, and it was one of the greatest birthday parties I have ever attended. It was at the cottage, of course. Mickey produced a marvelous cake frosted in white with three red frosting stars and a candle in the center of each star. And there was champagne. As soon as Ike had blown out the candles and we had toasted him with champagne, Telek trotted out—a red ribbon around his neck, a wag to his tail and all the charm in the world. He saluted Ike with another puddle, and someone suggested that Ike change the puppy's name from Telek to Puddle, and Butch said Piddle would be even better. The General shook his head. "Telek it is and Telek it's going to be," he said firmly.

"Telek." Butch shook his head disgustedly. "It sounds like the name of a toothbrush."

"Could be," the General said mysteriously. "His tail looks a bit like a toothbrush."

"But it's a ridiculous name for a dog," Butch persisted. "Why not call him Blackie or Rover or something like that? What does Telek mean, anyway?"

"That would be telling," Ike said. "It's top secret. Just like Telegraph Cottage. Maybe when the war is over I'll explain it."

The party broke up early, and the General and I had a last drink in front of the fire. Telek fell asleep in my lap. Ike came over and scratched the puppy's ears, and Telek opened his eyes, gave one little wag of his tail and went back to sleep. We smiled at each other. "Thank you, Kay," Ike said, "for bringing so much gaiety into my life. I don't know what I'd do without you."

The next morning Telek accompanied us to Grosvenor Square, sitting in front with me. He behaved like a perfect gentleman. From that time on, we were three. Telek went almost everywhere the General and I went. In the office he had his own little box with a pillow, where he snoozed most of the day. He even accompanied the General to Buckingham Palace when he went to pay his farewell call on the King before leaving for Gibraltar and North Africa. Telek did not go inside, of course. He stayed with me; but he did manage to leave his signature on a few inches of the Palace courtyard in a most disrespectful manner.

Telek had a pedigree a mile long. He was a true aristocrat. He was also spoiled rotten—and utterly, endearingly lovable. Once Admiral J. H. D. Cunningham of the Royal Navy took Ike to task for not training Telek properly. Not normally the kind of person who would venture to tell someone else how to train his dog, the Admiral simply could not refrain from speaking up when he noticed that Ike was feeding Telek bits from his plate at the luncheon table.

"That dog is spoiled," the Admiral said. "It's a mistake to feed dogs at the table. Gets them to thinking it should happen all the time."

"It does, Admiral. It does," Ike assured him.

The Admiral, who was really a very nice old boy, frowned, but Ike simply grinned and shook his head.

"If you want me to train Telek, someone has to train me first," he said. "There isn't very much I can do that's fun, but I can spoil this dog, and he enjoys it as much as I do."

When Telek was still a puppy, Ike would often say, "Hand that little black tramp over to me. I think he needs a little man-to-man talk." And he would hold him and talk nonsense to him and scratch his ears and his fat little stomach until Telek would curl up and go to sleep snuggled up to the General. Many a night we would lie on the floor in front of the fire, our drinks on the floor beside us, and roll a golf ball back and forth for Telek to chase. He would pounce on it as if he had captured a tiger. Another game he loved was tug-of-war. Ike would hold one end of the old leather belt he had donated to Telek's toy box and Telek would give a baby growl and grab the other end between his teeth. He used to shake the belt as if he were shaking a rat and growl ferociously all the time.

We were like two children with Telek—or perhaps doting parents might be closer to the truth. All we had needed to complete our little wartime family and make Telegraph Cottage a real home was a child. And Telek, for us, was a reasonable facsimile. Every dog lover will know how we felt.

9

M EN and women who are immersed in a creative process, whether it be waging war or making love or painting a picture or carrying a child in the womb or what I have come to think of as the ultimate creative process—dying—exist in their own special dimension. Their preoccupation is so great, their commitment so complete, their energies so all-absorbed that it is as if their days were being lived out in a tunnel. A transparent, invisible tunnel.

They seem just like their neighbors—eating and sleeping, walking and talking, catching colds in their heads and losing fillings in their teeth—but they are people apart. The invisible tunnel encloses them as surely as the medieval convent held its nuns or the amber its fly. The fervor of commitment has the same high-tension euphoria as a butterfly-brief love affair. For all tunnels come to an end. Wars are won. Orgasm is achieved; a vision captured. A child is born. The gates of death open—and close. Then one must emerge. Into what?

General Eisenhower and I were embarked on a voyage through a tunnel of war. It was a just war, a crusade against "the evil things." Never did we have to question the righteousness of our cause, nor did we consider ourselves as noble or self-sacrificing. We had a job to do. That was all. A war to win.

Like any job, war had its own routine. The General's responsibilities seemed to be a mishmash of this and that, but no matter how his day was splintered into a thousand little and big responsibilities, the Boss's only real concern was the war. And again as with any job, there were parts of it that he disliked. More and more he was having to grapple with the political as well as the military aspects of Torch, something that did not appeal to him at all. "Christ on the mountain," he burst out one night on the way home, "I'm a military man, not a politician!" He spent the rest of the drive to Kingston telling me how he had been taught at West Point that the military should not get involved with politics. "It's as important as the separation of church and state," he explained earnestly.

He was openly shocked at the country-club atmosphere at 20 Grosvenor. "Some of these fellows have been in London too long," he said darkly. Long lunches, early cocktail hours and three-day weekends had been taken for granted. But all that ended almost overnight. The General put an end to late arrivals and early departures by letting it be known that he expected everyone to report to work when he did—shortly before eight—and that he considered it very poor form for anyone to leave before the Old Man left.

Another problem was trying to establish harmony between the American and British soldiers. England is such a small country that the hundreds of thousands of Americans pouring off the troopships presented serious problems. There were all kinds of incidents that exacerbated the war-weary English, and the General spent hours smoothing these out. I remember one case well. An American officer, much the worse for drink, called a British officer a son of a bitch. The General ordered the American sent back to the States. The British officer asked the General to reconsider. "He only called me a son of a bitch, sir," he told the General. "We have learned that this is an American expression that should not be taken too seriously, that it is often a term of affection."

"I have been informed," Ike said, "that he called you a *British* son of a bitch. That is different. My ruling stands."

The General used the term often enough himself. I remember when he heard about an American officer who was boasting that his men would show the British what fighting men really were. Eisenhower's voice came blistering through the walls of his office. "I'll make that son of a bitch *swim* back to the States!" he shouted.

It was not only the officers who struck the wrong note. The English used to say that the trouble with the GI's was that "They are oversexed, overpaid—and over here." The Americans were paid nearly three times as much as their British counterparts, and many girls were swept off their feet by the attractive, free-spending Yanks. Eisenhower sent out several memos urging the men to save their money, buy bonds or send it home, but he was never able to make much of a dent in their extravagant ways.

He also worked hard at turning his draftee army into proud fighting men. He started at the top, with the commanding officers, demanding that they insist on spit and polish, on salutes and military discipline. If a soldier did not behave in a disciplined manner, he would not make a good fighter. But he was not content with simply issuing orders. One afternoon he said, "Kay, get the car. We're going to take a little ride." Before he got into the big Packard, he said, "Uncover the stars." The three silver stars on a red plate attached to the Army license plate were usually concealed by a little canvas slipcover, since Eisenhower did not care to call attention to himself. But this day the stars were shining silver bright, and his flag flew from the radiator cap, as he directed me to drive slowly down Audley Street past the Officers' Club and an enlisted men's canteen. The General sat erect and observant in the back.

"Around again," he ordered. So around I went past the club again at something like ten miles an hour; then we cruised into and out of the other West End streets around Grosvenor Square, passing hundreds of officers and enlisted men, until he ordered, "Back to headquarters." His face was turkey red. In twenty minutes only one man had saluted—and he was a British officer. Ike stalked into 20 Grosvenor, his jaw thrust out and his eyes cold in anger. He marched up and down his office dictating a memo for distribution to all commanding officers. From now on, he told them, whenever he spotted any laxity in saluting, he himself would ask the name of the offender—and that of his commanding officer. He would hold the commanding officer responsible. He got his point across. A week later we made another test drive along Audley Street. This time there was a satisfactory flurry of salutes.

There were also great flurries of VIP conferences. General Marshall came to London. And so did Admiral Ernest King, his Navy counterpart. Harry Hopkins and Steve Early seemed to be continually flying back and forth between London and Washington. Even Eleanor Roosevelt came to see things for herself. And scores of top American politicians followed her example. There were meetings at the War Office, at 10 Downing Street, at Chequers, at 20 Grosvenor. The olive-drab official cars shuttled back and forth with their important passengers.

It was truly a star-spangled time. I was meeting people I would never have expected to meet, let alone be on friendly terms with. The most impressive was Prime Minister Churchill himself. The General met with him at least twice a week—once for lunch and once for dinner—and usually more. One day I was sitting in the car waiting for the General in front of the building near St. James's Park where he often met with the P.M. I looked up to see him walking toward the car accompanied by a familiar figure. The P.M.! I hopped out and stood at attention. Churchill looked just like all the photographs and cartoons—that same baby bulldog face, with eyes as blue as Eisenhower's. He wore his famous siren suit. This was his own wartime uniform and of his own design. The best way I can describe it is to say that it was very similar to a baby's one-piece sleeping suit. He liked it because he could thrust his stubby legs into it, pull it up, push his arms into the sleeves—and zip, he was dressed. He usually wore slippers with it when he was indoors.

The General introduced us, and the P.M. was absolutely charming. He told me that he had heard what a good driver I was and said, "Now, I want you to take good care of your general. We need him."

I could hardly believe it. The Prime Minister telling me to take good care of the Commander. I managed a weak "Yes, sir." This was the beginning of a long acquaintance. One day I was asked along with Ike to lunch at 10 Downing Street. It was far more informal than one would have thought. The Churchills were living in the basement, because a bomb that had exploded down the street had damaged the upper floors. But it was cozy, with chintz-covered chairs and sofas. There were a number of paintings, and fresh flowers everywhere. That made a great impression on me, because flowers were one of the casualties of wartime, one of those pleasures you don't realize you miss until you are reminded. Mrs. Churchill was there, and so was their daughter Mary, who was in the ATS (Auxiliary Territorial Service—the women's branch of the British Army). There were a couple of young men, I think, but for the life of me I can't recall who they were. That is not so surprising, because the P.M. was such a spellbinder that he was always the center of attention. He was more like a guest than a host, but Mrs. Churchill was extremely gracious and charming. We had sherry and chatted for a bit before we went into the dining room. I can't remember what was served for luncheon, but there was a great deal of liquid refreshment.

The General made a practice of introducing me to all his friends and many of his British military associates. It was very heady stuff. I could tell that he was pleased with—and possibly even proud of—me. At one point he said, "I want you to know all these people, Kay. That way you can be even more helpful. I need someone to talk to and sort out my ideas with. Someone who knows the people and problems involved."

I thought I understood what he meant. There were times when Beetle and Butch and Mark Clark and Tooey Spaatz and the others were inclined to push their own ideas instead of listening to Ike formulate his and following his lead. So just the fact of my knowing all these people and a little bit of how they would react to situations was useful. Ike knew I was utterly discreet, and he had slowly got into the habit of talking things over with me in the car or over a drink when we arrived at Telegraph Cottage after work. My contribution to these conversations was very limited. I rarely said anything more than, "Hmm. Yes, I see. Is that so? Oh, that *is* a problem, isn't it?" Noncommittal, sympathetic sounds, so that he had the feeling that there was someone responding to his thoughts. But I never disagreed. I never made suggestions. I was just there—like a hum in the background.

Our life was quite different from other people's lives—even though everyone was concerned with the war in some way. We worked seven days a week, and often twelve hours a day, in a quickening rhythm, on a task whose climax would affect the whole course of the war. The North African operation had to be successful. When you work this way with someone, no matter in what capacity, nothing else seems to matter.

No one outside the handful of people at headquarters, the top generals and statesmen and the members of the "family" could share our world. It seemed calm, but only because the General imposed a calm on his surroundings. Although Butch and I and the rest of the little family shared only part of the General's crushing responsibilities, we were closer to his concerns, his moods, his physical ups and downs than we were to those of any other person.

The complete absorption of my time and energy disturbed my fiancé. Dick felt left out in the cold. "My God," he said one day, "you know all those top generals, the ones the rest of us only hear about. And Winston Churchill calls you Kay."

"It's only because of my job. It has nothing to do with me."

Dick sighed. He was really upset. "You know," he said, "when the war is over and we are living in the States, you won't be associating with prime ministers and three-star generals."

"Well, that will be another phase," I said. "Naturally I wouldn't expect to be popping in on General Eisenhower for breakfast or playing cards with General Gruenther when we are in America. The circumstances will be completely different."

The fact was that at this time I simply could not imagine leading any other life. I was completely caught up in the moment. I loved Dick. I really did. But at the moment, I felt closer to Ike. This was not a time for love, I felt. We all had a mission that was far more important than our personal lives and desires.

This knowledge was something that the General and I shared. His own family was far away. He rarely mentioned them. This was not through lack of caring. It was simply that we were in another world. And one could not share it with outsiders. The war was an irresistible catalyst. It overwhelmed everything, forced relationships like a hothouse so that in a matter of days one would achieve a closeness with someone that would have taken months to develop in peacetime.

Our nightly bridge games did a lot to bring Ike and me together. We had an almost telepathic relationship. From the very beginning we played well together, and we soon became so attuned to each other's thinking that we were a very effective team. I had never experienced such intuitive communication with anyone. Being bridge partners helped us transcend the boss-and-chauffeur relationship. One morning driving into London, I remarked on how uncannily we seemed to be able to read each other's minds at the bridge table. "That's strange," Ike said. "I was thinking the same thing. You know, even if you hadn't ruled out postmortems after a game, I doubt if we would ever have had any problems. We never disagree."

He was right. I could not imagine us disagreeing. The discovery that there was someone who could share my thoughts and feelings made me feel secure, just the way one feels crawling apprehensively into bed on a cold, damp night—only to discover that someone has tucked a couple of hot-water bottles between the sheets. You immediately relax and bask in the unexpected warmth.

By this time we had traveled deep into that invisible tunnel that separated us from others. Other people's ways, other people's lives were different from ours. We had a job to do. A crusade to make. And we were already very close to each other.

10

Four buzzes. That was my signal. The secretary was one buzz, Tex two and Butch three.

"Sit down," said Ike. "I've been meaning to talk to you."

Meaning to talk to me, I thought. What else has he been doing every day? What else was he doing on the way to work this morning? We'd reached Grosvenor Square only half an hour earlier. It must be something unpleasant. I rather suspected he was going to tell me that I would be transferred back to the motor pool when he left for North Africa. He had never followed up on that earlier hint that I might be going along.

"You know we'll be packing up and leaving for North Africa one of these days," he said. There was a pause. He put his hands on the desk and leaned forward a bit. "Kay, would you like to come along?"

I was practically jumping up and down in my chair. I wanted to go along. Badly. I would have felt simply terrible if I were left behind—although I would have understood.

"I'd give anything to go," I said.

"It's settled, then." He slapped his hands on the desk and leaned back. "You'll be following us. It will probably be a month or so before the situation is stabilized. And Kay, you don't have to be told this is top secret. Not one word to anybody."

"No, sir." I stood. "Thank you, sir," I said, "for asking me." I saluted.

"And one other thing," he said.

"Yes, sir?"

"You've got the sloppiest salute in the whole Army."

I laughed. "But General, you forget. I'm a civilian."

And I was. The uniform did not mean a thing. And that added to the red tape, because I had to have a passport to go to North Africa and passports were not being given out freely in those days. Tex finally pulled all the right strings and I got one, good "for one journey only." From that time on, I felt as if there were clouds under my feet instead of pavements or a gas pedal.

There was still the here and now to cope with, including the business of throwing the press off the scent of the coming invasion of North Africa. We indulged in all sorts of subterfuges. I kept an old guide to Finland on my desk. Butch tacked a huge map of Norway on his wall. When a journalist would look at it questioningly, Butch would lean back, puff on his cigar and say, "Great country, Norway. I understand they have some of the best fishing in the world." I don't know if Butch ever convinced anyone that our first thrust would be to the north, but he had a great time trying.

The real business of headquarters proceeded at its usual grueling pace. The General, who had tried to visit every military installation in Britain, scheduled one last inspection tour before taking off for Gibraltar and North Africa: an expedition to Scotland, where the First Division was practicing disembarking and storming the beaches, capturing "enemy" positions and grouping inland prior to embarking for North Africa.

We went up to Scotland in the General's private railroad car, *Bayonet*. It was quite elegant, paneled in teak, with a little sitting room, a private office for the General and sleeping quarters. Ike and I settled down in the office to catch up with some paperwork, and then we spent the rest of the day playing bridge and napping. Midnight found us deep in Scotland—and it was Scotland at its most typical. Abominable. It was not only cold but wet, not only wet but windy. And it was dark, dark, dark. A car was waiting. I drove as close to where the practice landings were being made as I could; then the General and Butch would get out in the rain and tramp across fields, down cart tracks and onto the rugged beaches to talk to the men and the officers. Ike not only wanted to show himself and demonstrate his concern for American soldiers; he also wanted to brief himself on the level of competence of these troops, most of whom had never taken part in any military action in their lives. He would stay at each position for half an hour or so, then plod back to the car, and we would go on to the next maneuvers area.

The driving was sheer hell. Not only were blackout conditions rigidly observed, but on those rural Scottish roads there were no white lines painted in the center. In London, blackout driving was feasible because except in the densest fog one could follow the white line. Here I could see nothing. I pushed ahead, daring to go only ten or twelve miles an hour, not even that. Ike was impatient at my snail's pace, but there was nothing else for it. Finally, the somber gray dawn found us in Inveraray at Admiralty House, where we were given breakfast.

The General was disturbed by the lack of experience and leadership that he had observed during the night. "They'll be sitting ducks if they don't sharpen up," he said. It was a very weary and worried man who got back on the train at midday. We were all tired. Five minutes after *Bayonet* was under way, we were all stretched out on bunks, where we stayed until we pulled into London. We were a sad-looking group. Ike had a cold. Butch had a cold. Mickey had a cold. And I felt absolutely terrible.

It was a time when a million little things—and a number of big things—seemed to be going wrong. Everything became much worse when Ike's fantastically competent and hard-working chief of staff, Beetle Smith, fell ill. An old ulcer kicked up, and he looked like a ghost, he was so pale. He looked so awful, in fact, that one night when Ike and Beetle had dinner with the P.M. Churchill took Ike aside and told him that he thought Beetle was going to die on his feet, right then and there. Ike immediately ordered Beetle to bed and then ordered Butch to find a nurse for him. Butch found the most beautiful nurse in the whole European Theater, Ethel Westermann. She looked like a Madonna, with big dark eyes and lovely skin. She was not only gorgeous, she was bright and funny—and an excellent bridge player. We soon were seeing as much of Ethel as we did of Beetle.

The pressures were getting to Ike. He was impatient, tired and nervous, his temper at the ready. Butch reported that the Boss was not sleeping—not even at the cottage, where it was usually easy for him to relax. The General was worried about himself. "I've got to get in shape," he kept saying, "before North Africa." But he was drinking more coffee, smoking more cigarettes and getting less sleep than ever. He could not stay still for a moment. And when he did, his fingers would be tapping on the table.

One afternoon Butch got him to leave early to play a little golf, but that did not help much. Ike walked into the house and said, "I've had it. Butch just beat me. That duffer beat me." They had played the thirteenth hole and Butch had taken eleven strokes, the General sixteen.

"Oh, that's bad," I said sympathetically.

"Let me tell you something," he snapped. "That's not bad. That's disastrous." It was the kind of incident that he would have laughed about normally, but now it got under his skin.

Finally it was time. Everything that we had been working toward since the first of July was ready. This was it. It was hard to realize that one phase was over and another beginning. We had a final dinner at Telegraph Cottage, just family and friends. The eve of battle is an eerie time. There were a few toasts drunk to a successful operation, but no one felt like talking. We did not even play bridge, but simply sat around the living room making remarks now and then, almost like courteous strangers in a waiting room.

Butch turned on the radio, and my mood brightened immediately. A whole string of Noël Coward songs was being broadcast, including my very favorite, "I'll See You Again."

"Oh, I love that song," I said.

"It's pretty," Ike agreed.

"Pretty!" I exclaimed. "It is the most romantic song in the world." I had seen *Bittersweet* the season it opened, and that song had been the hit. All London used to hum it, dance to it, sing it.

"What's *your* favorite song?" I asked Ike.

Butch answered for him: "The Beer Barrel Polka."

"Not at all," Ike said indignantly. "My favorite's the one I hum all the time, 'One Dozen Roses' "—and he started singing it.

"It's nice," I said, "but it's not as romantic as mine." And I started singing "I'll See You Again." And that was the way the evening ended. We sat around and sang a few songs and then said good night.

The next evening, after a day crammed with conferences and last-minute paperwork, Ike came out of his office and said, "Well, let's go." I drove him, General Clark and Butch to the out-of-the-way railroad spur where *Bayonet* was waiting to take them to Bournemouth. From Bournemouth they would fly to Gibraltar in the General's B-17.

"Well, Sunday's the day," Ike said.

"Good luck. And please take care of yourself." I meant it. I had grown tremendously attached to this man.

"Don't worry. It's going to be all right. I'll be seeing you soon. Take care of the little fellow." He gave Telek one last scratch under the chin and boarded *Bayonet*. I stood there waving, Telek in my arms, as the train chugged out of the freight spur and disappeared.

Forty-eight hours after General Eisenhower arrived in Gibraltar, the invasion was on. It had been scheduled for one o'clock in the morning of Sunday, November 8. And it went according to schedule. I spent all that night and the next day wrapped around my radio. It was so exciting that I could not sleep. There was a message from President Roosevelt, then a proclamation by General Eisenhower (but in such beautiful French that I knew it was not the General speaking), the stirring strains of the "Marseillaise" and reports of the assault on the beaches. The invasion was on. The Torch had been lit.

I can't say that I felt triumphant or relieved. Mostly I felt worried. What about Ike? Was everything going according to the plans he had made? According to his hopes? When would he join the troops in North Africa? I also felt sorry for myself. I wanted to be there too, sharing the danger.

11

Now it was my turn. The departure date had been set and I was packing for North Africa; in truth, I thought of it more as packing for the rest of my life. I had heard from Dick. He had been in the North African invasion. He was fine, he wrote, and was temporarily stationed in Oran. And there was good news: he had received word that his divorce had gone through. "It's signed, sealed and delivered," he wrote. My own divorce would be granted in a couple of months, and then we would be free to marry. Dick, of course, had no idea that I was going to Algiers. It would have been breaking security for me to tell him.

I was lightheartedly packing for the future in two Vuitton cases that had been part of my mother's trousseau. She had given them to me years ago when I went on my European tour. They were terribly elegant, with gleaming brass corners and locks that I polished just as carefully as I polished the buckle on my Sam Browne belt. I could never afford such luggage today.

Two cases were more than enough. It was wartime, and my trousseau was nothing like the one I had accumulated for my first marriage; in fact, it was practically nonexistent. Before I married Gordon, I had spent weeks shopping. I had bought nightgowns that were all lace and froth, and the most romantic, crazily impractical negligees I could find. One was white velvet trimmed with marabou, if you can imagine; another was of the palest green silk chiffon, so light that it floated behind me as I walked. My wartime trousseau was a bit different. An old blue flannel robe with white piping was the closest thing to a negligee, but there was a bit of luxury all the same. My old friends in the workroom at Worth had hand-stitched me a gorgeous wedding present: two satin nightgowns and three sets of marvelous silk crepe de chine undies. I cannot convey how creamily smooth good silk satin used to be. It seemed to melt on the body. There is nothing like it today. As I was tucking sachets scented with Je Reviens into the silken folds, I could not resist. I stripped and slipped into one of the nightgowns. It was breathtaking. It could have been an evening gown. It slithered down to my ankles, outlining my body in what I considered a very seductive way. I took out the two barrettes that held my hair back and brushed my hair until it was loose and bouncy, just touching my shoulders, and admired myself in the mirror. I have to smile—sadly—when I think of myself posturing in front of the mirror in that fantastic gown, smoothing the creamy satin down over my hips and twisting about. Smiling into the mirror, pretending I was smiling at my lover. Flirting. Turning my head. Lifting my chin.

Suddenly I was embarrassed at such nonsense. I was no tremulous virgin, but a woman about to enter into her second marriage. I should have acquired a certain sophistication. But the truth was that I had not. I was still a harum-scarum Irish girl. Forget my London gloss. Forget those years of modeling at Worth. I was still Kathleen in her corduroy bloomers with a runny nose and chilblains—finding it hard to believe that I was really the glamorous woman posing in the mirror.

I took off my satin nightgown, folded it in tissue paper with a perfumed sachet and got back into the old sweater and tweed skirt that I wore around my flat. Wisdom comes with age, they say. God knows if it is really true, but one thing I do know now is that one should always indulge those foolish fancies. If I had not had those romantic, slightly ridiculous moments in front of the mirror, I would never have enjoyed the silken luxury of my capsule trousseau stitched by loving—and very skilled—fingers. One has to savor every moment. But I did not know that then. I just thought that I was a terrible idiot to carry on that way.

I packed my few bits and pieces of jewelry. The pearl necklace that had been my sixteenth-birthday present. A pair of diamond earrings my grandmother had left me. A few gold bangles. I packed dozens of snapshots of my family. I packed my new summer uniforms and all my woolies. I was very proud of my store of woolen underwear, odd as that may seem today. For the last three years, every English house and office had been freezing cold in winter, since there was practically no fuel available. Most women wore woolies a good nine months of the year. I wore what they called combinations: knee-length pants and a vest—an undershirt with shoulder straps and a scoop neck. When I joined the Motor Transport Corps, I had refused to buy the regulation underpinnings. They could not have been uglier —a seasick green—or scratchier. I rushed out instead and bought half a dozen combinations in lacy blue wool with pink ribbons and another half dozen in pink with blue ribbons. When you get up day after day and month after month and put on the same uniform every blessed morning, it is a great morale booster to know that you have something on underneath which is pretty and soft and feminine. I knew that Algiers was not all sunshine and orange blossoms. At headquarters we were hearing a lot about the raw climate and the mud.

Mummy dropped by that afternoon. "Oh, you're packing," says she. "Yes," says I. And we hugged each other and cried a bit. Nothing more was said. She had been a soldier's wife and knew better than to ask questions.

It was only a matter of hours now. I was packed and ready. I had been desperately lonely in London these last few weeks; although I had a lot of friends and had gone out almost every night to talk and drink and dance until dawn, I was not in the mood to be part of the gaiety as I might have been a year earlier. I missed Dick. I missed the General and Butch. I missed being part of things—and I missed Telek. It had been decided at the last moment that a dog had no place on a crowded troopship and that there might be some unpleasant publicity, so Telek had been flown to Gibraltar, where Mickey took care of him in Ike's subterranean headquarters deep under the Rock of Gibraltar, and now he was in Algiers.

The next day I boarded a troop train for the overnight trip to Scotland. It was a far cry from the luxurious journey in *Bayonet*, with Mickey there to take care of our every need; but when we arrived at Greenock on the Clyde the next morning, it was the same Scottish weather—gray, cold, rainy—that had met us on the first trip. We were queued up for hours in the drizzle waiting our turn for the tender that chugged back and forth between the dock and the ship—the *Strathallen*, a hideous tub that had been converted to a troopship—at anchor in the harbor.

Life aboard ship was so awful that it was funny. Fortunately, two good friends were sharing the cabin with me: Ethel Westermann, the nurse, and Jean Dixon, an American. When the three of us crowded into the cabin with our baggage, it was like fitting sardines into a can. The first morning when we tried to get dressed, it was something straight out of a Marx Brothers comedy. Three women trying to put on stockings. Six legs waving in the air.

No sooner had we squeezed ourselves into the cabin than the alarm sounded for lifeboat drill. The commander wanted us to get used to the procedure before we hit the rolling troughs of the December Atlantic. The next thing we were instructed to do was prepare our torpedo bags. This became a nightly, before-bed chore. These musette bags were to be filled with essentials— official papers, medications, warm clothing, et cetera—just in case. The three of us were rather frivolous, however, when it came to packing our torpedo bags. I for one would not dream of abandoning ship without such necessities as my nylons, my grandmother's diamond earrings or my little silken trousseau. Those were my essentials, along with a few cosmetics and a clean shirt.

It was strange traveling in convoy. As we steamed away from Scotland, two ships accompanied us, but later as we plowed through the stormy gray Atlantic, other ships loomed up out of the fog and took their positions. There were ten or twelve, I believe, when the convoy was complete. The *Strathallen* was the only ship with women aboard. There were WACs, nurses and a few civilians like me. On our first day out, Ethel and I discovered to our great joy that Margaret Bourke-White, the famous *Life* magazine photographer, was on board. Peg had taken pictures of the General and the headquarters staff just a few months before, and we had liked each other. The four of us turned the voyage into one continuous bridge game. There was really very little else to do—eat, sleep, gossip or play bridge. Besides queuing, that is. Queuing was the principal shipboard activity. It was so crowded that there were three sittings for each meal and we had to line up for them. We also had to line up for the toilets.

It was a very rough trip, but there came a night when the winds died down, the ship stopped rocking and we all ran on deck to get some fresh air. Then we heard a cry: "Lights!" And there were. In the distance was something I had not seen for years: the starry lights of a city spread out along the coast like clusters of diamonds. After three years of blackout, this was something to exclaim over. Lights! There were still places in the world where the lights had not been pinched out.

It was dawn when we realized what it meant to be in the Mediterranean. The sun came up rosy and bright. The sky was blue. The sea was blue. It was intoxicating. And very rough. German submarines had been reported in the area, and the *Strathallen*, like its sister ships in the convoy, dropped a succession of depth charges, which frothed up the blue seas like a giant bubble bath. But after the winter gales we had been through, bouncing about in the sunshine seemed a minor irritation. In twenty-four hours we would be landing.

All that night there were last-night parties. In our joy at the prospect of landing, we forgot the crowding, the petty gossip, the discomfort and the dreary boredom of life on a troopship. It was close to one-thirty when we got back to the cabin, which looked almost shipshape for once. Before starting our round of partying, we had prepared for the morning. I had unpacked my torpedo bag for the last time and carefully tucked my treasures back into the Vuitton cases. All that had to be done was get some sleep. We would start disembarking at dawn.

I perched on the edge of the bunk, kicked off my shoes, loosened my tie and was about to start polishing my shoes and buttons for the morning when a tremendous explosion threw me off the bunk. Ethel and Jean had fallen on the floor too. Then the lights flickered and went out. The ship was shivering as if it had a monstrous chill and then began rocking ominously back and forth. "This is it," Ethel said. "Let's get going."

I can't die now, I thought, and grabbed my shoes, my life preserver and my handbag. Ethel and I followed Jean, who had a flashlight, to our lifeboat station. We had done this drill every day, every single day, three times a day, and it had become second nature, just as it had become second nature to wear one's life preserver everywhere, even to the loo. We clambered into our lifeboat, I still clutching my shoes.

Everyone in our boat started leaning over the edge looking down. "Don't do that!" I shouted. "Sit still in the middle, goddamnit, or we'll all drown!" It was pure Eisenhower language—and it worked. I can still hear myself shouting, "Goddamnit, sit still!" But someone had to. The crew, mostly lascars, did not know what to do. And I had been in boats all my life. The boat was lowered safely over the side, and there we were—adrift in the moonlight on the Mediterranean. Not as romantic as it sounds. Not romantic at all when the sea around you is filled with soldiers and nurses swimming about trying to find something to hang on to. Not every group had been as fortunate as we had. Several lifeboats had capsized. We pulled a good number of people into our boat, and Ethel went straight to work. Several had broken legs or arms. The boat was bobbing madly about as depth charges exploded far below. We could see the convoy silhouetted against the sky, our sister ships steaming past, seemingly aloof and uncaring. I felt very much alone. The *Strathallen* was in the distance now, settling lower and lower into the water.

Very soon, I thought, it's all going to be at the bottom of the sea. My little trousseau, the precious diamond earrings, the snapshots of my family. A British destroyer came up, and a megaphone voice told us that we would all be picked up in the morning. It was too chancy to try rescuing us at the moment because there was a pack of German submarines in the area. The sun eventually rose and helped dry us off and raise our spirits. Peg immediately went to work photographing the survivors and the other lifeboats surrounding us. Two cameras slung about her neck and a bag of film over her shoulder, Peg was oblivious of everything except her work. Many months later I saw one of her photographs. It brought the whole experience back very vividly. We were all sitting there, handkerchiefs over our heads as protection from the sun.

The destroyer steamed back in midmorning and started picking us up. Climbing that rope ladder and finally feeling a solid deck under my feet—well, it was then that I realized how terrified I had been. I began to cry, but I stopped immediately when I realized I had nothing to blow my nose on. The handkerchief that I had used to cover my head had disappeared in the scramble up the ladder.

They landed us at Oran. We had been so trim, so pressed and polished, during the trip out; now we were waifs. My stockings were in tatters. My shoes were an utter disaster. My hair was hanging down. Fortunately, I had a lipstick and comb. They helped a bit. I decided the thing to do was report to headquarters in Oran. Ethel went along with me. One thought was going through my head: Dick was in Oran—or he had been when he wrote me. Wouldn't it be wonderful if . . . ? When we got to headquarters, I went in and asked for Lieutenant Colonel (he had had a promotion) Arnold. The guard looked at me rather oddly, then admitted that there was such an officer there and agreed to call him for me.

I stood and waited. And waited. The soldiers looked at me as if I were very peculiar. I could understand why. My uniform skirt was stained from the salt water and terribly wrinkled. My shirt was torn. I had thrown away my stockings. And my hair was a mess. Suddenly I realized that my first order of business was to let the General know that Ethel and I were safe. I asked the guard if I could telephone Algiers. He looked uncomfortable and called a lieutenant, who came out to take a look at me. The lieutenant called a major, who also took a look. And the major summoned a colonel. By that time I was fed up with being treated like some strange exhibit in the zoo. My Irish temper was up.

"Look here," I told the colonel. "I was on the *Strathallen*, the troopship that was torpedoed last night. I am a member of General Eisenhower's personal staff. I want to call him and tell him we're safe. I want to get his orders as to what to do next." I was blazing with fury, clipping my words as if they were machine-gun bullets. But it was not my anger that got results; it was Eisenhower's name. Suddenly I was ushered into an office. Suddenly coffee was being offered. Suddenly I was shown a washstand where I could tidy up. Suddenly the operator announced that she had Algiers on the line. And suddenly there was dear, dull Tex's voice booming over the phone as if he were in the next room.

"Tex," I said, "we're here." It was a bit inadequate, I suppose, but it was all I could get out.

"Oh, that's great," he shouted. "We heard about the *Strathal-*

len. We have all been worried sick. I'm going to put you on to the General. He wants to talk to you."

The next voice was Ike's. "Thank God you're safe," he said. "Are you all right?" I told him I was fine, although a trifle out of uniform. "Great," he said. "Now you tell headquarters to find a place for you to spend the night and I'll send a plane for you and Ethel tomorrow."

I felt a lot better when I hung up the phone. Just hearing Ike's voice was comforting.

12

WHEN I turned, there was a tall, dark-haired lieutenant colonel standing in the doorway looking at me as if I were some apparition.

"It's me, Dick!" I cried. "I'm here! I've been torpedoed!"

He almost fell over. He was in such a state of shock that I will never forget it. Absolutely stunned. He had not the least idea that I was coming to North Africa. Now, seeing me this way, my hair in tangles and my clothes in tatters—well, it was hardly what he had expected when the guard had summoned him, saying merely that he had a visitor.

"Kay!" In one step he was beside me and I was in his arms. He held me so close it hurt, but it felt good. Even those brass buttons sticking into me. After a minute he held me away, took a long look at me and said, "Good God! Are you really all right?"

"I'd be all right if I had something to eat," I said, feeling rather faint suddenly. I had not had anything to eat for what seemed like a very long time.

"Wait here," Dick ordered, and I sat obediently while he loped down the hall. He was back in seconds with a chocolate bar—one of those wonderful American bars with nuts.

"I have to find a place to stay tonight," I said between bites.

"What do you mean? You're staying with me. You need

someone to take care of you." In no time at all I was soaking in a hot bath in the apartment Dick was sharing with another officer. When I got out, all scrubbed and shampooed, there was a strange wardrobe laid out on the bed: a T shirt, a pair of Dick's pajamas, some socks. Everything miles too big. I rolled up the sleeves and pant legs and made do.

"You look like a refugee from a Charlie Chaplin movie," he said when I emerged in my makeshift outfit. No matter how I looked, I felt marvelous. Clean and dry and terribly, terribly hungry. Dick rummaged around to provide a meal: rations, some cheese his mother had sent him and a bottle of local red wine. It was delicious. I do believe, though, that even my water-sodden shoes would have tasted good.

Then we talked. And talked. And talked. That is, I talked. I had so much to tell him. How the General had asked me if I wanted to go to Algiers, how I hoped we might be able to get married in North Africa, how I had packed my little trousseau and how it had gone to the bottom of the sea. He let me talk myself out, and whenever I paused for breath, he would say that he could not believe I was there. He just could not believe it.

I was with Dick. I was safe. I was well fed—and well wined. It was all I could ask for, except just possibly a few hours' sleep. It was agony to keep my eyes open, but I fought to stay awake. This was just about the longest time I had ever spent with Dick. Our time together had always been terribly limited. I saw more of the General in most weeks than I had seen of Dick in all the time I had known him. I yawned. I couldn't help it. Dick picked me up and tucked me into his bed. "Go to sleep, precious. I'll be in the next room if you want anything."

When I woke up, I found a note from Dick and a musette bag on the bedside table. The General's plane had arrived and I was to leave for Algiers at noon, Dick wrote. He would be back to drive me to the plane—and the musette bag held some things I might need.

Sitting up in bed, I dug into the bag and discovered a treasure trove. A toothbrush. And toothpaste. Two handkerchiefs. A uniform tie. Cold cream. A cake of soap. A nail file. It was one of those times when one could say, "Just what I wanted" and mean it. When Dick arrived to pick me up, I was back in uniform—what was left of it. The only thing that looked decent was my new tie.

I hated to leave, but the General's B-17 was waiting. There were tears in my eyes when the plane took off. On the way to the airfield, Dick had told me he was doing everything he could to get transferred to the front. He wanted a regimental command. This terrified me, but naturally I did not say so. What could I do? Dick was a career man, a West Pointer, doing what he had been trained to do, and war was the big proving ground. It did not occur to me for one moment to protest.

That afternoon I walked into headquarters in Algiers. The General's office was in the St.-Georges Hotel, one of the oldest and most elegant hotels in North Africa—or so I was informed; the elegance had to be taken on faith. The sprawling structure was cold and dreary. The bright mosaics of the lobby floor were hidden under the mud that everyone tracked in. In Algiers, I soon discovered, it was either mud or dust.

I reported to Tex, who told me that the General and Butch had left for the front that morning to spend Christmas with the troops, so there was really nothing for me to do. "Why don't you do some shopping?" Tex suggested. "You look a mite untidy. I'll get some ration coupons for you and Ethel."

My billet was about five minutes away from the St.-Georges in what appeared to be a very large, gleaming white villa set in spacious grounds. What it was—and I laughed when I saw the name on the entrance—was a maternity hospital, the Clinique Glycine. It was a pretty place. Glycine means wisteria, and there were great vines of it everywhere. The quarters were what one might expect—white, bare, utilitarian—but for the moment it was heaven.

Within a few days, at Ike's suggestion, I was to move to a

small house shared by five WAC officers* whom I had known in London. We called ourselves the Powerhouse, because we all worked for top brass. These women became my very close friends, and from then on we shared living quarters throughout the war—in London, in France and in Germany.

After a good night's sleep, Ethel, who was also billeted in the Clinique Glycine, and I set off on a shopping spree. It was not much of a spree. The Germans had occupied Algiers and left nothing behind. The cupboards were bare.

In one shop we thought for a moment that we had struck it rich. The proprietress assured us that she had some *magnifique* brassieres. And indeed they were. They were for a woman with a *poitrine magnifique,* someone along the lines of a super Jane Russell. Neither of us filled the bill—or the cup. Finally we found a boutique with some stock—enough so that we could buy two pairs of panties and two bras apiece. But such underpinnings! They had obviously been designed for ladies of a certain calling. Ethel and I giggled when we saw them and asked to see something else, but when the very charming saleswoman told us that there was nothing else, we did not hesitate for a moment. We bought. The panties were black mesh with a satin vine leaf strategically placed. The brassieres, also black, were cut out at the nipples. Ethel whispered, "How did they know we were at the Clinique Glycine?" I assure you, however, that these were not for nursing mothers.

I seem to be dwelling at quite some length on the matter of underwear, but there are times when it is very important. To finish with the subject once and for all, I would say that of all

---

* One was Ruth Briggs from Rhode Island, a witty, brilliant woman and a superb bridge player, so good that when Ike returned to Europe after the war to head SHAPE, he would send a plane to wherever Ruth was stationed to bring her to Paris for an evening of bridge. Once she was flown in from Turkey, she told me. Mattie Pinette, Ike's secretary-stenographer, was from Maine and a very pleasant, bright woman with whom I worked closely. Then there was Martha Rogers, a beauty from Mississippi, Louise Anderson from Colorado and Alene Drexel from Minnesota.

Kay Summersby as a member of Britain's Motor Transport Corps, 1941.

Major Dwight D. Eisenhower, shortly before World War II. **U.S. ARMY**

The General's Driver

Kay adjusts the flag of Eisenhower's car. UPI

The General speaks his mind to Kay in an unguarded moment!

BLACK STAR

The Supreme Commander

Ike strolls with King George VI of England, who neglected to greet his loyal subject Kay Summersby. **U.S. ARMY**

Ike and his Commander in Chief, Franklin D. Roosevelt, who took Kay on the most thrilling picnic of her life.

U.S. ARMY

Ike in conversation with Field Marshal Sir Bernard Montgomery—the one person who could always provoke his wrath, and whom Kay described as "a pain in the neck." U.S. ARMY

Ike and Prime Minister Churchill, who always ordered Ike to bring Kay to dinner with him at Number 10 Downing Street, and whose table manners surprised Kay considerably. WIDE WORLD

On the left, Eisenhower at work, U.S. ARMY; above, Kay at her desk, with Telek.

North Africa, 1942–1943

Kay at the wheel of Ike's car, Ike in the rear for formal purposes —he preferred to sit beside her in the front seat.   U.S. ARMY

my torpedoed treasures, I probably missed my woolies the most. Algiers was hellishly cold and damp most of the winter. I was able eventually to get replacements from the States—delivered courtesy of a very high-ranking officer. He would have been more than disconcerted, I suspect, if he had known that the package he dropped off at General Eisenhower's office contained half a dozen snuggies with matching vests—in blue.

Headquarters, when I came back from shopping, was all doom and gloom. Admiral Darlan had just been assassinated. I no longer remember all the ins and outs of the Darlan affair, but its political repercussions had been enormous. The General had appointed the Admiral head of the French military forces in North Africa. Although Darlan had been a German sympathizer, even a collaborator, the General had thought him the best choice under the circumstances. It was a choice, however, for which he was bitterly criticized by many people. Now Darlan was dead, shot by a young Algerian, and even more problems loomed. Ike was rushing back from the front.

When the General arrived at the office late the next day after something like thirty hours of nonstop driving through rain and sleet, his face wore that familiar gray pall of exhaustion. He was in a dismal state of mind. At the front he had seen for himself that mud was as brutal an enemy as the Germans. Torrential rains had turned the ground everywhere into mud, immobilizing the big tanks and even the jeeps so that attack was impossible. Now he had this Darlan affair to handle.

Only the inner circle was allowed to see how depressed he really was. To the rest of the world, he was his usual brisk, charming and confident self—just a bit weary, that was all. Now that he was back, headquarters seemed to become electric. Cables were coded and shot off to Washington and London. The switchboards were constantly lit up. Memos were dictated and rushed to various commanding officers, both British and American. Consultations were set up. It was the same frantic pace I had become accustomed to at Grosvenor Square.

Along about eight or nine, Ike slapped his hands on his desk and said, "Well, I've done all I can do here. Kay, get the car."

"Where is it?" I asked.

That did it. He leaned back in his chair and laughed. "My God, welcome home, Kay. It seemed so natural to have you here and I had so much on my mind that I forgot you just arrived. Let me take a look at you."

He stood up, put his hands on my shoulders and turned me around. "Well, no damage that I can see. You're here. And you're safe. When the news came through that the *Strathallen* had been hit, well, I don't mind telling you I never did get to sleep that night.

"Now, let's forget this mess for a few hours. Even a general is allowed to celebrate Christmas."

Christmas! I had not realized what day it was. "Merry Christmas," I said, and the two of us walked out of the St.-Georges. Ike wished all the guards a Merry Christmas and he returned their salutes. He seemed to have cast off his fatigue.

"Come on, Beetle is holding dinner for us," he said. "He's having a real American Christmas dinner—roast turkey and the fixings. Georgie Patton sent him two live turkeys. God only knows where he liberated them."

Suddenly Ike was in great spirits. Five minutes later, we walked into Beetle's villa and Ike started caroling, "God rest ye merry, gentlemen, let nothing you dismay. . . ." Everyone was there, and we all hugged and kissed each other. It was great to see them again. Beetle's villa was gorgeous—practically a palace, with gardens and terraces and two vast drawing rooms. Some of the floors were covered with mosiacs of intricate design. There were lots of Oriental rugs and paintings.

Christmas dinner was just as it should have been: turkey and plum pudding and champagne. Beetle was a marvelous host. He was really at his best on occasions like this. At headquarters he was often a cold curmudgeon. He had to be. He was the Boss's other self. While Ike exerted his charms, Beetle played the role of villain—tough, obsessed with his job, driving others to the same point of exhaustion that he drove himself to. But at Telegraph Cottage and now here in his own villa in Algiers, the real Beetle was allowed to surface—witty, thoughtful, kind and with as much charm as Ike.

It was like being home again after all those weeks. Tex was there. Butch was there. Ethel was there. And best of all, the General was there. We talked a mile a minute, busy trying to catch up with all that had happened. Ethel and I described how it felt to be torpedoed, and we heard how Ike had caught a terrible cold in Gibraltar because his headquarters, deep inside the Rock, was cold and damp. "The walls dripped so that there were puddles everywhere," Butch said.

And that brought us to the subject of Telek. "You should see that scamp," Ike said. "He's not housebroken yet."

"Not housebroken yet!" I yelped. "He was perfectly trained when he went off with Mickey. Well, almost perfectly. You just haven't been paying attention to him."

Ike defended himself. "I've had a couple of other things on my mind, you know."

I felt like an idiot. I had not really expected the Boss, who had a war on his hands, to concern himself with the walking of a very small black Scottie. I apologized. Ike laughed. "Don't worry. Now that you're here, Telek will straighten out."

"I'm dying to see your house," I told Ike. "Is it as splendid as this one of Beetle's?"

"God, no!" he said. "But it's still too splendid for my taste. You will see it tomorrow. You'll be over for breakfast, won't you?"

It all felt so right, so natural. "Yes, thanks. I'll be over for breakfast," I said happily. I was back where I belonged.

13

LIFE in Algiers was not too much different from life in London. It was only the landscape that was different, and at that we still had those familiar barrage balloons dotting the sky. The weather was much like that of a late December or January in London—raw, gray, rainy—although there were occasional bright blue Mediterranean days when the breezes were deceptively balmy. Headquarters routine was almost exactly the same. The General still had to spend much of his time and energy forging a unified command. He was still inundated with paperwork. He still made constant inspection tours—of battlefronts now, rather than training camps. And my job was still the same. The only difference was that in the car's glove compartment I not only kept the usual maps and supply of cigarettes and a Western in case of delays; I also had a bottle of paregoric—the panacea for Algerian tummy.

But the first morning I drove up the long palm-lined driveway to Villa dar el Ouad, the most modest house in a compound of luxurious villas, it seemed as if I had been transferred to some exotic paradise. The villa was high on a hill above the city. Far below, the Mediterranean stretched sparkling blue to the horizon. There were sentries on the terrace who saluted smartly as I walked in. Unlike the Dorchester or Telegraph Cottage, this residence was heavily guarded. One had to show a pass before being allowed to enter the compound. There were guards patrolling the driveway and the grounds. Anti-aircraft guns were dug in here, there and everywhere.

The moment I walked through the door all this was forgotten as a ball of black fur came rocketing at me, barking furiously and wagging his tail with joy. Telek! He remembered me! Breakfast was a long and happy party that day. Telek sat in my lap and had half my bacon. Moaney and Hunt told me that I had better get cracking and start housebreaking him. I cheerfully scolded everyone, including Mickey, for having spoiled Telek. Ike growled that he would like it if just one morning he could get his coffee the way he liked it. Hot, goddamnit! Butch said all he wanted for breakfast was a bowl of cold aspirin. He had gone out for a second Christmas celebration after we had left Beetle's the night before. It was nearly nine before Ike said, "Well, we better get going. We've got a war to win." I could not have been happier as I drove off with Telek at my side.

By the time I drove the Boss home that evening, I felt as if I had been in Algiers for months. "You're staying for supper tonight," he told me. "We've got a lot of bridge to play." Before supper Butch gave me a tour of the villa. Villa dar el Ouad, he informed me, meant Villa of the Family. The name was appropriate, I agreed, but the house had no family feeling about it. It lacked the coziness of Telegraph Cottage on the one hand, and on the other it seemed drearily middle class compared with Beetle's beautiful place. When I mentioned this to Butch, he groaned dramatically. "If you only knew," he said. "I had a terrible time getting Ike to go this high. He kept barking at me that he wanted something small and simple. I kept telling him that this was not London. He had to have a place that was compatible with his rank."

Just as we finished dinner, we heard the old familiar air-raid noises. German planes were bombing the harbor. We rushed out to the terrace. It was like some giant fireworks display. Streamers of lights streaking the sky, arcing up at the planes overhead;

monster explosions below. We had snatched up our helmets as we went out, but when the shrapnel started clattering down on the terrace helmets did not seem like much protection, and we retreated inside, where Telek, the wisest of us all, had stayed whimpering under the sofa.

Our retreat was only as far as the bridge table, which had been set up in the small sitting room as close to the fireplace as possible. Ike had the place of honor in front of the fire, and although he complained that his backside was getting roasted, he was obviously glad of the warmth. He was developing another of his colds. Sometimes it seemed as if his colds had colds. The night before at Beetle's, he had been sneezing and complaining of a raw throat. Tonight he was a disaster area. His nose was running and so were his eyes. There were great puffy bags under his eyes. He was obviously feverish. But woe to the person who dared mention his condition or suggest he might be better off in bed with a hot toddy and some aspirin.

Ike detested being ill, and he detested even more having anyone comment on his health. Every once in a while, Butch would take his life in his hands and tell the Boss that he should get some rest. Ike would practically bite his head off. This particular cold turned into the flu, and Ike was really miserable, miserable enough to stay in bed for four days before crawling back to the office, still sick and ashen pale. There was no point in even hinting that he go home. I knew just how he felt—there was so much at stake and he was responsible for all of it.

The North African operation was not going well. In fact, things were very bad. There were defeats—and glum expectations of more defeats. The walls of Ike's office were covered with big maps showing our positions and those of the Germans. Time after time during the past week I had gone into the office to find Ike sitting in his chair in front of the smoky fireplace, the only source of heat in the whole office, a long pointer in his hand, staring at situation maps. Sometimes he would lift the pointer and trace a tentative shift of position, then impatiently tap it on the floor as he dismissed the idea and slump back again in his chair.

"It's bad, Kay," he would say. "We weren't prepared for these rains, this mud." He would fret about the quality of the leadership at the front. "Our officers don't have the experience. Don't know how to handle their men or their weapons." These were not criticisms, just statements of facts. Facts that had to be faced. The British complained that the American soldiers were green— "apple green" was the way one general described them.

On top of that, the Boss was involved in the preparations for the Casablanca Conference. As the "guest list" firmed up, I got very much excited. The P.M. and President Roosevelt would be there. So would General Marshall, Admiral Lord Louis Mountbatten and just about all of the top Western statesmen and military brass (Stalin had sent his regrets). The security arrangements alone were staggering. It was easy to understand why Ike did not want to sit home by the fire with hot lemonade and take care of his health.

I was far more interested in the conferees than I was in the agenda. I have never been politically minded, and in those days I was more than a trifle star dazzled. Working with great men, men whose actions affected people's lives all over the world, has a very seductive glamour about it. The men themselves were very seductive. I don't mean that in a sexual sense, but they would not have had the power they possessed if they did not also possess this magnetism. And the great men I met while working for the General all possessed it. Even untidy, unprepossessing Harry Hopkins, who seemed to be President Roosevelt's unofficial envoy to almost everyone and every place; even cool, aristocratic Mountbatten—and most definitely President Roosevelt and the P.M. They had what people today refer to as charisma—lots of it.

Tex stopped by my desk one morning and said, "The General laughed twice. Guess that means he feels better." Tex adored Ike, but somehow he always managed to rub him the wrong way

—mostly through his eagerness to do a perfect job. His overwhelming preoccupation with detail made him seem officious, but it was the very quality that made him indispensable, if a bit of a pest. Whenever Ike did not feel up to snuff, it was always Tex who got the brunt of it, and he could never understand why. He would have done anything to lighten the Boss's load. But nobody could. There was nothing any of us could do. Ike's blood pressure went up so sharply during this difficult January that we were very much worried. It wavered between 175 and 185. He was working long hours, looked ghastly—and there was absolutely nothing we could do to help him.

His healthy constitution and his determination pulled him through, but the Casablanca Conference did not do much for his state of mind. The war news was bad, and the top leaders, while not criticizing Ike openly, were not praising him either. "The Boss's neck is in the noose. If anything more goes wrong, he's had it," Butch said. But the General's neck was not the chief item on the agenda. Casablanca was the place where President Roosevelt and Prime Minister Churchill agreed that they would accept nothing less than unconditional surrender from the Germans.

There was one participant in the Casablanca Conference who was absolutely wholeheartedly behind Eisenhower, and that was General George Catlett Marshall, Chief of Staff of the United States Army—Ike's boss. He terrified me. He was cold and austere and terribly, terribly formal. He came to visit Ike in Algiers after the conference, and Telek and I immediately got off on the wrong foot with him. I had driven the two men to Ike's villa, where Marshall was going to spend the night. When we arrived, Eisenhower said, "Come on in, Kay. I know you're dying to see Telek." I followed the generals in, and Telek came running. He had just discovered that he had a tail, and his favorite game was to chase it around and around. I soon got the very strong impression that General Marshall was not as charmed by his antics as

Ike and I were, so I disappeared into the little sitting room with Telek while the generals adjourned to the drawing room.

Soon I overheard Ike say, "Let me show you to your room." The two men started up the stairs, and Telek, who never wanted to be left out of any excitement, jumped out of my lap and followed them. Butch told me the rest of the story when he came downstairs, red faced, Telek firmly under his arm.

"You know what this beast just did?"

I lifted my eyebrows.

"He peed on the General's bed."

"I don't believe it," I said.

"He did. Ike was leaning over, pushing down on the mattress to show Marshall how comfortable it was, and Telek jumped up on the bed. He went right there on the spread, and then before I could grab him, he trotted up to the head of the bed and lifted his leg on the pillow."

"Oh, my dear God!" I said. "What did Ike say?"

"'Get that goddamned dog out of here'—that's what he said."

Telek was in deep disgrace for a few days. I took him home with me and did not allow him to show his nose at the villa until General Marshall was safely out of Algiers.

I don't know whether this incident had anything to do with it, but I always had the distinct impression that General Marshall would have been just as happy if I did not exist. He always shook hands when we met, but there was never any indication that he saw me as a person. Certainly he never addressed a personal word to me. This was not at all out of character. He was the only person I ever knew who worked closely with the General and never, ever, once called him Ike. It was always General Eisenhower. I thought Marshall was a cold fish.

Butch insisted that I did him an injustice, that while Marshall had a stiff exterior, he was very fond of the Boss. I snorted, but he may have been right. I know that Marshall spent an afternoon with Butch discussing the Boss's health. Marshall did not approve of Ike's regimen. He was working too hard, spending too much time in the office. Four hours a day should be sufficient, according to Marshall. "I'm charging you with seeing that General Eisenhower cuts down," he told Butch.

When Butch told me about this, he said, "How am I going to persuade Ike to work a four-hour day? And how in holy hell am I going to get him to have a daily massage?" That had been another of General Marshall's orders. Butch was really in a funk. "Why don't *you* tell Ike he has to have a massage?" he suggested. I begged off. Eisenhower could not have been more charming and kindly toward us, but he was not the commanding general for nothing. He was tough and he was in charge. No one was going to tell him what to do. Not Butch. And certainly not Kay Summersby.

We decided that the only thing to do was report General Marshall's instructions to the Boss and then see what happened. As it turned out, General Marshall had told Ike himself that he should use a masseur. Butch managed to come up with one and even managed to pin Ike down to a time and place for his first massage—his bedroom at six in the evening. Afterwards, Ike came down to supper saying that it had been very relaxing indeed—but that first massage turned out to be the only one. Somehow he never managed to be able to find the time again. Ike would faithfully carry out any of General Marshall's orders concerning the conduct of the war, but when it came to what he considered "sissy stuff," Ike simply dug his heels in.

He was willing to concede that he needed some exercise to work off his nervous tension. "I need another Telegraph Cottage," he said longingly one night. "Well, that's easy enough," Butch said. And it must have been, because it was only a few days later that we drove ten miles outside the city to inspect the new secret hideaway. This one was a white stucco farmhouse with a red-tiled roof—rather shabby, but quite comfortable, and there were tennis courts and stables on the property. It had its charm, including a view of the sea, and it was private. Butch informed us that it was called Sailor's Delight (I'm inclined to think that the General's naval aide christened it himself).

It was at Sailor's Delight that Ike and I went riding together for the first time. Ike was an excellent horseman. "West Point," he told me when I remarked on it. "I used to ride farm horses bareback when I was a boy in Kansas, but at the Point they taught us to ride like gentlemen."

Butch had arranged for three magnificent Arab stallions to be put at the General's disposal. I had never been on anything like these beasts. They were chestnut in color, with flowing manes, and truly beautiful. The only horses I have ever seen that were more impressive were those ridden by the spahis who guarded General de Gaulle's palace in Algiers. The spahis were mounted on pure white Arab stallions that looked like the horses one sees in a dream. Our horses were practically wild. If we allowed them to touch each other, they would rear and snort and go to it. You had to hit them with your riding crop as hard as you could to get them to obey you. The first time it happened, I was scared to death. My horse was dancing about on his hind legs, and I was not sure that I was strong enough to control him. What if one of those great hooves should strike the General in the head? I finally summoned every bit of strength I had and got the horse into a gallop across the fields. It was a good while before I dared to come up to Ike and his mount again that afternoon.

It was not the best riding country. It was stony underfoot, even in the wooded areas. The Army had cleared the area and there were guards posted—it seemed as if they were behind every bush—so we felt quite safe. We also felt as if we were on parade. There was always a security man riding discreetly behind us, in addition to the sharpshooter guards. It is an eerie feeling, knowing that your every move is being watched. Ike often complained about it, not only while riding, but as it affected every phase of his life.

"I live in a goldfish bowl," he said. "There is never a moment when I don't feel that someone is peering at me." He was right.

Someone always was peering at him. And it had to be that way.

We were a strange couple. Ike was very correctly dressed, and he looked fabulous. I, on the other hand, had a hit-and-miss outfit: jodhpurs that had been sent from the States, Army shoes, a uniform shirt and a kerchief over my hair. We would leave the office in the middle of the afternoon several days a week, drive out to Sailor's Delight, ride for a couple of hours, shower, have a drink and supper and then drive back to Algiers. Once in a while we would spend Saturday night and all day Sunday, doing all the things we had done at Telegraph Cottage. We played bridge, sat outdoors when it was warm enough, knocked a few golf balls around on the grass and practiced target shooting. My little Beretta had gone down with the *Strathallen*, but Ike had got me another, which he insisted I carry with me at all times. I used to sleep with it under my pillow.

While Sailor's Delight was never the real home that Telegraph Cottage had been, it did more for Ike than any number of massages ever could have done.

14

O NE night as I was driving Ike home, there, standing in the drive, was a familiar figure in a familiar costume. Winston Churchill in his siren suit.

"Jesus Christ!" Ike said. "What's he doing here?"

The General jumped out of the car, and after a moment's hesitation I followed. It was hard to know whether to behave as an impersonal driver or as a pleased and surprised acquaintance. Churchill settled that question promptly. He waved his big cigar at me and said, "Well, Kay, I thought I might find you here. How do you like driving on the wrong side of the road?" It turned out that the P.M. had been meeting with President Roosevelt in Turkey and had decided to drop in on Ike on the way home. This was to be the first of many visits from the P.M., who enjoyed what he referred to as "lolling around" in Algiers. He definitely liked the warmth and the sun. Now that the season had changed, it was a far brighter world than that of gray, austerity-ridden London. Churchill and the General were always openly happy to be together, laughing and chatting like two old school chums.

Eisenhower immediately went to work planning a luncheon in the P.M.'s honor. It turned out to be the luncheon of luncheons. As Ike worked out the guest list, he said, "Do you realize, Kay, that almost all my guests will outrank me?" There were the

Prime Minister; General de Gaulle; Sir Alan Brooke, who was Chief of the Imperial General Staff; Admiral Cunningham, who had been named Allied Naval Commander for the Mediterranean, and half a dozen others who boasted more stars and stripes than Ike. The protocol people were in a tizzy trying to work out a seating plan.

I don't know whether it was a result of this luncheon party or not—I suppose it really had nothing to do with it—but just a few days later Ike got his fourth star, the one that made him a full general. That night Ike broke out the champagne and we had an impromptu party just for our headquarters group. He was very, very happy that evening. I'll never forget the sheer pleasure that radiated from him. I remember thinking, There's a man who has never had very much fun in his life. The General was always very charming, always had that grin at the ready, but underneath it all he was a very serious and lonely man who worried, worried, worried. I used to feel that it was a real achievement whenever we were able to divert him so that he forgot his problems for a little while and was able to have fun.

Life in Algiers was not all promotions and parties. Not at all. I learned what life was like at the front. Miserable. My first combat drive was to Constantine, Tebessa and the Kasserine Pass. Things were very bad up there—so bad that just a few days after our visit, we suffered one of the great defeats of the war at the Kasserine Pass. The trek to the front was nothing like our carefree drives through the English countryside en route to a training camp or base. Now we traveled in convoy—a scout car leading, then the General's big car with the flag flying, a weapons carrier, a backup car in case something happened to the General's car and finally a second scout car bringing up the rear. The highway was two lanes wide, and the traffic was remorseless, all of it military. Trucks highballing it up to the front with supplies; more trucks racketing back empty to pick up more supplies. Coping with those trucks on that narrow, potholed highway was an exhausting experience. The drivers were hard-boiled men, and the General's flag meant nothing to them. I was constantly terrified of being forced off the road and either being up to my axles in mud or tilted at a forty-five-degree angle in a ditch.

In addition to the driving problems, there was the everpresent danger of strafing attacks. I said to the General, "If we're strafed, it's every man for himself. I'm going to stop and run as far away from this car as I can. Don't expect me to hold the door for you."

"Fine," said Ike. "Agreed." I looked up in my rearview mirror and I could see the corners of his mouth twitching. It struck me how ridiculous I must have sounded, and I started to laugh. We got into one of those fits of laughter that children sometimes enjoy, when it is next to impossible to stop. There were laughter tears in my eyes by the time we finally sputtered into silence. After that, whenever we set off on one of these trips to the front lines, Ike would say, "Now it's every man for himself. Right?" It was a bit silly, but silliness helps—especially when you are scared to death.

The truck drivers saluted me with whistles, wolf calls and all kinds of interesting proposals, completely uninhibited by the presence of my backseat passenger. This used to make Ike absolutely livid. I assured him that it did not bother me in the least, but he still became very rigid and red when he heard the remarks that were tossed my way from the cabs of the trucks. I felt it was rather flattering, particularly considering that I was no longer the trim, tailored driver I had been in England. Driving in the combat zone, I wore boots, slacks, a man's battle blouse and an old Air Corps flying jacket that I had managed to scrounge. To top it all, I had a steel helmet. Ike used to tease me about trying to look like General Patton.

It took us about twenty-six hours to reach the front. At Tebessa we picked up a scout car to guide us to the command post. Ike went straight on up to the front to see conditions for himself and talk to the men. He always felt that it was very im-

portant for the men to see the commanding general and know
that he did not spend all his time safely behind the lines.

I stayed at the command post. No one paid any attention to
me as I watched and listened. The situation could not have been
worse. There were bad casualties and talk of retreat. As the
hours wore on I realized that they were all concerned about the
General and that no one knew exactly where he was. The battle
lines were fluid and it would have been very easy for his driver
to mistake the enemy's patch of mud for our patch of mud. I decided to get some sleep so that if anything happened, I would be
rested. They put me in the VIP tent, which differed from the
others only in that it had a pebble flooring instead of the usual
wall-to-wall mud. I spread out my sleeping bag on a cot and
wriggled in completely dressed—boots and all. At one point I
woke up and heard the General's voice outside. He was back
safe, then. I heard him tell someone that he wanted to get a couple of hours' sleep before starting back.

"Your driver's in there," someone said. "We'll wake her."

"Jesus Christ, don't do that. Let her sleep," Ike growled. The
next thing I knew, he was in the tent, spreading out his sleeping
bag on another cot. In minutes he was snoring like a one-man ar-
tillery bombardment.

A few hours later we were ready to leave. Ike had on his
heavy cold-weather gear and a wool hat pulled down over his
ears, but he looked pinched with cold. He was very tired and
very depressed. The commanding officer was anxious to get us
out of there. A German breakthrough was expected within
hours. He urged Ike to fly back to Algiers rather than risk driving into a German-occupied zone. Ike refused. We needed all
our aircraft for fighting, he said, not for ferrying generals about.

There was a somewhat amusing sequel to this particular trip.
When we were back in Algiers, Tex said, "I think you ought to
know, Kay, that there's a lot of gossip about you and the Boss.
People are saying that you—uh—uh . . ." He was too embar-

rassed to continue. "That we what?" I asked. "That you, uh—well, that you sleep together when you go on trips."

I stared at him and then burst out laughing. "We did, Tex. We did!" Poor Tex looked completely bewildered until I told him what had happened. Then he shook his head. "Don't worry, Tex. If anyone says anything more, just tell them that I'm engaged to be married and that the General and I are certainly not interested in each other that way. It's ridiculous," I said. At the time I thought it was all very funny.

Sharing the hardships and the dangers of trips like this to the front actually did bring Ike and me closer together, although never as close as gossip would have it. His worries were my worries. Being at the front with him, seeing his utter frustration over losing a battle because of inexperience and weather increased my understanding of the pressures on him—including the pressures he put on himself. And he knew that I understood. He would often look over at me in the course of a conversation and say, "Kay knows what I'm talking about." And I did. I did indeed. I also recognized the emotional and physical toll these trips took of him.

I got my first gray hairs in Algiers, and Ike lost a lot of his hair there. People who think war is glamorous and exciting are people who believe what they see in the cinema. It is not. It is dirty, tiring, frightening. Ask the men who spent that war in the mud. They know. Eisenhower knew. And so did I.

15

My divorce papers were on the way. In one of his typically thoughtful gestures, the General had instructed London that the documents were to be sent to Algiers by diplomatic pouch, which meant that they would arrive in a matter of days rather than weeks. The next time I saw Dick, who had just been promoted to full colonel, I was able to say, "Now you're in for it. I'm a free woman."

"Well, you'll just have to hold your horses," he laughed. "I'm busy right now." He was in Algiers for a few hours on his way to join his regiment. This was the first time I had seen him in months, and Ike had given me the day off. The fields outside Algiers were bright with poppies, and the air was filled with the scent of jasmine. We had a marvelous time at Sailor's Delight, swimming and playing tennis and making plans for the future. It would be a June wedding, we decided—if conditions permitted.

Things could not possibly have turned out any better, I thought. I no longer had to worry about Dick's being at the front. After the disastrous winter, spring had brought a change in Allied fortunes, and for all practical purposes the North African campaign was over. There had even been a victory parade in Tunis. The parade had been a terrible ordeal—hours in the blazing heat and smothering dust. I had thought I would pass out, but there had been one wicked pleasure that had kept me on my feet. General Montgomery was also on the reviewing stand. He deserved every salute that was flung at him. His Eighth Army had fought well. Monty was a shrewd, careful strategist, and his men were tough. But he was also a pain in the neck. Worse—he hated women. He was squirmingly uncomfortable in their company. My very presence on the reviewing stand took the edge off his pleasure. And I was bitchy enough to be glad of it.

Monty was the only person in the whole Allied command whom I disliked. Not only was he a supercilious, woman-hating little martinet, but he did things that used to make me so indignant that I would say to the General, "How can you stand it? Why don't you tell him off?"

Ike would shrug his shoulders. "Don't let him bother you. He just can't help it," he would tell me. I thought he jolly well could help it. He used to do mean, petty things. For example, when the General visited Eighth Army headquarters, Monty would ask him to bring along American cigarettes. He would also try to mooch the very last packet the General had in his pocket. Then Monty, the great nonsmoker who would never allow Ike to smoke in his presence, would distribute the cigarettes to his men, never giving Ike or the Americans any credit. He was a perpetual thorn in Ike's side. That is exactly how the General used to describe him. "He's a thorn in my side," he would say wearily, "a thorn in my side." And he was to become even more infuriating after we left North Africa.

Apart from Monty, everything seemed to be coming up roses. Or orange blossoms. Every day was full of sunshine. Algiers gleamed, and the Mediterranean seemed to dance in the sun. Romance was in the air. Even Telek had been bitten by the love bug and become a husband and father. I was a bit jealous of Telek's romance. Butch had gone to Washington for a few days, and when he returned he had brought a surprise: a wife for Telek. A terrible little bitch, I thought. Her name was Caacie (for Canine Auxiliary Air Corps), pronounced "Khaki," Butch announced. "Stupid," I said. "Any stupider than Telek?" he asked. "Much stupider," I said firmly. But Caacie she was, and Caacie she remained.

Her first act on meeting Telek was to bite him, which did not endear her to me, but she soon accepted him, and he, the idiot, adored her. He was the very kindest of husbands, and she rewarded him with a litter of three of the most adorable jet black puppies I had ever seen. Telek was not one for humdrum domesticity, however. His idea of the good life was to go off to the office every morning with the Boss and me, sleep under my desk during the day and snuggle up to Ike for ear scratching and stomach rubbing when we drove back home again.

Headquarters routine continued at a somewhat less hectic pace, and despite the fact that Ike had started working on the invasion of Sicily in real earnest (the code name of this operation was Husky), there was a bit more time for bridge, for riding, for just sitting in the sun and talking. It was a time to catch one's breath before the next big push. One day I became very much concerned about Ike. He was all tied up in knots about something. As the day wore on, he became terribly withdrawn. I was truly worried when I drove him home from the office and he just sat there, slumped in the back seat. Ike was a master of small talk and always enjoyed chatting when we were going back and forth, but now he was silent. When we reached the villa, he got out heavily like an old man. I was positive that he was ill.

"Kay, come on in," he said, just as he said it every night. We went into the little sitting room. Ike lit a cigarette. I asked him if he would like me to make him a drink. "That would be a good idea," he said. "Make one for yourself, too." I was about ready to beg, "Please, can't you tell me what's the matter?" when he said, "Kay, I am just going to give this to you straight. Dick has been killed."

I looked at him. I heard the words, but they had no impact. Very calmly I asked what had happened. "It was a week ago," he said, "but the news just came through this morning. It got lost at the message center. Dick was with another officer, inspecting a minefield. There was no danger; the mines had been marked. But the other man stumbled and caught his foot on a trip wire. Dick was killed. The other man was badly wounded.

"I am very, very sorry, Kay."

I said nothing. I walked into the hall and paced up and down listening to my heels thud on the tiles in a mournful rhythm. "Dick has been killed. Dick has been killed." After a while I went back to Ike. "It's all right," I said. "I'm all right." And I burst into tears.

Ike put his arm around my shoulders and led me over to the sofa. "Go ahead," he said. "Go ahead and cry. It's the only way. Just let it out." And I did. I cried and cried. All the time Ike was there holding me, saying soothing things, not really saying anything, just making noises. "There, there," he'd say, and pat me. "You'd better blow your nose," he kept telling me, and would hand me a handkerchief. I would obediently stop for a moment, blow my nose and then start bawling again.

Finally Ike said, "You'll make yourself sick. Come now, blow your nose again." He was so kind, so gentle. I tried to do exactly as he told me. My sobs died down to sniffles. He handed me a fresh handkerchief. I looked at the pile of crumpled handkerchiefs on the floor and, curious, asked, "Where did you get all those?"

"I called Mickey before we left headquarters," Ike said. "I told him to leave a dozen on the table.

"I'll be back in a minute," he told me, "and then we can talk." I stayed there huddled into a corner of the sofa, stunned. He came back with a cup of tea and spooned it into me as if I were a baby. And in between hiccups and sobs, I managed to get it down.

"Now let me tell you what I think," he said. "I think you ought to go out to Sailor's Delight for a few days. There's nobody there. You can be alone. Get yourself straightened out a bit. Go riding. Activity helps. I have learned that myself."

That seemed like a good idea, and Butch drove me out there that night. I walked back and forth on the terrace for hours and finally went to bed. I lay there listening to the rustlings and chirpings around that rustic Algerian house, and when the sun rose I was still lying there listening. My love was dead. And I was all alone.

This self-pity made me suddenly angry. Who was I to feel sorry for myself? I was alive. I should be thinking of Dick, not myself. And at this, I plunged even deeper into misery. I realized in the bright light of morning that I knew very little about Dick. I could think about the way his eyes crinkled when he laughed, the way he walked, about his devotion to the Army, the way he called me "precious," but not much more. Ours had been a wartime romance. There had been weeks and months when we had not seen each other. Each time we met it had been as exciting as a first date, and probably for that very reason our knowledge of each other had not progressed much beyond the first-date stage. Ike knew more about me and had seen more of my family than Dick ever had. I knew very little of Dick's family. It was as if we had met and loved in a vacuum. Now when I tried to mourn him, I discovered that I did not really know the man I was grieving for.

I dressed hurriedly and had one of the stallions brought around. That day I rode until I was exhausted. I was full of the most immense sorrow—for Dick, for myself, for all that might have been. But I had touched bottom. The realization that I had never really known him was as shocking as the knowledge that now I never would.

16

A FTER a few days, I came back to Algiers. Ike had given me valuable advice the evening that he broke the news that Dick had been killed. "Activity helps," he had said. "I have learned that myself."

He did his best to keep me busy. When I think back on everything that he did for me in those first days, I wonder how he found the time to be so supportive. "Kay, I've got a job for you," he told me one morning. "I know you can keep secrets, so I'm going to tell you a big one." And he paused. Ike was always very good at leading up to something. He would have you sitting on the edge of your chair, holding your breath, waiting for him to come to the point. And he would sit there throwing out tantalizing little hints, building up to the climax.

"We're going to have a very important person visit us. The biggest VIP you can imagine." He paused again. I was thinking furiously. The biggest VIP? Who could be bigger than the ones we had had? Bigger than Winston Churchill?

"The King of England!" he announced. "King George the Sixth is coming to North Africa," he said. Ike was always enchanted by royalty—kings and queens and princes and princesses, palaces and crowns. They had a fairy-tale aura for him. When I had told him once that I had met the then Prince of Wales at a dance during my first season in London, he was fascinated and asked all kinds of questions about him.

"I'd like you to drive me to meet His Majesty, Kay. If you feel up to it, that is," the General said. "The British will be escorting him about most of the time, but when he is in Algiers I will be his host. And I'd like you to be his driver."

The King of England! That was exciting. In those days, there was still a tremendous amount of glamour attached to the throne. The then Duke of York had been forced onto a throne he had never wanted when his brother abdicated to marry Mrs. Simpson. The shy new King had won the hearts and support of his subjects during these very difficult times by the example he set.

I had hero-worshiped the Prince of Wales. I had made him into a superman—handsome, democratic and very wise—and I was not alone. The whole kingdom was charmed by him. But when as King Edward VIII he decided that he preferred one woman over all of us, we were hurt. I was, at least. It was terribly romantic, the idea of a King of England giving up his throne for the woman he loved, but what about the rest of us? As the General had said once, "He lost sight of his duty."

Oh, yes, I felt up to driving King George. There was no question about it. "That would be smashing," I said. "Oh, I'd like that. I'd like that very much. Thank you so much."

"Well, that's settled," Ike said. "You better go see the security people. You'll need to be briefed." The security measures were fantastic, all designed so that no one would think that any extraordinary security measures were being taken. Algiers was teeming with spies and informers, so the whole operation had to be carried out as if nothing, absolutely nothing out of the ordinary were going on.

The King was traveling as General Lyon. General Eisenhower would pick up General Lyon at the airport, welcome him and escort him to General Gale's villa, where he would be staying, in his big armor-plated Cadillac. I hated that car, and we rarely used it. The armor plating made it so heavy that not only did the tires blow out all the time, but one had to really know the car in order to apply the brakes effectively. It was so heavy that the momentum would carry it three times beyond usual braking distance. But it was just the right automobile for the King. It was bulletproof and practically bombproof, barring a direct hit. I sighed when I realized that it was the logical car and prayed that my braking would have the necessary finesse. I practiced for a couple of mornings in the compound to make sure I had the feel of the unwieldy vehicle.

When the day came, the Boss got into the car just a little more pressed and creased and polished than usual, if that was possible. Butch was going to accompany us. His job would be to hold the door for the King, who would sit in Ike's customary seat—on the right in back. After the King was comfortably settled, Ike would go around and get in on the left side of the car, where I would be holding the door. Then Butch and I would scramble into our seats in front, and off we would go.

We had rehearsed this, enlisting two of the sentries on duty at the villa to play the parts of King George and General Eisenhower. As we drove through Algiers, Butch said, "I'm as nervous as if I were going to open on Broadway with only one rehearsal." As we drove through the city, the customary two-motorcycle escort rode ahead of us to clear traffic; there was absolutely nothing visibly different about this trip. Butch often accompanied the General on his trips here and there, and no one could possibly spot how extra clean and smart we all were. I had spent the night before washing my hair and polishing my shoes and buttons. I was squeaky clean—or as squeakily clean as it was possible to be in dusty, gritty Algiers.

Just as I drew up in the designated far corner of the airfield, there was the King's Lancaster dropping down out of the blue. It was one of the fastest landings I have ever seen. All the top British brass were there to greet the King, having come by different routes and in a variety of vehicles so that there would not be an obvious concentration of high-muck-a-mucks.

The plane door swung open. The King appeared, came rapidly down the steps, returned the salutes of the welcoming committee and smiled. Movie cameras were whirring away, salutes were being snapped off and there was an air of great, although sedate, excitement. Eventually Ike escorted the King to the Cadillac, and everything went just as we had rehearsed it with our sentry stand-ins. The King seemed very cheerful, even rather excited. He told the General that it was the first time he had been out of England in years. He remarked on the warmth and said that he was looking forward to spending some afternoons on the beach, swimming and soaking up the sun. He talked about his two daughters and said he wished he could give them the opportunity to get some of this sun.

All this time, as we wove our way back through Algiers, the King kept saluting as British soldiers would do a double take and snap to attention when they recognized the man in the car with General Eisenhower. The General also saluted. Butch muttered to me out of the side of his mouth, "What do you think? Should *I* salute?" I whispered back, "Of course—you're an officer. Go ahead." So he did.

When we arrived at General Gale's villa, Butch rushed to open the door for His Majesty and I did the same for the General. Then, quite unexpectedly, "Your Majesty," said the General, "I would like to present my naval aide, Captain Harry Butcher." Butch got red in the face, but drew himself up stiffly and saluted. The King smiled and held out his hand.

Then Ike beckoned to me and presented me to His Majesty, saying that I was a British subject who was on loan to him. I was petrified. I did not know what to do. I was a civilian, so it would not have been correct for me to salute. On the other hand, I was in uniform, so I did not think it would be correct to curtsy. I would have given anything to have an Emily Post at my elbow to whisper instructions. I finally bobbed a half curtsy and stuck out my hand, saying, "How do you do, sir?" but the King stood there like a statue. Whether he was struck speechless by my impudence or simply, like me, did not know what to do, I'll never know.

"Your Majesty," Ike said, trying again. "This is Miss Kay Summersby, who is a British subject and now on duty at my headquarters as my personal driver."

The King nodded and turned to General Gale, and they started toward the house. I felt frustrated—and a little hurt.

When the King came back from his tour, I drove him on the return trip to the airfield. This time he was not the chatty, confiding, enthusiastic man we had picked up two weeks earlier, but utterly silent and glum. There was a reason. He had been stricken by Algerian tummy, sometimes known as the GI's—an undignified ailment that was no respecter of rank or royalty. We all carried paregoric to gentle its ravages.

I had hoped that as he left, he might shake my hand, bestow a smile or even a few words on me, but he departed without ever having recognized one of his most loyal subjects. I did not feel as crushed as I might have felt: during the ride to the airport, the King had not said one single, solitary word to the General either.

THE summer rolled on. War has its own kind of accelerated time, and the sad days of early June began to fade into the past. Even the first precarious months in North Africa, now that we were involved with the Sicilian invasion, seemed ancient history. It was today that counted. The momentum increased, slackened, picked up again.

I was spending more time than ever with Ike. Even in London with our seven-day weeks, I occasionally visited Mummy and Evie, lunched with friends, went to the odd cocktail party. But now I trod a very narrow path. From breakfast to the final nightcap, I went where Ike went. Once when Omar Bradley was coming to dinner, Ike and I were a bit late. When we walked in, Brad said, "Here they are. Ike and his shadow." After that, whenever he saw Ike without me, he would ask, "Where's your shadow?" When the General had an official engagement in the evening and did not need me, I would go straight home, wash my hair and go to bed. I never went out.

All of us in Ike's little wartime family felt very, very close. There was an intense quality to our relationships. And an idealism. There was no place in our group for pettiness or selfishness or any of the other less pleasant aspects of human nature. We all had a sense of working together for a better world. We were not the least bit cynical. We believed this, and we talked about it. Not that there was not a lot of savage political infighting, but that was on another level. In the little family that Ike had created, peace and trust and love prevailed. Our relationships seemed deeper, more meaningful and richer than any we had known before.

Butch and I were talking about this one day sitting on the terrace with our sundown drinks. We agreed that there was a sweetness about our relationships that was quite extraordinary. Ike came out and asked, "What are you two being so serious about?" When we told him, he nodded. "I know what you mean," he said. "There are times when we demand the best of ourselves," I remember him saying. "We're always better than we think."

I was a better worker, at least, than I had ever believed I would or could be. Ike had recently given me a new responsibility: answering his mail from the public. "I just can't keep up with this mail," he complained. "How would you like to take it over? How about it?"

"I'll have a crack at it," I told him, "and if you think I can handle it, I'll consider it a privilege." I had occasionally helped him with some of his personal correspondence. One day he had asked apologetically if I would mind typing a letter to his wife for him. "I've got so much on my desk that I'll never get to it today," he said, "and she gets upset if she doesn't hear from me."

Naturally, I agreed. He told me briefly what he wanted to say, and I went back to my desk and typed it out. When I brought it in, he read it through carefully and nodded. "That's fine, Kay. Thank you. You sound more like me than I do myself." He picked up a pen, added a few lines, folded the letter into the envelope I had prepared and sealed it carefully. I heard later that Mrs. Eisenhower had taken exception to this. No more typewritten letters, she had informed him.

All kinds of people wrote to the General. There were letters with suggestions for horrible weapons that would end the war—and the world—promptly. From young mothers complaining that they had no place decent to live and bring up their children. From wives who had not heard from their husbands in weeks and were sick with worry. From mothers. Some letters reported injustices, family problems, all kinds of things that had to be investigated and then acted upon. Then there were the presents. Cookies and candy (lots of homemade fudge), games and books, just about everything that could be knitted or crocheted. The General insisted that every letter be answered and every gift acknowledged. "They wouldn't take the trouble to write," he said, "if they didn't have something that seemed important to them to write about." He had answered the letters himself up to this time, but now there were fifty or sixty a week and he just did not have the time.

I enjoyed my new chore. I would show Ike a few of the interesting letters, because he wanted to have a sense of what the writers were concerned about. If I read one and thought, Oh, this will amuse him or This will make him feel good, I would set it aside for him to read. Most of the letters required nothing more than a courteous acknowledgement, but some required research and a final decision on some kind of action. I also saw that every present went to a hospital or rest center or a local orphanage.

There were also hundreds of requests for the General's autograph, and I used to get him to sign his name thirty or forty times at a crack, but it became impossible to keep up with the demand. He insisted that I practice his signature so that I could sign the letters I wrote over his name. "I'm damned if I'm going to sign them," he said. "I'll get writer's cramp." Later on, I autographed most of the photographs he sent out, too: *Dwight D. Eisenhower, D.D.E.* or *D.E.*, depending on whether they were for GI's and their families or for personal friends.

17

ONE morning when I went into the General's office at the St.-Georges to consult him about something or other, he grinned and said, "I have a surprise for you."

"Oh," said I. "You do?"

"Yes," said Ike. "I do. How would you like a new uniform? Seems to me you could use a couple."

He was right. I had been re-outfitted after my woebegone arrival in North Africa, but my two uniforms were now sadly worn. This was not the kind of life in which one came home from the office and changed into something comfortable. It was your uniform from the time you got up until you went to bed—seven days a week. My skirts were not only baggy, they had a shine on the seat, a shine polished to a high gloss from sliding in and out under the steering wheel. We had been at war for a long time now, and the "wool" in our present uniforms was ersatz stuff for the most part, which did not wear well and did not hold its shape at all. My "good" uniform was a far cry from the elegantly tailored outfit I had acquired for the Military Transport Corps in 1939.

"I'm having some made for myself," Ike went on, "and I've told the tailor to measure you for a couple too. I think you deserve a little wardrobe freshening."

"I'd absolutely adore a new uniform. Thank you."

"Uniforms," he corrected me. "Plural."

"That's too much," I protested. "You do so many nice things for me. How can I ever thank you?"

"You can't possibly know how much I would like to do for you," he said. There was a strange quality to his voice. He was looking at me, his teeth clenched. That kind of look from which you cannot tell if a person is going to laugh or cry. Startled, I sat there at his desk looking at him. Neither of us said a word. Then Ike took off those reading glasses of his and stretched out his hand. "Kay, you are someone very special to me." I felt tears rising in my eyes. He was someone very special to me, too. I had never realized how special before. But he was. Very.

He laid his hand over mine. And he smiled. This was not the famous Eisenhower grin. This was a tender, almost tremulous smile, even a bit rueful. And full of love. I could not return it. I felt shaken, timid, almost as if I were undressing in front of him very slowly. In my face, in my eyes, there was nothing but absolute naked adoration. I could not hide it.

We just sat there and looked at each other. I felt overpoweringly shy. We were both silent, serious, eyes searching eyes. It was a communion, a pledging, an avowal of love.

And it was an absolutely shocking surprise.

So this is love, I thought. I had been in love before, but it had never been like this—so completely logical, so right. For over a year, Ike and I had spent more time with each other than with anyone else. We had worked, worried and played together. Love had grown so naturally that it was a part of our lives, something precious that I had taken for granted without ever putting a name to it.

Yes, I loved this middle-aged man with his thinning hair, his eyeglasses, his drawn, tired face. I wanted to hold him in my arms, to cuddle him, delight him. I wanted to lie on some grassy lawn and see those broad shoulders above me, feel the intensity of those eyes on mine, feel that hard body against mine. I loved this man.

Ike and General George S. Patton, whom Kay found "sweet and affectionate," but who caused Ike "a lot of grief."   U.S. ARMY

Kay arrives in North Africa, after the sinking of the Strathallen *and the loss of her trousseau. On the left, Kay in the lifeboat, wearing a checked head scarf,* BOURKE-WHITE/TIME . *Above, Kay in a borrowed British Army Warm arrives in Oran,* UPI .

Ike and General George C. Marshall, who resisted Kay's charm.

An angry Ike lays down the law to Admiral Darlan, who shortly afterward was assassinated by his own countrymen. To the right, General Mark Clark looks on.

Kay tries out an Army motorcycle in the North African desert.

Oujda, Morocco: Ike at the front observes machine gunners in action.

Ike, Telek and Secretary of the Navy Frank Knox.

WIDE WORLD

Ike is greeted by a jubilant George S. Patton, as Generals Omar Bradley and Courtney Hodges smilingly look on.

U.S. ARMY

Overlord, 1944

At Ike's secret retreat outside London, Telegraph Cottage, Kay gets ready far their daily ride together.

June 5, 1944: Ike visits the paratroopers of General Maxwell Taylor's 101st Airborne Division just before their D-Day drop. He told Kay, "It's really very hard to look a soldier in the eye when you feel you're sending him to his death." U.S. ARMY

Ike at headquarters with General Mark W. Clark.
U.S. ARMY

No wonder I felt shy. This was all in my eyes as I looked help-lessly at Ike. I don't know how long we sat there without speaking. Not too long. Tex burst in with a file of papers for the General. "I'm next, Kay," he boomed cheerfully. "That's fine, Tex," I told him. "I was just going." And I picked up whatever paper I had come in with and left the office.

Back at my desk, I pretended to sort out some papers, not knowing what I was doing, but trying desperately to appear busy. It would never do for anyone to note how moved I was. Oh yes, I loved Ike. I had loved him for a long time without ever being aware of it. Ike was the person around whom my world revolved and had been revolving for many months now. Ike was the person whom I admired more than any other. For whom I felt an aching tenderness and concern. With whom I always felt comfortable, at home.

I thought of all the times our eyes had met across the bridge table as we shared an unspoken comment on one of Butch's girl friends or an instant of glee over a bluffing bid that had suc-ceeded. Our communication was always instant and complete. I thought of how easy it was to work with him, knowing just what he wanted and how he wanted it. I thought of how unreservedly kind he had been to my mother and brother, how he had given me Telek, of the uncounted and uncountable ways he had befriended me, comforted me and involved himself in my life.

I thought, too, of the silly excuses we had made for touching each other all these weeks and months, excuses I had never ad-mitted to myself before. A touch of the fingers as I handed him his appointment schedule for the day. His hand on my shoulder as he leaned over to look at some letter I had called to his atten-tion. The occasional (was it really accidental?) touch of foot and knee at the dinner table. The times when, as we sat together on the sofa, our hands had slid together and touched without either of us seeming to notice—or moving them apart.

That morning, life took on a sweetness that was almost un-bearable. I floated on a cloud of happiness, delighting in my secret, exploring the feelings I had hidden from myself for months. I felt peaceful and fulfilled.

I had no thought for the future, but went over and over exactly what had happened in that emotional interlude—what he had said, what he had done, how he had looked. But the day-dreaming had to end. This was headquarters. There was a war. The General's mail was stacked on my desk, waiting to be read and answered. And in just a few minutes it would be time for me to drive him home for lunch.

I went into what I can only describe as a girlish panic. How was I going to face him? What should I say? What would he say? There was no time to think about it. Ike came striding out of his office with his usual "Ready, Kay?" and I jammed my overseas cap on my head and ran for the car. It was a silent drive back to the villa. Usually we had so much to talk about that we were still chattering as we walked into the house. Today—not a word.

The sentries on the terrace saluted as we walked in. Mickey was at the door to take the General's hat, and he followed us to the dining room, where Hunt and Moaney were waiting for the signal to put lunch on the table. This was the goldfish bowl that Ike was perpetually complaining about. Moaney came and went, serving lunch and clearing away. Mickey poured the coffee. Now that I was aching for privacy, I understood what a burden it was to live one's life under constant observation. There was not a moment, not one single moment when we could exchange a private word, a meaningful look. We sat there mute and poker faced, completely caught up in thoughts and feelings that could not, should not be expressed. As we were leaving to go back to the St.-Georges, Mickey beckoned surreptitiously, and I stepped back into the dining room.

"The General isn't himself today," he whispered worriedly. "Bad news this morning?"

"I don't know," I whispered back. "Hope not. I haven't heard any," and I rushed after Ike. As we were driving out of the compound, Ike said, "I'm sorry about this morning, Kay. That shouldn't have happened. I spoke out of turn. Please forget it."

Forget it! Impossible. I was a woman caught up in a dream of love. This man was the center of my existence. It had taken me long enough to realize it, but now—how could I forget it? I could not. Absolutely could not. If I cry, I thought, I will never be able to live with myself. I willed the tears to dry up. It was like willing the waves to stop breaking. One after another, the slow tears slid down my cheeks.

"Goddamnit!" Ike's voice crackled furiously into my ears. "Don't you understand? It's impossible. I was a damn fool. I'm asking you to forget it."

I did not say a word. There were no words.

"Goddamnit, stop crying," he ordered.

I took a deep breath. Swallowed. Managed to say, "I'm not crying. And furthermore, I do not understand what you are talking about." I stuck my chin up in the air, clamped my lips shut and drew up at the side door of the St.-Georges with a flourish. I would have given anything to be able to indulge in the old childish gesture of wiping my sleeve across my eyes to brush away the tears, but grown women in their thirties don't do that. I simply borrowed the General's favorite word and said, "Goddamnit, I've got some of this bloody Algerian dust in my eyes." If General Eisenhower regretted his words and his show of feeling, I regretted my reaction to them even more. I had made a fool of myself—a transparent, bloody fool of myself. That afternoon I applied myself to the typewriter with a vengeance.

Tex came out of Ike's office and warned, "Watch out. He's a real bear this afternoon."

Butch asked, "What's up, Kay? Did he say anything at lunch? He was in a fine mood this morning."

"No," I answered honestly. "He didn't say a word at lunch."

Butch whistled. "Hmmm—it's either Monty or the French. Can't imagine anything else that could have come up." I could imagine something else, but I was not volunteering.

Suddenly, four buzzes. That was my signal. I took a firm clutch on my newfound poise, grabbed a pencil and pad and marched in.

"Just wanted to tell you that the tailor will be at the villa first thing tomorrow morning to take your measurements. Butch can drive me to the office and you can come along later when you're through." The General did not look at me. He was flipping through a folder as he spoke.

"Oh, I think not," I said coolly. "What I've got will serve perfectly well. Thank you, but I think I should say no."

He got so red in the face that I thought he would pop a blood vessel right then and there. He stood up and walked around his desk. "You are a goddamned stubborn Irish mule," he said between his teeth. "You're going to get measured for those uniforms. And you're going to get measured tomorrow. That's an order." He glared at me. I was just as angry as he was. We stood there like two fighters, each daring the other to make a move.

"Goddamnit, can't you tell I'm crazy about you?" he barked at me.

It was like an explosion. We were suddenly in each other's arms. His kisses absolutely unraveled me. Hungry, strong, demanding. And I responded every bit as passionately. He stopped, took my face between his hands. "Goddamnit," he said, "I love you."

We were breathing as if we had run up a dozen flights of stairs. God must have been watching over us, because no one came bursting into the office. It was lovers' luck, but we both came to our senses, remembering how Tex had walked in earlier that day. Ike had lipstick smudges on his face. I started scrubbing at them frantically with my handkerchief, worrying—What if someone comes in?

Ike put his hands on my shoulders. "We have to be very careful," he said. "I don't want you to be hurt. I don't want people to gossip about you. God, I wish things were different."

"I think things are wonderful," I whispered. I knew what he

was talking about. I understood the problems. And I did not believe for a moment that love conquers all. But still—everything *was* wonderful. I did not expect anything to be easy. But I was not one to deny love. I could see no reason to deny it. This is part of the business of living in that special dimension, in our case the tunnel of war, where all your feelings, all your energies are absorbed by one great purpose. Your world is different from that of other people, divorced from the world outside the tunnel. What was important here and now was that there was love—pulsating, irrepressible love.

When I came out of Ike's office, everyone looked up at me. I almost panicked, thinking that my hair was untidy or there was some other telltale sign. Then Tex asked, "Well, how is he? Did he bite your head off too? Did you find out what was wrong?"

"No," I said. "He seems to be over whatever it was. He was cheerful enough."

I wanted to stand in the middle of the office and laugh and say, "Listen, everyone, we're in love. *Love!*" But as Ike had warned, we had to be careful. Very, very careful. And until now, I have lived up to that bargain. I have lied and dissimulated to do it. But it's true. We were in love. And it was glorious.

NOTHING had changed. Everything had changed. The acknowledgment of our love heightened the pleasure of every moment Ike and I spent together—and heightened the frustrations as well. As long as we were in Algiers, all we could hope for would be a few stolen moments of privacy—to talk. No more mad embraces. That initial passionate encounter could not be repeated. There were eyes and ears everywhere.

Many, probably most, of Ike's top staff officers had mistresses, but that was different. They were able to meet for assignations in hotel rooms, in rented or borrowed apartments or even in the officers' own villas, where there were always obliging, discreet orderlies to smuggle the lady out before dawn. But nothing and no one could slip discreetly into or out of Villa dar el Ouad. There were guards patrolling the grounds and sentries at the door twenty-four hours a day. Furthermore, this kind of liaison, this kind of behavior was not possible for Ike. First of all, and most important of all, it was not in keeping with his character. Dwight David Eisenhower was a man of the utmost integrity. I have never known him to act with less than complete honor and fairness. He could not have acted otherwise. He did not possess the capability. And second, it simply would not have done for there to be gossip about the General. There were too many people who believed in him and looked up to him. He had caught the imagination of Europe and Great Britain as a man who represented all that was best about the American character. This was a tremendous responsibility for one man to carry, a man already burdened with staggering responsibilities. A man who was a man like all others—possibly more disciplined and more scrupulously honorable than some, but certainly no less human. Ike had always led a life that was above reproach—and it had to remain that way. I would not have had it otherwise. He *could* not have had it otherwise.

For all these reasons, love made no visible change in our lives; the change was all within. We picked up the threads of routine as if they had never been broken. The next morning when I arrived for breakfast, Ike was well into his first pack of cigarettes and badgering Mickey for more coffee—"Hot, this time." His coffee complaints were pure habit, just like brushing his teeth and polishing his spectacles.

"Go on upstairs," he said. "The tailor's waiting for you."

There, spread out on Ike's big bed, was the material for my new uniforms. Marvelous, gorgeous, wonderful real wool worsted. Simply beautiful fabric, the same cloth that Ike's uniforms were being cut from. I asked to have mine made just like the General's with what we called the Eisenhower jacket. Actually, the jacket was borrowed from the British—Monty used to wear similar blouselike jackets; but Ike was the one who started the fashion among the Americans. It was a neat, trim look and much more comfortable than the standard coat. It was short—came to just below the waist, and gave you plenty of room to move. Every morning when I put on those uniforms I used to feel loved. I still have one of them. After the war I had it cleaned by the best cleaner in Washington; then I put it away in camphor. It has been in one of the packing cases that have followed me here and there for close on to thirty years.

As I went upstairs to be measured that morning, I overheard Butch saying, "Well, what does one have to do around here to get a new tailor-made uniform?"

I stopped and listened for the reply. "All you have to do," Ike said brusquely, "is work day and night, seven days a week, always be obliging and cheerful and get paid less than half of what the lowest-paid American clerk gets. That's all."

Butch apologized. "I shouldn't have said that, even joking. I keep forgetting that Kay's a civilian. She must have a hard time getting along."

I didn't really. My pay was laughable, but there was nothing to spend it on. There was nothing to buy in Algiers and nowhere to go, so I always had money left over.

Ike tried hard to arrange his schedule so that we could go out to Sailor's Delight and ride every afternoon. This caused no comment, since it was known that Marshall had ordered him to get more exercise and spend less time in the office. Most of the time driving back and forth to the farm, we were alone, but the car was as much of a goldfish bowl as the villa or the office. The only difference was that it was on wheels. There was no stopping and parking by a secluded beach, no shifting of seating arrangements possible. Ike always sat in back on the right. Everyone knew the General's car with the big star stenciled on the side, the four-star plate and his flag.

I craved privacy now as I never had in my whole life. I said as much to Ike one day. "I know. I know," he said impatiently. "So do I. But it's the one thing that I can promise you that we will never have." It was relatively easy to find time to talk. It was hard to believe that there was anything about ourselves that we had not told each other already, but there were many things.

Ike was adept at small talk, but while seeming to be very candid, he rarely revealed much of the man within. He would tell fascinating stories about growing up in Kansas, about his mother and father, about his brothers, about how he used to work at a creamery. He was a delight at the dinner table and even his most aristocratic guests enjoyed his tales of an American boyhood. He never concealed his simple origins. "I'm just a country boy," he would say. "I grew up poor." And he seemed completely open. But he never discussed his feelings and one never knew what was going on inside this man.

One day when we were riding, I teased him about this. "I know more about how you felt about the Belle Springs Creamery Company in Abilene than I do about how you feel about me." I was half serious, but I did not expect to raise the storm that I did. Ike hit his horse with his crop and they went tearing over the rocky fields as if ghosts were chasing them. He was back in minutes, coming around in a wide circle and slowly gentling his horse down to a sedate walk.

"I'm sorry," he said. "Let's stop and walk awhile." We tethered the horses and walked along the cliff above the beach. "I'm sorry," he said again. "It's hard for me to talk about things . . . about people . . . that mean something to me. I have always kept my feelings in check. Not talked about them. Not even thought about them much. I'm not used to talking about love. It makes me uncomfortable."

This came out slowly, a few words at a time, as if he were trying to explain himself to himself as well as to me. We were walking along, both of us looking down at our feet. I would have given anything to be able to hold his hand, put my arm around him, pat his cheek—just touch him. I wanted to comfort him. He was upset, and he had always struck me as a man who had had very little comforting in his life. But I could not touch him. There were all those hidden eyes. We scuffed along silently. "Your boots are getting dusty," I said irrelevantly. He grunted. Eventually we turned back. He helped me mount, and we headed back toward Sailor's Delight. Every once in a while we would turn and smile at each other, but I was very thoughtful.

We stayed at the farm for supper that evening, sitting on the terrace during the long sunset, nursing a couple of drinks, not saying much, just enjoying the calm and the view until Mickey came out in exasperation to report that he could not keep our meal warm much longer. "It will dry up," he warned.

The cocktail hour was often a time we could count on for ourselves. In Algiers we would sit on the high-backed sofa in the living room, listen to some records, have a couple of drinks, smoke a few cigarettes and steal a few kisses—always conscious that someone might walk in at any moment. We were more like teen-agers than a woman in her thirties and a man in his fifties. We were certainly a curiously innocent couple—or perhaps it was simply the circumstances in which we found ourselves. But we were neither forlorn nor mopish. I was happy just to be with Ike. To be working with him and to know that he loved me. That was enough.

Telek and his offspring also gave us an excuse to be together. The three puppies he had sired were growing up to be fat little dumplings, full of mischief and personality. We would bring them into the living room and get down on the floor and play with them, the way we had played with Telek when he was a puppy. Telek still liked to rollick around chasing balls and playing his old tug-of-war game. One afternoon in the car, Telek gave me the fright of my life. The windows were open, because it was blisteringly hot, and Telek saw a dog—one of those poor Arab mongrels, all skin and bones and sores. It must have been a female, because Telek got terribly excited and jumped out the window. Fortunately, I had been going very slowly. The road was rotten, and I didn't want to give Ike a bumpy ride. I jammed on the brakes and jumped out. Telek was lying there in the roadway perfectly still; then he got to his legs and shook himself in a very bewildered manner. He was a bit stunned, that was all. I picked him up in my arms and ran back to the car crying, "He's all right! He's all right!" I had been terribly scared. Ike took him in the back seat. He checked him for broken bones and pronounced him whole. "He'd better stretch out quietly for a bit," he said, and he kept him quiet for the rest of the drive, scratching him behind his ears and telling him that he should not be such a woman chaser.

Later on, Ike said, "When I saw your face, I felt sad. I don't think I could ever show as much feeling over a person as you did over a dog. I'm so used to concealing my feelings that there are times when I don't know what I feel—only what I think I ought to feel.

"And Kay, I don't think I'll ever change. I'm too old. It's too late. I've lived this way for a long time now. But I want you to know that I love you. There's nothing else that I can give you." He sighed. "If only things had been different," he said. That was a phrase that he was to use over and over during our relationship.

"I've loved you for a long time," he said huskily, "and I'm going to tell you something so you'll never have to doubt my feelings. The night the signal came through that the *Strathallen* had been hit, I felt as if the ground had been taken away from under my feet.

"You don't know how much I was looking forward to seeing you again. I followed the progress of that convoy as I followed no other convoy. And then the bottom fell out of my world. I spent that night worrying about you, cursing myself for not having had you fly to Algiers. I went through hell that night.

"If there was ever any question in my mind as to how deeply I felt about you, that night answered it. I had never let myself realize quite how dear you were to me before. But for God's sake, I never thought that I would be talking to you like this. Never. I was never going to tell you how I felt. And sweet Jesus Christ, I don't know how I ever had the guts to."

There was no mistaking his sincerity. Or that these words cost him a great effort. There was no reply possible.

"I'm very out of practice in love, Kay," he said after a silence. I read no signficance into this. For a man out of practice in love, Ike did many loving things.

One day he gave me a card with a four-leaf clover on it. "I have two four-leaf clovers someone sent me from home," he said. "I'd like you to have one. They bring good luck, you know." Ike believed in luck. He had some lucky coins that he used to rub during bridge games. He'd reach his hand into his pocket and smile and I would know that he was fingering his lucky coins. This day he told me, "Maybe they'll bring us both good luck and happiness." He had pasted the four-leaf clover on a little card, and on the back of it, he had written, *Good luck to Kay*. And then, *Africa* and his initials, *D.E.* I have always carried that card in my wallet. For all these years. I have it still.

He liked to come up with little surprises. One night before dinner, he said, "I've got some new records. Tell me what you think of them," and he placed a couple on the turntable. They were all currently popular songs, but when the last record dropped down onto the turntable, he said, "I think you may like this one." It was "I'll See You Again," the waltz from *Bitter-*

sweet that I had told him was my favorite song many months ago in England, just before he left for North Africa.

> When I'm recalling the hours we've had,
> Why will the foolish tears
> Tremble across the years?
> Why shall I feel so sad,
> Treasuring the mem'ry of these days
> Always?
>
> I'll see you again
> Whenever spring breaks through again.
> Time may lie heavy between,
> But what has been
> Is past forgetting.
> This sweet memory
> Across the years will come to me;
> Tho' my world may go awry,
> In my heart will ever lie
> Just the echo of a sigh,
> Good-bye.

The needle started spinning in the empty grooves. "Oh, it's so beautiful, so romantic," I sighed.

"It's pretty, but it's too sad," Ike said. "I don't like good-byes and sighs and all that."

"But it *is* romantic," I protested.

"Romantic," he scoffed. "Women!"

I didn't care. When a man carries the name of a song in his head for months and then produces it at the right moment, that is romantic. I felt wonderfully cherished. Perhaps it was because of this song that I always thought of these early days, when our love struck us like a kind of thunderbolt, as a kind of bittersweet honeymoon. Bitter only because unconsummated.

18

G ENERAL Eisenhower had much more than me, Kay Summersby, on his mind. World War II was an enormous enterprise. He not only had to work out strategies and determine priorities and make all the other decisions involved in waging war; he had to handle excruciatingly sensitive personnel problems. Probably no high executive is more of a prima donna by nature than a general. I say this as the daughter and sister of army officers. The top brass tend to be a prickly, arrogant lot. Eisenhower's unassuming, considerate ways were most exceptional.

The most difficult man that Ike had to cope with—always excepting Montgomery, who was in a class by himself—was the flamboyant General George Patton. They were old, old friends, and Ike had great respect for Patton, but that man caused him a lot of grief.

I had met General Patton in London and driven him about occasionally. I'll never forget my first meeting with him. Ike had suggested that I give him "the dock tour"—the same tour I had given Ike and Mark Clark when they first visited London. General Patton reacted very emotionally as I drove him around the East End dock area and showed him site after site that had been a grammar school, a warehouse, a cinema, a tenement or whatever and now was a heap of rubble. He would burst out with "The bastards! The dirty mother-fucking bastards!" He would apologize immediately. "Excuse me, Miss Summersby. I beg your pardon. My tongue ran away with me." Seconds later he would be at it again. "The sonsabitches! The bloody sonsabitches!" he would curse—and then apologize.

Despite his profanity, he was by no means coarse or crude. He was a gentleman, terribly courteous and very proper, with great respect for and consideration of women. I am not saying that the legendary "blood and guts" George Patton did not exist. He most definitely did. But there was another side to the man, a rather sweet and affectionate side. He was very strange—and very endearing. He loved the Army. He loved pomp and spit and polish. He was always ramrod stiff, whether standing or sitting, and always a military fashion plate. I had never seen as many decorations as he used to wear. They stretched from armpit to armpit. He should have been a general in the time of the Romans when he could ride around in a chariot. And he had the world's most unfortunate voice, a high-pitched womanish squeak.

Georgie was amazingly childlike in some ways. One day he pulled out one of his guns and waved it under my nose. "Look at that," he commanded.

"It's very handsome," I commented, wondering why he was showing it to me.

"People always talk about my pearl-handled revolvers," he complained. "That's not pearl. That's ivory. Good solid ivory," he said with satisfaction. "From an elephant," he added a few seconds later.

We used to talk a lot about horses and polo. Patton had his own string of polo ponies in the States, he told me, and he had once been Master of Foxhounds of the Rappahannock Hunt in Virginia. A consummate horseman, he was always at ease with a fellow equestrian. When he learned that my father had been a cavalry officer, he was delighted. I remember his striding into Ike's office at 20 Grosvenor and demanding excitedly, "Ike, did you know Kay's father was in the cavalry?"

Ike looked up at him and said, "Seems to me I heard something to that effect."

"Well?"

"Well what?" asked Ike. "Are you suggesting I put her on a horse?"

"Well, no," George squeaked. "No, I just wanted to be sure you knew."

"I know," Ike said drily. I had no idea what had got Georgie so fired up about that bit of my background. It may simply have been that he felt a kinship to any horseman. But it was typical George Patton. You never knew what was coming next. Unfortunately.

Patton had played an important part in the fighting in North Africa; and in Sicily, his Seventh Army had made Montgomery look like a cautious fuddy-duddy. Ike regarded him as one of his most valuable generals, and all the time we were in Algiers, he was a frequent guest. We always had a good time when he came to dinner. He was amusing and had an unending string of anecdotes. Ike used to tease him a lot. After Patton had finished telling some long, involved story, Ike would say, "Come on, Georgie. I don't believe a word of it." And Georgie would get all flustered and indignant.

After dinner, when the men started swapping off-color stories, Patton would always shoo me out of the room as if I were his daughter, saying, "Kay, it's time for you to leave. You tell one of those handsome aides of mine to play Ping-Pong with you." Ike would wink. I'd excuse myself and off I'd go. I always appreciated his thoughtfulness. Georgie was really quite prudish. He could be very charming, and I liked him.

But now I was furious with him. Georgie had visited a field hospital just behind the lines in Sicily—one of the routine vists every commander makes. He chatted with the men, told some stories, and then he came upon a soldier who was sitting alone and shaking. Georgie asked what was wrong. The soldier told him that it was his nerves, that he could not stand the constant shelling anymore. That set Patton off. He started ranting that there was no such thing as nerves, called the man a coward—and slapped him in the face. The incident had been kept under wraps for a while, but it was bound to get out, and it did. It was a terrible shocker.

Eisenhower wrote Patton a very severe reprimand and ordered him to make a public apology, but there were many people who criticized Ike for being too soft on the General. They thought that he should have court-martialed him or sent him back to the States in disgrace or both. The whole affair was very distressing. Ike did not condone Patton's behavior for one moment, but on the other hand he did not want to lose a valuable general just because of one mistake. He lost many nights' sleep over this. Finally, "I'm going to stand by Georgie," he told us. "I think we need him." Patton was not abashed in the least when I talked to him about the incident a few weeks later. "I always get in trouble with my goddamned mouth," he said, "but if this sort of thing ever comes up again, I'd do it again."

One day when Georgie was lunching with us, he turned to me and said, "You should get Ike to bring you over to visit me next time he comes to Sicily. I'd love to show you around." I said something about being sure that Georgie was too busy to entertain guests, but he insisted. "It's only a hop, skip and jump from here. Ike," he said, "you bring Kay along. I owe her a sight-seeing trip." Ike thought it was a good idea, and the visit was scheduled for the next day. Ruth Briggs, one of the Powerhouse WACs, went along with me.

Unlike Ike, General Patton believed in nothing less than the very best for himself. He was living in a palace that had once belonged to the King of Sicily. It suited Georgie's grandiose style very well. After lunch, he took us on the promised sight-seeing trip. He was an enthusiastic and well-informed guide. Our final stop was a medieval church just outside Palermo. He gave Ruth and me a short lecture on medieval architecture and then sank to his knees and prayed aloud for the success of his troops, for the health and happiness of his family and for a safe flight back for Ruth and me. He was completely unself-conscious and did not care who listened in on his prayers.

When I told Ike about our day, he smiled and shook his head. "Georgie is one of the best generals I have," he said, "but he's just like a time bomb. You never know when he's going to go off. All you can be sure of is that it will probably be in the wrong place at the wrong time."

Later on, when Patton's Third Army romped through France and Germany and across the Rhine, Eisenhower's decision to keep this master of military pursuit on his staff was amply vindicated. I think Patton, despite his bravado, was always truly appreciative of Eisenhower's forbearance. But he never did learn to keep his "goddamned mouth" shut. And he caused Ike a lot of grief.

19

I T used to be said that if a person sat on the terrace of the Café de la Paix in Paris long enough, everyone he had ever known would pass by. North Africa was something like that in the autumn of 1943. Our life seemed to consist of a round of luncheons and dinners for the most important men in the Western World.

First and foremost, there was the P.M. One never knew when Winston Churchill would pop in. Sometimes his visits were scheduled, and other times he just appeared—like a little boy who could not stay away from the action. Once he told Ike that the reason he came to Algiers was to take a bath. He reveled in long hot tub baths, which had become a delight of the past in England because of the stringent fuel rationing. The General would be invited to join the P.M. in the steamy bathroom for long talks, sitting on the toilet seat while Churchill soaked and smoked his cigars and discussed the state of the world. Ike would always have to change into a fresh uniform afterwards, because the steam was murder on trouser creases.

Ike really liked Churchill. They disagreed on a number of things, matters of strategy and military priorities, and had some very spirited arguments, but this did not affect their relationship. The only thing that Ike really deplored about the P.M. was his habit of staying up until all hours. By nature Ike was an early-to-bed, early-to-rise man; the P.M. was the opposite. He was at his best from dinnertime on and would keep a party going well into the wee hours without the slightest compunction for the other guests who would be in agony trying to stifle their yawns. Since the P.M. was always the ranking guest, no one could leave until he was ready to call it a night.

The P.M. was a menace at the dinner table in more ways than one. His table manners were atrocious, especially in contrast to Ike's, which were neat and unobtrusive, once I got used to the American way of handling a knife and fork. At the beginning, I used to say, "Listen, I can't understand you. Here you are—cutting a piece of meat. After I cut mine, I simply raise my fork to my mouth. You have to switch your fork to your other hand. I thought Americans were supposed to be so efficient."

I always used to think how shocked the P.M.'s nanny would have been if she could see the way he behaved. He would slurp his soup, spill things, pick up food with his fingers. He would pick his nose while listening to the rare person who managed to get a word in edgewise and would quite uninhibitedly unzip his siren suit to scratch his crotch. I remember once at dinner he interrupted himself in mid-anecdote, banged his fist on the table and demanded, "What happened, General? Did you run out of claret?" Mickey rushed to fill his glass. At that moment the P.M., engrossed in his story again, made a sweeping gesture and knocked the glass to the floor. He paid no attention to what he had done. No attention whatsoever. Simply went on with his story. Ike and I exchanged a glance and a grin. Mr. Churchill, you really had to acknowledge it, was adorable—but his manners were horrifying. The truth was that it did not matter. He was absolutely brilliant, and all these possibly purposeful gaucheries seemed trivial when he started talking. He had the most fabulous command of the English language. I could have listened to him forever.

Whenever he was coming to dinner, he would instruct Ike, "Now, tell Kay to come. I want to see her." And Ike would buzz

me and say, "You're invited to dinner. The P.M. wants you." I
don't know whether Churchill sensed the special feeling Ike and
I had for each other or was just being gallant, but either way I
appreciated his courtesy.

At one period, it seemed as if we had dinner parties almost
every night. Ike entertained Lord Louis Mountbatten, whom he
now knew well enough to call him Dicky, when he came by on
his way to India. Then Averell Harriman, who had just been
appointed American Ambassador to the Soviet Union, dropped
in on his way to Moscow with his daughter Kathy. I had known
Kathy in London, so this was a particularly welcome visit.

The Harrimans arrived on the General's birthday, and Ike
said, "Now, I don't want my birthday mentioned. You tell
Butch that, too."

"Fine," said I. "In that case you won't want your present, I
suppose."

He grinned. "Well now, I don't remember saying anything
about no presents." So I whisked his birthday present out of my
pocketbook—one of those dreadful Western magazines that he
liked.

"You must have had to grit your teeth to buy this," he said.

"You're right," I told him. It was not much of a present, but
there really wasn't anything to buy. It had been a toss-up between the magazine and a package of chewing gum.

Henry Morgenthau, the Secretary of the Treasury, and Cor-
dell Hull, the Secretary of State, flew in while the Harrimans
were there. This involved a series of back-to-back, high-level
luncheons and dinner parties. And there were what seemed like
a constant stream of American Congressmen, all of whom
wanted to pay their respects to the General.

Then there were the theater people and other entertainers
who came to North Africa to perform for the troops. Whenever
possible we would invite them to the villa for a buffet supper. I
can't remember all the stars, but there was Vivien Leigh, who
was even more beautiful in person than she had been on the

screen as Scarlett O'Hara. There was Bob Hope, who was able to make the General double up with laughter. There were Kay Francis and her troupe. And Bea Lillie. The high point for me was Noël Coward's visit. The General told him that I had worn out his recording of "I'll See You Again," and Mr. Coward said that it was probably the most popular song he had ever written. He told us that he had been in a traffic jam in New York City when the theme had come to him. I can remember just the way he described it—"It was in the air waiting to be captured." Just to convince the General that he was not planning to entertain the troops by singing romantic waltzes, Mr. Coward sang that marvelously funny song, "Mad Dogs and Englishmen Go Out in the Midday Sun," doing a soft-shoe routine at the same time. Ike loved that. He slapped his knee and beamed and said, "That's great. That's swell. That's the stuff."

One day Ike asked me, "Can you keep a secret?"

I was reproachful. "I never breathe a word of anything," I said. "You know that." And I never did.

"Well, do you want to know what I know?"

I was ready to wring his neck. Of course I did.

"President Roosevelt is going to visit us."

Franklin D. Roosevelt. I had listened to his radio broadcasts and seen his pictures with that cigarette holder jutting out at a cocky angle. This was a man I would love to meet. He had been in North Africa at the time of the Casablanca Conference, but I had not gone to Casablanca. I was aware that he had been crippled by polio, but the image he projected—even in newspaper photographs—was so vital that one did not think of him as having any disability.

The King's visit and the frequent descents of the P.M. had not prepared us in any way for the security arrangements that prevailed for the President of the United States. They were incredible. The advance visits of the Secret Service people were responsible for several memorable eruptions of the Eisenhower temper. I wonder how he would have felt if he had suspected

then that someday they would be performing the same services
for him.

The Secret Service people were so powerful that they over-
ruled the General's wishes—temporarily, at least—in the matter of
who would drive the President. When the day came and I drew
up beside the President's plane on the airfield in Tunisia, the
Secret Service chief started shouting at me. I had met him
earlier, when he was making the advance arrangements. His
name was Mike Reilly, and he was as stubborn an Irishman as
ever was born of Irishwoman. We almost got into an old-
fashioned shouting match when he told me that "No woman
will ever drive the President." He banged on the top of the car
to make his point. "No woman ever has—or ever will as long as
I'm boss here," he shouted.

The President and the General got into the car while all this
fuss was going on—a far cry from the decorum that had obtained
when we welcomed the King. The whole thing ended up with
me driving Butch back to the villa just outside Tunis where the
President was staying. When we got there, I jammed on the
brakes. I'd never seen anything like it. The house was ringed
with soldiers as if they expected an immediate attack in force. I
was about to pull the car around in the driveway when one
of President Roosevelt's aides came over and said, "Miss Summersby, the President has asked to meet you."

The President and General Eisenhower were in the library.
Two of his sons, Elliott and Franklin, were with him. Ike
walked over as I came in and took me to where the President
was sitting in front of the big window. "Mr. President," he said,
"this is Kay Summersby." The first thing the President said was
not "How do you do?" or anything like that, but "Why didn't
you drive me? I'd heard you were going to be my driver and I
was looking forward to it."

"Mr. President," I said indignantly, "your Secret Service
wouldn't let me drive you." Everyone laughed. There was no
formality after that. The President said he would like it if I

would drive him during his stay, and I said that there was nothing that I would like better.

As I left I ran into Reilly again and could not resist telling him that I had just been presented to the President and that he had asked me to drive him. Reilly scowled. I pointed out that the President would be safe with me. "I'm as Irish as you are, Mike," I told him. He looked at me disbelievingly. "Now, are you?" he said. "I wouldn't know with that Limey accent." I convinced him, and peace was declared.

When Ike and I arrived the next day to take the President on a tour of the Tunisian battlefields, we were amazed at the scene that greeted us. They had assembled what seemed to be a small army—jeeps, weapons carriers, half-tracks, truckloads of armed MP's—to accompany us. The President was tucked into the car. Two men simply picked him up out of his wheelchair and set him down on the back seat with no to-do whatsoever. Our cavalcade got off with a roar of engines. A radio car led the way, then there were a couple of jeeps full of soldiers and then our car. Beside all those military vehicles bristling with armed men, our group looked like a family on a Sunday outing. Telek was sitting in front between me and a very quiet man in civilian clothes who was clutching a briefcase as if it contained the Crown Jewels. He was a Secret Service agent, and the briefcase held a machine gun. The President and the General were chatting, very relaxed, in back when there was an unscheduled incident that not even the almighty Mike Reilly could have foreseen. Telek, who had made it clear that he did not care for the Secret Service agent, turned himself into a flying missile and launched himself directly at the President. Ike managed to grab Telek in midair before he landed on Roosevelt. The President just laughed. He took Telek on his lap, and as we drove along he scratched our bad Scottie under his chin and told us stories about Fala, his own Scottie.

Suddenly he broke off and said, "Child." He meant me. I discovered later that he called most young women "child." I liked it. Nobody else had ever called me that. "Child," he said. "That's a pretty grove of trees there ahead. Let's have our picnic there." That particular grove of trees was not on the schedule. Reilly had given me a program that called for the President to have his lunch forty-five minutes later in a completely different locale. But I decided the President was boss and turned off the road onto a track leading into the trees. It was a pretty place, rather like an oasis in the barren country we had been driving through. I braked and started opening the picnic basket.

"No, let me do that, Kay," Ike said. "I'm very good at passing sandwiches around."

All the time there was a grinding of gears and the noise of engines in the background as our escort vehicles lumbered after us. Soldiers jumped out and completely circled the car, elbow to elbow, their backs to us, bayonets fixed.

The President said, "Won't you come back here, child, and have lunch with a dull old man?" Tremendously flattered, I got in back and sat beside him while Ike took over the front seat and the picnic basket. The Secret Service man had disappeared. "I have a delicious chicken sandwich here that I can let you have," he told the President as he peeked between the slices of bread. Roosevelt asked how he knew it was delicious and Ike said it was because of all the Sunday-school picnics he had gone to as a child. "I got to know who made the best sandwiches pretty fast," he said.

Roosevelt was enjoying himself immensely, laughing and telling stories. He had the gift of putting a person completely at ease, and I soon got over my awe of him and was chatting away as if I had known him all my life. I told him about London in the early days of the war, about the trips the General and I had taken to the front. I told him about the WAC officers with whom I shared the villa in Algiers and how much I liked them.

"It seems to me that you might like to join the WACs," he said.

"There's nothing I'd like more, sir," I told him. "But it's impossible. I'm a British subject and I'd have to become an American citizen to be a WAC."

"Well, who knows? Stranger things have happened," he said.

It is hard for me to imagine it now, but it seemed completely natural for me to be sitting in the back seat of a car parked in a grove of trees in Tunisia eating chicken sandwiches with the President of the United States—and having those sandwiches served to us by a four-star general who was in love with me—and I with him.

20

THERE had been a reason for the flurry of VIP visitors. Two major conferences took place that autumn—the Cairo Conference, starring President Roosevelt, Prime Minister Churchill and Generalissimo Chiang Kai-shek, and the Teheran Conference, where Roosevelt and Churchill met with Stalin.

When General Marshall informed Ike that he was to attend the Cairo Conference, Ike said to me, "Well, here's a chance for a little holiday. How about coming along?" I would love to, I told him, but how in the world could it possibly be arranged? "No problem," Ike said, "I'll ask some of the other headquarters staff too. There's plenty of space in the plane." And that's the way it worked. Ruth Briggs and Louise Anderson were delighted to have a chance to visit Cairo. Even ultraconscientious Tex decided to go.

We all trooped into the big C-54 General Marshall had sent for Ike and settled down to a few rubbers of bridge just as if it were any other night. Mickey hovered about serving drinks and passing peanuts. After the game we all settled ourselves for the night. One by one the others dropped off to sleep, leaving Ike and me the only ones awake. Tex's snores drowned out our whispers, and we felt completely unobserved. I suppose it seems ludicrous to think of two adults necking in a darkened plane, but we were dreamily content. Reality took precedence over romance, however. We were dead tired and did not want to risk falling asleep in a compromising position. We moved apart and went to sleep. I kept waking up and looking over at Ike. Every time I turned my head and saw him there in the dim light, his mouth slightly open, his tie loosened, I felt a surge of tenderness. Even when the sun showed every weary wrinkle and line, I could not imagine anything better than seeing that head on the pillow beside mine every morning. It was good just to have been close to him for those few hours.

Today, when sex seems to be so matter of fact, it may be hard to realize how wonderfully romantic and rather innocent people were only thirty years ago. To me, that night was as much an act of love as a more physically intimate encounter.

The appearance of three women with the General threw the welcoming group into a panic. Where would they put us up? "That's no problem," Ike said. "They can stay with me." There was plenty of room in the luxurious residence he had been assigned, and Ruth, Louise and I had our own private suite. It was a long time since we had lived in such comfort. We were all so used to our family-style life that the rank-conscious scruples of our conference hosts struck us as amusing and old fashioned.

The General went off to his conference, and the three of us headed straight for the famous Shepheard's Hotel. After a marvelous lunch, we set out to sight-see and shop. Cairo was hot and dirty, but luxurious beyond belief. Store windows were full of fruit and clothing and jewelry. It was a whole other world. Unfortunately, almost everything was far too expensive for us. All I bought was some fruit.

That afternoon there was a huge cocktail party, and Ike was easily the most popular man there. That grin of his never faded as people kept pushing their way up so they could exchange a few words with him. I tried not to look in his direction too often. I was resolved that I would never give anyone reason to gossip.

Eisenhower dined with General Marshall that evening. Ruth and Louise went on to dinner from the cocktail party with a group of friends. I went home alone. Later that evening, Mickey knocked on the door. "The General asks if you'd join him in a nightcap," he said.

Ike was walking up and down the long drawing room. "Did I hear something about a drink?" I asked.

"Correct. Come on in. And Kay, close the door." I closed the door softly and ran straight to him. We stood there, our arms around each other, his cheek on my hair. "Oh, that's good," he said. "This is where you belong." We stood there. Making cozy little noises. This was no passionate embrace. Just two people who ached to hold each other close and never got a chance.

After a few minutes, we drew apart and I opened the door again. There was no point in arousing anyone's curiosity. Ike sighed and reached for my hand. He sat there smoking one cigarette after another. He always smoked them right down to the stub. I used to say, "You're very conservative. Just like me. You don't want to waste anything."

"General Marshall has ordered me to go on vacation," he said after a while.

My heart sank. In the last few weeks, rumors had been flying, rumors that struck panic into my heart—rumors to the effect that Ike would be recalled to Washington to serve as Chief of Staff and General Marshall would come to Europe to take over the Allied command of Overlord, the code name for the projected invasion of the Continent across the English Channel. In recent weeks one important personage after another had told Ike about these rumors. One day he exploded. "Goddamnit, I've had a bellyful of every Tom, Dick and Harry coming here from Washington and telling me I'm about to be stuck behind a desk in the Pentagon."

"What do you want me to do?" I asked. "Gag every visiting fireman before he comes into your office?" But I did not feel at all flip. At headquarters, the whole staff felt that such a move would be shabby recognition of the Boss's achievements in putting together a truly unified Allied command and conducting the successful Mediterranean campaigns. But like Ike, I did not want to hear about those rumors. As far as I was concerned, they were bad news. If Ike was recalled to Washington, there was not a chance in the world that I would ever see him again. He might be able to take other members of his personal staff with him, but there was no way that he would be able to bring a British civilian into the Pentagon as a member of his entourage. It was simply out of the question.

This was the first time I had ever had a glimmering that there would be an end to this wartime world of ours. I had come to think of it as a way of life; but now intimations of the future were being forced on me—and the future held changes that I did not want to face.

When Ike told me that General Marshall had ordered him to take a vacation, I caught my breath and very hesitantly asked, "They're sending you back to Washington?"

"No, just a couple of days off. That's all. Damn it! I don't know. It may be a way of preparing me for the news. He didn't say. I didn't ask." Ike shook his head. "There's no point in worrying about it. They'll tell me when the time comes."

I was not so sure. And no matter what he said, Ike was worried. I could tell. I remembered the typical Army snafu when he got his fourth star. The news had been on the BBC and the American radio hours before Ike had been notified. It did not seem inconceivable to me that they might send Ike away for a short vacation and announce that General Marshall would be the commander for Overlord in his absence. Not out of malice. No one held any bad feelings toward Ike, ever. Just out of the utter and incredible inefficiency of Army bureaucracy.

I said as much to Ike. "No, there's too much involved," he said. "The British. The French. The Russians. It will be a big formal announcement when it comes.

"Don't look so upset," he said. "If it has to be Washington, I'll find a way. I'm never going to let you go." I smiled a little trembly kind of smile. I knew he meant it. But I was a realist.

There was no way he could ever manage to bring me to the United States.

"All we're talking about is a couple of days off," Ike said. "Marshall says I look tired. And I am. I'm very tired." This was the first time I had ever heard him admit such a thing. He usually blew his top if anyone so much as intimated that he looked tired.

"I'm leaving tomorrow," he said, "and you're coming with me."

"Me? I can't believe that's what the General ordered."

Ike laughed. "I thought I'd go take a look at the pyramids. I'll probably never have another chance. We could take the girls and Tex with us. What do you think? It would mean a lot to me to have you along."

The next afternoon we were all in Luxor, a city built on the site of ancient Thebes. Elliott Roosevelt had come along too. That night we went out to view the crumbling temples, the huge statues of pharaohs and the rows of sphinxes in the moonlight. It seemed like a dream. This was such a tremendous experience that there was very little talk. Each person was concentrating on his own impressions. We wandered about quietly, separating, then coming back together. Ike pressed my hand. "You have to know how much it means to me to be seeing this with you," he said softly. Subdued and impressed, we eventually sauntered back to the hotel, the desert moon lighting our way. We had a drink and then said our good nights. Ike tucked a piece of paper into my hand as we walked down the hall. A few minutes later, alone in my room, I read, *You know what I am thinking. Good night. Sweet dreams.* I went to sleep thinking how much I loved him.

A caravan of decrepit cars awaited us the next morning to take us across the Nile to the famed Valley of the Kings. On the way we got a look at the very primitive life of the fellahin. Water buffalo plodded about in circles to pump water. Donkeys looked out of doorways. And everywhere there were hordes of grimy little children and flies, flies, flies. It was blazing hot, and the cars kept breaking down, but when we reached the desolate ravine that was the Valley of the Kings, we forgot about the discomforts. We spent the whole day exploring the tombs, learning about life in ancient Egypt as our very learned guide, a personal friend of Air Chief Marshal Tedder, explained the significance of some of the tomb paintings and translated the hieroglyphics. When we emerged from the last tomb in the late afternoon, we shook our heads as if we had jumped across hundreds of centuries.

Back in Luxor that evening, there was nothing any of us wanted except a cold drink, a warm bath and bed. It was a grand kind of tiredness. Ike went straight to bed and slept for fourteen hours. The next morning he looked like a different man.

General Marshall was so pleased when he saw how much better Ike looked after his two-day vacation that he insisted on his taking another short trip immediately. When Ike came back after meeting with General Marshall, he asked, "Have you girls made any plans for today?" We had nothing special planned, but we were looking forward to more window-shopping and sight-seeing. "Oh," he said, feigning disappointment. "I was thinking of going to Jerusalem for lunch. I'd hoped you would join me."

"You are thinking of *what?*" I shrieked. "Jerusalem! For lunch? We can go?" Ruth and Louise were equally enthusiastic, and Ike was highly pleased with the effect he had produced. At noontime we were lunching at the King David Hotel in Jerusalem, none of us quite believing it. After the pyramids, the Holy Land was a bit of a letdown. Nothing was the way we had imagined it. It was terribly commercial and not at all impressive. Even Bethlehem was a disappointment. We were going to visit the manger where Christ was born. I suppose it was utterly idiotic of me to expect to see a wooden manger filled with straw. It was an ornate hunk of marble, and I was absolutely repelled by it.

For me, and for Ike too, a stroll in the Garden of Gethsemane was the high point of the visit. None of Christ's long-ago agony communicated itself to us; it seemed, rather, more peaceful than the other religious landmarks we had visited, a place where meditation seemed natural. Our voices were hushed as we wandered along the paths. I felt that our visit was a form of prayer. And I was praying very hard. "Please God, don't let them send him back to Washington."

Ike collected a lot of postcards, and when we were wandering through the bazaars in Jerusalem, I saw some good-looking sheepskin coats. I tried on one coat after another. There was one I liked particularly, and it cost only twenty dollars. I didn't have that much with me, but Ruth Briggs lent me a few dollars. "You're crazy, you know," she told me. "You don't need that. When will you wear it?" "After the war," I said. "I'll never find a good warm coat like this in England—not at this price." I was very proud of my foresighted practicality.

Our next stop was the airport. We all agreed that we'd had enough of the Holy Land. We were playing cards on the way back when Ike wrinkled his nose. He sniffed and sniffed and then he said, "What's that goddamn smell?"

"Smell? Smell?" I said. "I don't smell anything." And then I got it. The most disgusting rotten stink was wafting up from the back of the plane. "Oh my dear God," I said. "It's my coat. It's my bargain." As the interior of the plane warmed up, it had brought out the worst in my coat.

"For Christ's sake, you mean we're going to have to fly with that stink?" Ike was disgusted. It got worse and worse. Fortunately, it was a short flight. It was the only purchase of any size I made during the war, and it was a disaster.

Before we went to bed, Ike took the postcards he had been collecting out of his pocket. "Here," he said as he handed one to me. "You liked the Garden of Gethsemane. This will be a little

Ike in France, conferring with General Omar Bradley, Commander of the U.S. First Army.
U.S. ARMY

BELOW
Ike takes a break on the Riviera, at the villa Sous le Vent, near Cannes. Kay is on the left as Ike (center) sips a preluncheon aperitif.

Ike visits Hitler's retreat at Berchtesgaden in 1945, with Kay beside him in the back seat of a jeep. U.S. ARMY

Ike stands between Bradley and Patton in the ruins of a liberated continent. U.S. ARMY

*Ike attends a theater party in London, with Kay by his side (cen-
ter front) and his son, John (at far left).*   UPI

Ike greets his new Commander in Chief, Harry S. Truman, who later commented about Ike's affair with Kay: "He wanted to come back to the United States and divorce Mrs. Eisenhower so that he could marry this Englishwoman."　　　U.S. ARMY

Victory in Europe: Kay stands behind Ike as they celebrate the surrender of the German Army. In some official versions of this photograph Kay's presence has been removed. TIME/LIFE

Kay poses for a glamour leg shot on her arrival in the United States with Telek beside her. UPI

Telek poses on Ike's desk. Ike said about the dog's name, "It's a combination of Telegraph Cottage and Kay. Two parts of my life that make me very happy."

The Conquering Hero: General Eisenhower returns home.

Toward the Presidency: On the steps of Columbia University Eisenhower gives the famous victory wave and the smile that carried him to the White House for two terms.

Kay Summersby Morgan, 1908–1975

SOUVENIR

FROM

THE GARDEN OF GETHSEMANE

Photo. ALBINA-BROTHERS
APPROVED MILITARY
PHOTOGRAPHER NO. 74

COPYRIGHT

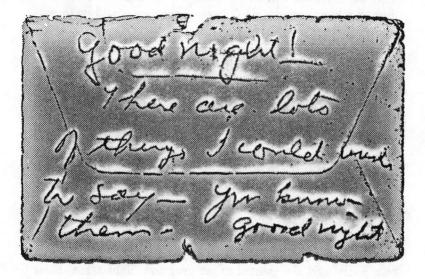

souvenir." It was a postcard with its own envelope. On one side
was printed, SOUVENIR FROM THE GARDEN OF GETHSEMANE. And
on the other side, Ike had written, *Good night—there are lots of
things I could say—you know them. Good night.* I tucked it into
my bag and said very briskly, "Oh, thank you, General. Thank
you so much. And thank you for a lovely day." He spread the
rest of the cards out on the table and said, "Now Ruth, Louise,
take what you want. You should have some remembrance of the
trip besides that unholy stink from Kay's coat."

Back in Algiers, headquarters was practically afloat with new
rumors that Ike would be leaving for a post in Washington the
first of the year. This really got him upset. He had come back
rested, with a fresh perspective on things, and now, after just a
couple of hours back at his desk, he was getting tied up in knots
again.

"I don't see how they can send you back to Washington," I
told him. "No one else can do the job you did in London and
here. And Overlord will be the same job, the same kind of thing
—just on a bigger scale. I don't know what they would do if anything ever happened to you."

He gave a noncommittal grin—more of a grimace than a grin.
"Let me tell you something," he said. "There's no such thing as
an indispensable man."

"They couldn't get along without you," I insisted stubbornly.

"Sure they could. Don't kid yourself. It might be difficult for
a few days, even a week. But then everything would fall into
place."

There was nothing to do but wait. Not even Ike could make a
guess as to how long it would be before the announcement was
made. In the meantime, there was plenty to keep us all busy.
Ike's mail had stacked up on my desk while we had been away,
and I was working late every evening. We were setting up a trip
to advance headquarters in Italy. The invasion there had bogged
down badly, and Ike wanted to get over and "light a fire under
Monty."

We were also preparing for the return visit of President Roosevelt on his way back to Washington from Teheran. This time we all took the Nervous Nellies of the Secret Service in our stride. We had become used to their ways. The President arrived on December 7: a rather grim date, the anniversary of the attack on Pearl Harbor—but he was wearing that sparkling Roosevelt smile. On the way from the airfield, he congratulated Ike on his new appointment. It was definite, he told him. Ike would be named commander for Overlord. The announcement would be made as soon as the President got back to Washington. And Ike would have a new title: Supreme Allied Commander. The General was so happy I almost thought he would burst. That grin never left his face.

That night Elliott Roosevelt gave a dinner for his father. Ike and Butch and I were invited. It was rations, but lots of fun, the most informal meal you could imagine. There was a lot of joking and laughing, and everyone toasted Ike. He was beaming and looked fabulous. It was as if a load had rolled off his shoulders. It would be presumptuous of me to say that I was even happier than Ike, but I may have been. For him it was recognition of his professional abilities and achievements; for me, it was a reprieve.

It was a good thing that Ike had the prospect of Overlord to buoy him up, because our trip to Italy was pure misery. One never expected life at advance headquarters to be comfortable. It had been rugged enough in Tunisia—but in civilized Italy it was unspeakable. Ike's headquarters in Caserta were in a huge palace that was about the dirtiest place I have ever seen. We spent very little time there, however. Ike visited Montgomery at his headquarters and conferred with the other commanders at their command posts. He always made a point of talking to as many officers and men as he could. The men were always glad to see him. They would shout, "Good old Ike!" and things like that. Despite the fact that the fighting was incredibly bitter, they were in good spirits. But Ike was depressed. The Germans were putting up an unexpectedly strong fight—and then there was

Monty. He was never willing to take a chance. "If I could only get Monty off his duff," Ike complained over and over.

The lowest point of the trip was the night we spent in what had been Prince Umberto's hunting lodge in the mountains. Butch had wanted the General to have one day of rest during the trip and had set this up. In good weather the lodge might have been pleasant enough, but in the cold December rain it was utterly depressing. And cold. And dirty. Our spirits were pretty low after we inspected it. Then we heard Mickey shouting, "There's a rat in the General's bathroom!"

Telek had been sniffing around, exploring his new quarters, and had flushed out a rat. All of us rushed to the bathroom. There was the rat. Sitting on his hind legs on the toilet seat.

"I can handle this," Ike said. He put on his glasses, pulled out his gun and took aim. And missed. The rat jumped up and clung to a pipe. Ike fired again, and this time he got part of the poor rat's tail. He finally tumbled him on the third shot, but the rat was still alive. One of the sergeants came running in with a log and slammed it down on the poor thing. The rest of us were bent over with laughter. Butch congratulated Ike. "Great marksmanship, Chief," he said. "Just what we'd expect from the Supreme Commander."

That was the highlight of the stay. None of us got any sleep that night. The place was full of hungry Italian bugs. We left early the next morning—not even waiting for coffee—all of us scratching our bites.

It was Christmas Day when we got back to Algiers. We lunched at our desks and in the evening played a little bridge and went to bed early. We were so busy winding up affairs in Algiers that Christmas seemed beside the point. Ike was going back to the States for a couple of weeks and then would fly to London to set up SHAEF (Supreme Headquarters Allied Expeditionary Force). I would be leaving for London myself very shortly. I was beginning to feel homesick for the first time, now that I knew I was going home. It would be good to be back—no matter how cold or rationed or bleak it might be. It was home. And Ike would be there.

IKE had left for Washington and I was alone, left behind in Algiers. All the energy had gone out of headquarters like air out of a balloon. Some of us were preparing to join the General in London; others would go to other posts. It was a sad time. We had all been so close for so many months. Although I was going to London, I may have been the saddest of all.

I was also jealous. Ike and I had carefully avoided one topic. He rarely mentioned his wife in my presence, only when someone asked after her. I never mentioned her. But I thought about her. For one thing, I thought her a fortunate woman to have this man as her husband, the father of her son. I had other thoughts, too. Some rather graceless ones. I kept them all to myself. It was anguishing for me to think of Ike going home, home to his wife.

For the first time in my life I had trouble sleeping. What lay ahead for us? For me? When I tried to look at our relationship objectively, it seemed like a schoolgirl crush on my part. But I was no schoolgirl. And my feelings were reciprocated. I was serenely certain of that. Ever since Ike had told me—hesitant, mumbling, embarrassed and utterly, tenderly loving—about his night of torment when he heard that the *Strathallen* had been torpedoed, I had never doubted his love. And I did not doubt it now. But . . .

This was a strange love affair, if one could call it an affair. Whatever it was, I have never had such a perfect relationship with anyone else in my life. Ever. Not with anybody. We were absolutely in love with each other. If he took my hand and gave it a squeeze, I knew everything that was in his heart. He was like that. He was never able to come right out and say, "I love you" after that first time. His way of telling me would be to say, "Kay, you know exactly what I would like to tell you. You have to understand." And I would say, "Yes, I understand." And I did.

Tossing about in bed night after night, unable to get to sleep, I went over and over Ike's last hours in Algiers. After breakfast on the day he left—it was the last day of 1943—we were drinking a last cup of coffee while elsewhere in the house Mickey attended to the packing. "I'm going to miss you a lot," I said. "Two weeks seems like a long time. Especially when you are going to be so far away."

"Twelve days," he corrected me. "You'll be with me all the time. Don't you know that, my darling? You know—you have to know—the things that are in my heart. You know what I want to say. I don't have the right. But think of me. I'll be thinking of you." It was a long speech for Ike, the most taciturn of men when it came to sentiment.

He held my hand and looked at me for a long moment. Then we were on our way to the airport. We must have looked like a kennel on wheels. Telek was in front with me, and in back with Ike and Butch were Telek's son and daughter, Junior and Rubey. The men had decided the puppies were the perfect late-Christmas gifts for their wives. A small crowd was waiting to see the General off. I was grateful that he had arranged for those few private minutes for us to say good-bye. He shook hands with all his staff. I was the last one. He took a slip of paper out of his pocket and said, "Kay, will you tend to this for me?" "Certainly, General," I told him. "Have a safe trip."

I stood on the ground watching until the plane disappeared into the haze on the horizon. Back in the car, I looked at the paper he had given me. *Think of me,* he had written. *You know what I will be thinking.* I cried. I simply could not help it. But that was a dangerous indulgence; someone might be watching. I sniffed and angrily scrubbed my fists into my eyes to wipe away the tears and turned the car around to head back to the St.-Georges.

After days and nights of heart searching, playing over scene after scene in my head, starting from the very first day I had set eyes on the unknown major general in Grosvenor Square, I finally became very calm and accepting. I loved Ike. That was all that mattered. I wanted nothing more. It was folly to think of the future. There was a war. If it had been peacetime, it would have been entirely different. An entirely different matter. Then, I believe, I might . . . after a certain time, I think I might . . . I might have said, "Make up your mind." But we were living in a different time. In wartime one has an entirely different approach to life, based on the here and now. After all, we were never sure that there would be a tomorrow. We had seen too much. Tomorrow would have to take care of itself.

I would follow my heart. And every one of my heartstrings led to Ike.

21

I flew to London in General Eisenhower's brand-new B-17. It was a fantastically luxurious plane, with wood paneling and comfortable seats upholstered in blue leather. After hitching rides in cargo planes where you were lucky if there was a bench or a row of bucket seats bolted down (and the toilet facilities were also of the bucket variety), I thought this plane, with its carpeting and bunks and a washroom with a flush toilet, was like a Claridge's in the sky. This time I was not traveling with Vuitton cases and silken luxuries carefully wrapped in scented paper. All my belongings were easily stuffed into a duffel bag, and I did not feel the least bit underprivileged. I had learned how unimportant possessions are.

As we drove in from the airfield, everything said home to me: the grimy London buildings, the double-decker buses, the very way the English held themselves as they walked. I was in a rush to go around and see my mother. I was spilling over with all the experiences of the past year—but the most important, I kept to myself. I could not tell even my mother about my feelings for the General. She asked after him with great interest, and I told her all about the suspenseful time when we had not known whether he would be appointed commander for Overlord or be called back to a desk job in Washington. I told her how we had gone riding together at Sailor's Delight. I told her how he had been very ill with the flu. But I never mentioned a word of the love that had grown between us.

The next morning, the world was invisible. I stepped out into such a pea-soup fog, the kind that left your throat raw and your eyes red, as would have done credit to the days of Charles Dickens. One could barely see an arm's length ahead. When I walked into 20 Grosvenor, Tex told me excitedly, "The Boss is on his way. You'll have to go get him."

"Marvelous," I said. "Where is he coming in?"—getting ready to scramble for the car like a firehorse responding to the bell.

"He's in Scotland," Tex said. "He can't fly in because of the fog. They've sent *Bayonet* up for him and he'll be arriving around eleven tonight." Tex looked concerned. "Do you think you can drive in this fog? What should we do if it doesn't lift?" I assured him that I could find my way around London blind-folded. "Don't worry," I said. "I'll be very careful. It will be a piece of cake."

Once I had the car out on the street that night, however, I had my doubts. The fog was thicker. The buses were proceeding at a walk. Literally: most of them were being led by a man going ahead on foot carrying a lantern. I would have to stop every now and then, get out and scuffle around with my feet to find the curb. I was scared silly of missing a turn and ending up miles out of the way. Even though I had allowed myself ample time, I began to wonder if I would reach the station before the train arrived. I did. Barely. I reached the platform just as the short little train pulled in. There behind the engine was old, fa-miliar *Bayonet*, the General's personal railroad car. And there was Butch. And Mickey. And the General. I felt like flinging my arms around him, but this was definitely not the time or the place.

"It's great to be back," Ike said. Then he stepped out into the night. "My God!" he exclaimed. "This is the worst one I've seen. How did you ever get here?"

"No problem," I said airily. "I just muddled through." I was praying that I would be able to muddle through again. I drove the return trip mostly by memory, but when I thought we must be close to 20 Grosvenor, there was no way to tell. The fog was that impenetrable. I stopped and got out, feeling for the curb with my foot, then I got down and crawled across the sidewalk until I came up against a building wall. I started forward, shuffling so that I wouldn't fall into an open areaway, feeling for a door. I came to one within a few feet—and it was 20 Grosvenor. I had been right on target. It is impossible to describe my relief. "Here it is!" I shouted. Ike insisted that we form a human chain reaching from the car to the door.

This was not the end of our travels that night. The General had only wanted to stop in at headquarters to check his messages. By the time I had washed the sidewalk grime off my hands, he was ready to go on. Because of his dislike for hotel living, they had found him a lovely town house just off Berkeley Square. Ike said, "Come on in, Kay. Let's see where they've put me." We went over the whole house from top to bottom. Ike even wanted to take a look at the basement. He liked the house. "I don't need a big place like this," he said, "but it's very pleasant. Very pleasant. Still and all, I think I would rather be back in Telegraph Cottage."

"Oh, my goodness," I said. "I don't think I could have found the cottage in the fog tonight." He laughed.

We were all tired. The General had had a long plane trip and the train journey from Scotland on top of that. And I had had a nerve-racking couple of hours driving through fog. It was well after midnight. Butch said that he was going straight to bed, but the General was too wound up to settle down. "Stay and have a nightcap, Kay," he said. "I'm too wide awake to go to bed."

Mickey had a drink tray ready in no time at all, complete with a plate of cheese sandwiches. I realized that I was starving and gobbled two of them down one right after the other. Ike told Mickey that that would be all for the night, not to wait up for him.

We were alone—or practically. No one was going to come wandering into this living room tonight. There were no peering eyes. This was no goldfish bowl.

"I've got a lot to tell you," Ike said. "Come here." I sat down beside him, and he put his arm around me. "I missed you," he said. "I missed you too." We sat and talked. I told him how we had been grounded in Marrakech on the way back to London and spent a couple of days sunbathing and sightseeing. And he told me a bit about his stay in the States.

"After two days, I started getting itchy," he said. "I wanted to get back here and get to work. But Marshall insisted that I needed the whole twelve days as vacation. Some vacation. I spent as much of it as I could in the Pentagon." He stopped and then said, "Oh my God, I almost forgot. I saw the President while I was in Washington and he asked after you."

"He did?"

"Yes, he did. He sent you his very best wishes and he gave me something for you." Ike went out into the hall and yelled for Mickey. "Where's that big envelope from the White House?" he asked when a sleepy Mickey came down the stairs. Mickey was back in a couple of minutes with the envelope. "Will there be anything else?" he asked. "No, no," Ike said. "Go to bed. Get some sleep." And poor Mickey trudged upstairs again.

I opened the big envelope. It was a photograph of President Roosevelt inscribed to me. I was very flattered. Ever since the war, I have had my own photograph gallery of heroes—autographed pictures of General Eisenhower, Prime Minister Churchill and President Roosevelt. No matter where I have lived, they have always hung in the place of honor in my living room.

Ike refilled our glasses several times and then, I suppose inevitably, we found ourselves in each other's arms in an unrestrained embrace. Our ties came off. Our jackets came off. But—

tons were unbuttoned. It was as if we were frantic. And we were.

But this was not what I had expected. Wearily, we slowly calmed down. He snuggled his face into the hollow between my neck and shoulder and said, "Oh God, Kay. I'm sorry. I'm not going to be any good for you." I didn't know what to say except "You're good enough for me. What you need is some sleep." It was a bit embarrassing struggling back into the clothes that had been flung on the floor. Finally we were dressed. Ike looked troubled. "I don't want to let you go," he said. "But you can't stay here. God, I'm sorry. I can't even drive you home."

"Don't worry," I told him. "I'll be fine. It's just around the corner." We kissed good night. As he let me out the door, I saluted. "Good night, General. I'll be here in the morning." One never knew who might be lurking in the fog ready to catch an indiscreet word.

I was ready to go to sleep then and there with my head on the steering wheel. Or was I ready to bawl my head off? I did neither; simply drove another few blocks through the fog and got myself to bed. My last thought as I dropped off to sleep was to the effect that things are never the way you think they'll be.

I was back at the house at breakfast time. "Come on, Kay," Ike said. "You better have an egg. We've got a big day ahead of us." He and Butch were very cheerful and energetic. The inner qualms I had had about seeing Ike this morning disappeared in the daylight. The fog had lifted. And life seemed bright again. Ike was discussing plans with Butch. He had decided to move SHAEF out of Grosvenor Square to Bushey Park, and take over the group of buildings where Tooey Spaatz's Eighth Air Force used to be headquartered. "I'm going to move the whole shebang out to Kingston," he told us. "That way we won't get caught up in all that la-di-da London society stuff, and the officers will be thrown together so they'll get to know each other and each other's ways fast. I want to turn this command into a very close-knit group. It's the only way."

I interrupted. "Does that mean we can go back to Telegraph Cottage?"

"You're damned right it does." Butch and I beamed at each other. "When?" I asked. "As soon as possible," Ike said briskly. "We'll keep this place for when I have to spend a night in London, but Telegraph Cottage is going to be home." He said this last with great satisfaction.

After outlining his plans, Ike dispatched Butch to Bushey Park to start setting things up, and I drove Ike around to Grosvenor Square. We slipped right back into routine. That afternoon I drove the General out to Bushey Park. "Let's make a detour," he said. "I'd like to take a look at the cottage. I've missed that little house." Nothing could have pleased me more. I took the familiar turn and soon came to the driveway with the white pole across it.

"Goddamnit!" I said as I got out to swing the pole aside.

"What was that you said?" Ike asked startled.

"It's that pole."

"Oh," he remarked. "I just wondered where you picked up that kind of language."

The house was just as we had remembered it. Adorable. "Okay, let's go," Ike said. I turned the car around to leave. Then he said, "Just a minute." I looked up at the rearview mirror to see what he wanted.

His lips were grim and straight. "I'm sorry about last night." He was talking into the air over my shoulder. "I told you a long time ago that I was out of practice in love."

"I'm the one who should apologize," I said. "I should have known how exhausted you were. I should have known better." I should have. It was not as if I did not know what he had been through in the last two weeks. Days crammed with family and military affairs. A long and exhausting air trip. On top of that, a twelve-hour train ride to London. He had been exhausted. Butch had been sensible and gone straight to bed. But we, the greedy lovers, had stayed up until after two in the morning. I was old enough to know better. I was sophisticated enough to know that a man in his fifties has only so much resilience.

"You're not terribly disappointed, then?"

"No, I'm not disappointed. Not a bit. Because now I know . . ." I hesitated. It was hard to say it. "Now I know that someday we . . . well, you know . . . someday we're going to," I ended rather incoherently.

"Maybe," said Ike. He did not sound convinced. But I was not worried. I only wished that we did not have to have our very intimate emotional exchanges in the car. It is very difficult to respond to a voice coming over your shoulder, to a face you see only in the rearview mirror.

22

I N no time at all, SHAEF was transferred to Bushey Park, and our little family along with it. Ike and Butch were back in Telegraph Cottage once again with Mickey and Sergeants Moaney and Hunt. I was about two minutes away, sharing a house with the five WACs. And Beetle flew in from Algiers to resume his duties as chief of staff, bringing Telek along with him.

Poor Telek had to go straight to a kennel for six months. The English quarantine laws are fantastically strict. They are not broken even for the Royal Family. The first time we went to visit him at the kennel, a crowd of journalists and photographers was lying in wait. Someone, probably the kennel people, had tipped off the press, and the result was a rash of cloying stories about Ike and Telek all over the London papers. Ike was boiling mad. In North Africa he had been well protected from the intrusions of the penny press, and he did not enjoy meeting up with them again.

The two of us sneaked back to the kennel the next day. I brought my old handbag for Telek so that he would not feel completely deserted. For the next six months, he always slept with his head on it. We went to see him at least twice a week, like visiting a prisoner. Telek would go wild with joy, but when we left, he sat there utterly dejected. Ike once said, "This is terrible. I feel as if I have locked up part of my heart." At first we saved all our beef bones for him, but this turned out to be a mistake. He got a stoppage, and the veterinarian told us very crossly, "No more bones."

Not everyone shared our love for Telek and his family. One evening I asked rather idly after Rubey and Junior. Were they thriving in Washington? "God only knows," Ike growled. Both Mrs. Eisenhower and Mrs. Butcher had been dismayed at the sight of the puppies, he reported, and doubly dismayed when the poor things made a puddle on the living-room Oriental. Butch had had to spend a good part of his leave finding homes for the cuddly black waifs.

Ike made himself a drink and settled down in his favorite big chair by the fire. I was sitting across from him, my feet on the brass fender. It was cold and dark outside, warm and cozy within. "There was the very devil to pay," he said, "from the moment we walked in with those two pups until I left. And it wasn't only the dogs."

His lips twitched. He finally gave in and grinned. "The big trouble was . . . I kept calling her Kay. That tore it."

"What?"

"I kept calling her Kay. Every time I opened my mouth to say something to Mamie, I'd call her Kay. She was furious."

I am ashamed to say that nothing could have pleased me more. No pity for Mrs. Eisenhower spoiled my enjoyment. Today I feel great sympathy for her. It must have been a cruel shock to realize that another woman was uppermost in her husband's thoughts. But at that time, she was far away. And I was a woman in love.

"I'm sorry about that," I said. "It must have been a bit upsetting for her. And for you too."

"Jesus Christ! You have no idea." Ike was smoking one cigarette after another—lighting one from the tip of the last, then throwing the stub into the fire. "I thought about you a lot," he said. "You know what I like to think about nights before I go to sleep?"

I shook my head.

"The first time I ever set eyes on you. I saw you walking along Grosvenor Square. You looked very glamorous. Beautiful. And all of a sudden, you started running straight toward me. It was as if you had read my mind. Then you stopped. All out of breath. And asked if one of us was General Eisenhower. Well! I thought I was dreaming. You would never believe how disappointed I was to discover that Claridge's was so close to headquarters. I wanted that drive to last forever."

"You never told me that," I said.

"You know me," he protested. "There are so many times I look at you and want to tell you how beautiful you are and how much you mean to me, but something always stops me. I suppose it's this stolid German-Swiss heritage of mine that makes me feel a man should not talk about such things. For God's sake, there were months when I could not let myself face how I felt about you. I used to think that if I had a daughter I would want her to be just like you. It took a disaster to ram the truth home to me. I had to nearly lose you before I could admit to myself that my feelings were more than paternal.

"And then there's something else. I just don't have the right to tell you what I want to tell you."

When I think about the long talks we used to have at Telegraph Cottage, I am overwhelmed with nostalgia. Not that we were ever really alone. There was never once that the two of us had the house to ourselves—but we had privacy. We began to feel quite relaxed, sitting quietly in front of the fire, or on our favorite secluded bench hidden in the shrubbery, hand in hand, my head on his shoulder—talking our hearts out. Just enjoying being together.

I suspect that over the years—long before Ike and I ever set foot in Telegraph Cottage—many couples had sat in front of its fire and whispered confidences to each other. There was something about the atmosphere of that little house that bred intimacy and trust. It was easy to talk about all the things that one had never spoken of before. Of secret fears. Of past mistakes. Of withering sorrows.

It was in that living room one sunny morning that Ike talked very seriously and at length about his relationship with his wife. There was deep hurt on both sides, hurt so deep that they were never able to recapture their earlier relationship—although it was not for want of trying. Ike had applied to himself the wisdom he had shared with me that "activity helps"; had thrown himself so completely into his work that there was room for nothing else. It was hard for him to tell the story, even in the benign atmosphere of Telegraph Cottage. He would say a few words, then halt. His voice was low. Most of the time he was leaning forward in his chair looking down at the floor.

"Kay, I guess I'm telling you that I'm not the lover you should have. It killed something in me. Not all at once, but little by little. For years I never thought of making love. And then when I did . . . when it had been on my mind for weeks, I failed. I failed with you, my dearest. Didn't I?"

I sat on the arm of his chair and cuddled his head against my breast. "It's all right. It's all right," I crooned to him the way my mother used to soothe me when I was a child. "I love you. It's all right."

He straightened up, took out his handkerchief and honked into it. His eyes were red. "I'm sorry. I'm a damned fool. But you know that. God, I don't know what's the matter with me."

"Nothing. Nothing at all," I whispered.

"Somehow I just lost the way," he said standing with his back to me looking out the window.

"Someday things will be different," I promised him. "I'm not Irish and stubborn for nothing."

It would be incorrect to think that the General and I spent most of our time exploring our emotions and feelings for each other. We were far too busy for that kind of introspective luxury. I was now acting as his appointments secretary. There could not have been a better job for me. I knew everyone the General knew and almost everything that was going on. And I knew the General—the people he liked, the people he tolerated and the people who drove him up the wall. I now had my own private office and my own secretary. I loved the job. It was a natural extension of our relationship.

No one could get in to see the General without going through my office first. I also took all his telephone calls. I would say, "General Eisenhower's office. Miss Summersby speaking." Then I would pop into his office and say, "General So-and-So is on the line," or "The P.M. is calling you." That way he was spared the jangling of the telephone and the irritation of the intercom buzzer. These were trivial annoyances, of course, but it was important to make his office life as smoothly efficient and pleasant as possible. He had enough problems without having to suffer avoidable irritation. When a visitor was staying too long or I thought that the General might want to cut a meeting short, I'd go into his office with a piece of paper in my hand and say, "Excuse me, General. This message just came in." Then whoever it was would usually say, "Well, I've got to be going." And if he didn't, Ike would say, "I'm sorry. It looks as if we're going to have to cut this short," and stand up so that his caller would have no choice but to rise to his feet as well. And that would be that.

Young officers who had been summoned to the Supreme Commander's office, usually to be congratulated on some achievement, would wait in my office. They would be nervous. Simply petrified. "What should I say to him?" they would ask. "What will I do when I'm in there?"

"Just be yourself," I would say. "Say what you have to say and you'll find out that you get along very well."

Afterwards, when they came out of the General's office, their faces would be glowing. Ike always knew exactly how to put people at ease, and he liked talking to these young men. It was a bit of relaxation for him. He was really very, very busy in those months preceding the invasion of the Continent. A typical day would have a string of appointments that would read like this:

    10:30   General Betts
    11:30   Conference of the Commanders in Chief
    12:30   General Prentice
     1:30   Lunch with the P.M.
     8:00   Dinner with Admiral Stark
    10:00   General Spaatz

Each of these conferences would be on some vital aspect of mounting the invasion, and Ike was the only man who had all phases of the operation in his head. Then, for two or three days at a time, we would leave SHAEF and travel all over England and Scotland visiting different bases. Every time we came back from an inspection trip, Ike would have another cold. He wanted to visit every installation—including hospitals and certain factories—before the invasion: an almost impossible task. He would talk with the commanding officers, inspect the men's quarters, tour the mess and then talk to as many men as he possibly could. He wanted the men to know that the Supreme Commander was concerned about them.

He liked groups of three and four, where he could shake each man's hand and say a few personal words. Then he would move on to another group. He was awfully good at this, and the men liked him. They weren't just putting it on. You could tell that they really liked him. But when we got back to headquarters, he would be so hoarse that Ethel would be popping into and out of the office all day long, spraying his throat, taking his temperature and scolding him that he should be in bed.

His office was probably the worst place possible for a man with Ike's tendency to catch cold. It was unheated, as were all the offices. And although, in deference to his rank as Supreme Commander, there was a carpet on the floor, it was a very thin

carpet and the damp chill of the concrete floor seeped right
through it. We all wore long underwear when we worked there,
and Ike often wore two pairs of socks to try to keep warm, but
he suffered acutely from the cold. He developed a cough that
lasted for months, and he was always getting little infections because he was so run down.

I still have my little blue leather appointment book for 1944.
It is very shabby now and rather hard to read, because I scrib-
bled everything down in a hurry and much of it is smudged. I
used to jot down his appointments and add a word or two about
the subject under discussion or Ike's comment on the meeting.
One Friday, for instance, the most important entry was *Lunch
with the King and Queen at Buckingham Palace, 1:30.* Later
that day, I added Ike's report on the lunch: *Most enjoyable 2
hours.*

Little by little, the small blue book turned into a combination
appointment book and diary. Ike would say, "Bring the book in,
Kay." He would leaf through it—sometimes to check on what
had been discussed the last time he saw a certain general, or
sometimes just to relax. He would say, "Oh, that was a great
day. We had a good time, didn't we?" and laugh. Then he
started writing in it himself. One Sunday he recorded the day's
activities: *Office until 1:30 p.m. Home to lunch, then went for
drive. Found very short way to kennels.* Another day he wrote:
*Terribly busy at office. Had lunch at desk. Worked late, but saw
Telek on way home. Beetle and Ethel came to dinner. To bed
early.* I was the driver, of course, who found the short way to the
kennels, and I was also there for dinner with Beetle and Ethel,
but we never wrote such things down, even though the diary
was kept safely tucked away.

I drew on the material in this little blue book when I wrote
my first book a quarter of a century ago, but I was very careful
about how I used it. In that book, for instance, I wrote: "On an
inspection trip to Scotland, he managed to get in an entire day
of salmon fishing at the lovely estate of Colonel Ivan Cobbald."

A bland enough, non-gossip-provoking report. But what I had written in the diary at the end of that day in 1944 was: *Started fishing at Cobbald's place at 9:30. No luck at all. Beautiful weather though. I caught a baby salmon—three inches. E. got a kelt, which was bad luck as he had to throw it back in the river. We all had a lovely time, wish we could have stayed longer.*

Ike needed every possible diversion like this fishing trip that he could possibly get. He was as nervous as I had ever seen him and was extremely depressed. There were times when the problems that faced him seemed insurmountable. It is impossible to list them all. There was the problem of getting enough supplies to mount the invasion. He kept pleading for more landing craft. There were the inevitable problems arising from the fact that hundreds of thousands of American and Canadian soldiers were now tucked away all over England. It did not seem possible that one more man could fit onto this island—but every day, troopship after troopship unloaded new units. There were rapes, thefts, fights—the same problems that have bedeviled every army in history.

There was General de Gaulle, proud and prickly, who became so incensed at one point that he stalked out of a luncheon meeting, threatening the intricately woven fabric of Allied unity. There was General Montgomery, who resisted each and every directive of Eisenhower's and always wanted to do things in his own way at his own chosen time. Even the P.M. was a problem of sorts. An amateur of war, Mr. Churchill had fresh ideas every day on how to conduct the invasion and insisted on imparting them to Ike himself. He often telephoned after midnight to discuss a new brainstorm. Ike could not simply tell the P.M., "That idea stinks." He had to point out to him exactly why such and such an idea would not work or would not be politic. This took a lot of time and an awful lot of patience.

Telegraph Cottage became more important in maintaining the General's equilibrium than ever before. It was so close that it was easy for him to go home for lunch. That little break in the day helped him relax. Many days, if he had no afternoon appointments, he would not return to Bushey Park, but would stay home and go over his papers, then get some exercise.

We spent many afternoons riding in Richmond Park, just minutes away from the cottage. This is an absolutely delightful spot, with miles and miles of bridle paths winding through woods, along lakes and past some very beautiful houses, many of them royal "grace and favor" dwellings in which relatives and friends live at the invitation of the Royal Family. We often rode past White Lodge, a royal residence that had been much favored by Queen Victoria. It was not what one ordinarily thinks of as a lodge, but a big stone mansion. Ike had learned that the King and Queen had spent their honeymoon here and that the Duke of Windsor had been born here. That made the place interesting to him.

When the weather was bad, Ike indulged himself in a favorite hobby: cooking. Actually, I think anyone would enjoy cooking Ike's way. He had Hunt and Moaney to do all the dirty work. They did the chopping and measuring, set out all the ingredients—and, of course, they washed up afterwards.

His beef stew was really very tasty, but one had to know how to eat his fried chicken. I remember watching him make it one day. He always insisted on an audience. Butch and I and Tooey and Beetle and Ethel all stood around while Ike presided at the kitchen table. Hunt and Moaney followed his orders just like two nurses assisting a famous surgeon. Moaney cut the chicken up in pieces, and Hunt produced the ingredients for Ike's coating mixture.

Ike would say, "Measuring spoon," and Hunt would hand him the spoon. He would say, "Chili powder," and Hunt would open the little tin and pass it to him. Ike measured out each ingredient and dumped it into a bowl. When he was measuring out the chili powder, Butch groaned, "There's not enough beer in England to put out that kind of fire." Ike rolled the chicken pieces in the mixture and then started instructing Moaney as to just how hot the fat in the skillet should be. At that point, Tooey and Beetle intervened. They had been through this before and insisted that Ike join us in the living room for a drink before dinner.

When we sat down to eat, Ike said, "Now, isn't this great?" And we all agreed that it was. I discovered that if I scraped off the coating, which was throat-burning hot, the chicken was absolutely delicious. Moaney really knew how to fry chicken.

When the ground got dry enough in the spring, we played a little golf, and we played bridge every night that Ike was home. We had a lot of visitors. One I remember very well was Averell Harriman, who arrived from Moscow one day with a huge tin of caviar. We all sat around the table piling great gobs of it on Melba toast and washing it down with champagne. Butch looked at the caviar and the champagne bottles and said, "Now I know what they mean when they say war is hell."

Mummy joined us several times for dinner at the cottage. Georgie Patton was a guest one night that she was there, and I was a bit apprehensive about how she would react to his profanity, but the evening went by with only the mildest of outbursts from the usually incorrigible general, who put himself out to be gallant. Ike was always extremely thoughtful of my family. Once during this period he invited my brother to accompany him on a tour of air bases. When the photographers clustered around, as they did at every stop, Seamus quietly withdrew to the sidelines, but Ike said, "Seamus, you have to be in this too" and drew him into the group. It was gestures like this that showed Ike's truly deep consideration. He did everything he possibly could to make people feel good.

Ike still tried to sketch Telegraph Cottage, but was never satisfied with the results. One evening he had his sketch pad on his knee and was busy drawing. I looked over his shoulder and discovered that he was drawing floor plans, not a picture.

"What do you think?" he asked, holding out the pad. "It struck me that if I owned this place, I'd want to make a few changes." He had designed a little wing with a new kitchen and a little maid's room and bath. He thought that the present kitchen should be turned into a big dining room and that another fireplace should be built where the old stove was. We had a lot of fun talking about the changes we'd like to make. After that, he would quite often pick up his pad and work out different floor plans for the cottage. He had a lot of very good ideas and would get completely absorbed in working them out. It was almost as much of an escape for him as playing bridge.

He also spent quite a bit of time planning the vegetable garden. He had had some gorgeous seed catalogs sent to him from the States, and he would go through them and make lists of what he wanted to plant. When he came to some vegetable that he particularly liked, he'd stop and read the description to me. It was impossible to convince him that even though my father had been quite a noted gardener in County Cork, I knew less than nothing about sticking seeds into the ground and having them come up to be something one could eat. But he persisted. He would read things like " 'Lima beans, the finest, meatiest, most delicious beans. Strong plants.' What do you think, Kay? Do you like lima beans? Here's another variety. 'Very large flat beans with pink spots.' "

"Oh," I remember saying once, "beans with pink spots. By all means. They should be very pretty."

"That's not the point," he snapped.

But there came a day when all this stopped abruptly. It was late May and the invasion was imminent. Everything we had been working for since the first of the year was about to be set in motion. The only major problem that still had to be resolved was —when? The invasion date had been narrowed down to a span of a few possible days when the moon and the tides would be on our side. Now everything depended on the weather. The General had the meteorologists on the telephone almost every hour, asking for the latest forecast. And at the end of May, we left Telegraph Cottage and moved to advance headquarters in the woods outside Portsmouth.

23

Ike was bleakly depressed. And I reflected his mood. Our advance headquarters, hidden in the woods at Southwick about five miles north of Portsmouth, were dreary beyond belief. It was raining on and off, and the trees were dripping onto the roof of the trailer we used as an office. I kept thinking of Telegraph Cottage as we had left it. The sun had been shining, and every flower of spring had seemed to be blossoming in the garden. Here there was nothing but gloom.

The story of the D-Day decision and how much depended on the one thing man could not control—the weather—has been told and told again. There was a certain combination of moon, tide and sunrise needed for the attack on the Normandy beaches, and there were three days in early June that would provide the combination: the fifth, sixth and seventh. But without good weather the attack could not be mounted, and it would be some time before the moon and tide and sunrise would be properly synchronized again. This problem had been hanging over the General's head for months. He consulted with the meteorologists almost as often as he consulted with his top commanders. Hundreds of thousands of highly trained soldiers, millions of tons of supplies, aircraft, ships—everything had been assembled for the invasion, all poised to go into action as soon as Ike gave the word. Sometimes it seemed as if Britain would sink under the weight of men and matériel. And everything hung on one unknown quantity: the weather.

On June 4, the forecast for the following day was heavy clouds, high winds and rough seas. It would be impossible to land the men if waves were pounding on the beaches and equally impossible to provide air support without good visibility. The General postponed the invasion.

The long-range forecast was for more of the same. Ike could not have been more anxiety ridden. There were smoldering cigarettes in every ashtray in the trailer. He would light one, put it down, forget it and light another. He was having blood-pressure headaches, and his stomach was giving him trouble too. Every once in a while he would bend over with a terrible gas pain.

He grumbled that military textbooks taught that the weather was neutral, but that in his experience—in North Africa, in Italy and now—the weather was always partisan, and on the side of the Germans. He marched up and down the trailer, stopping occasionally to stare out at the drizzle, his hands on his hips. Occasionally the sun would break through for a minute, and he would rush outside to look at the sky and tell me to get the weathermen on the telephone. He couldn't eat. He simply drank pot after pot of coffee and smoked.

At four o'clock in the morning of the next day, June 5, the meteorologists phoned through a report that there would be a break in the weather. It very much looked as if June 6 would be a fine, clear day—and possibly June 7 as well. This did not give Ike much leeway. There was no assurance that the weather would not change suddenly, capriciously—faster than the weathermen had predicted. There were no guarantees. He listened. And then—fifteen minutes after he got that early-morning report —Ike made the decision that only he could make. The invasion was on. D-Day would be June 6.

The General held a press conference that morning to brief the pool journalists who would cover the invasion. From then on, the pace was unrelenting. Orders were sent to ships already at sea and to those waiting in crowded harbors fringing the English Channel, to the commanding generals and to the Allied statesmen. The P.M. and his retinue arrived at the trailer. General de Gaulle came by. Field Marshal Smuts of South Africa dropped in, and so did a dozen others. There were messages from Washington and London. Messages from commanders. From Monty. It was a frantic day. At one point Ike said, "I hope to God I know what I'm doing. There are times when you have to put everything you are and everything you have ever learned on the line. This is one of them."

"I know," I told him, "and if it goes all right, dozens of people will claim the credit. But if it goes wrong, you'll be the only one to get the blame." I was wrong, as it turned out. Everyone gave Ike the credit he was due.

At six that evening he stopped everything. He had something important to do, something that turned out to be the most memorable event of the whole war for me. My little blue diary holds this entry: 6:30 *p.m., start trip to visit Airborne troops in the Newbury area. Gen. Taylor. Visited 3 airfields. Morale of troops very high. Watched some of them take off. Wonderful sight.*

This conveys no idea of the drama of that evening. The 101st Airborne Division, commanded by General Maxwell Taylor, was the key to seizing Utah Beach and the eventual capture of Cherbourg. Not everyone agreed with this aspect of Ike's battle plan. Some British commanders thought that he was sending these men on a suicidal mission and that the casualties would be crushing, as high as eighty percent. Ike never ignored dissenting opinions like this. He always sought and considered the views of his commanders, considered them very seriously. I think that was why he was so successful as Supreme Commander. He would not agree with the Americans just because he was an American. He would listen to the English, to the French, to the Czechs, to the Canadians, to the Poles. He would listen to the lot of them. And he was equally courteous to each. Then he would make up his own mind. Now he went over and over his

battle plan. He spent hours alone in his tent checking every cal-
culation he had made, taking everything that could possibly go
wrong into account—and decided to stick to his plan. But he was
worried.

And the night before D-Day, we dropped everything to make
the long drive to Newbury and visit the 101st Airborne. They
would be the first troops to land in Normandy behind the
enemy lines. Some would be towed over in huge gliders that
would settle down quietly in the darkness with their cargoes of
young fighting men. Others would parachute down into this
heavily fortified area. Ike's last task on the eve of D-Day was to
wish these men well.

There was no military pomp about his visit. His flag was not
flying from the radiator of the car, and he had told me to cover
the four stars on the red plate. We drove up to each of the
airfields, and Ike got out and just started walking among the
men. When they realized who it was, the word went from group
to group like the wind blowing across a meadow, and then everyone went crazy. The roar was unbelievable. They cheered
and whistled and shouted, "Good old Ike!"

There they were, these young paratroopers in their bulky
combat kits with their faces blackened so that they would be invisible in the dark of the French midnight. Anything that could
not be carried in their pockets was strapped on their backs or to
their arms and legs. Many of them had packages of cigarettes
strapped to their thighs. They looked so young and so brave. I
stood by the car and watched as the General walked among
them with his military aide a few paces behind him. He went
from group to group and shook hands with as many men as he
could. He spoke a few words to every man as he shook his hand,
and he looked the man in the eye as he wished him success. "It's
very hard really to look a soldier in the eye," he told me later,
"when you fear that you are sending him to his death."

The good weather promised by the meteorologists had arrived,
and all the time that Ike had been talking to the paratroopers

there was the most spectacular sunset—deep glowing colors stretching across the sky. As it faded and the light started to go, the men began to embark. General Maxwell Taylor was the last to leave. Ike walked him to his plane and shook hands with him, and then we went over to the headquarters building of the 101st and climbed up to the roof.

The planes were taking off, roaring down the runways and climbing, climbing. Soon there were hundreds circling above us. By this time, it was dark and the moon had come up. It was a full moon, so brilliant that it cast shadows. The planes, wheeling like some immense flock of birds, blotted it out from time to time. It was such a gigantic moment! My heart was pounding, and I was practically crying. I knew I had never seen anything like it before and never would see anything like it again. We stayed on the roof for a long time watching the planes. Ike stood there with his hands in his pockets, his face tipped toward the sky. The planes kept circling, and then they began tailing off and headed toward Normandy. We sighed. A lot of those men, men whom Ike had just been walking with, shaking hands with, were going to their deaths.

The General turned and left the roof without saying a word to anyone. I hurried after him, but then I stopped. He was walking very slowly, his head bent. I could not intrude. He needed to be alone. Before he got into the car, he turned to me and said, "Well, it's on. No one can stop it now." There were tears in his eyes. We were silent as we drove back along the moonlit road to the trailer in the woods at Southwick.

For the next few hours, we just sat in the trailer waiting for the first reports. There was nothing Ike could do. Just wait. The hours went by. Like everyone else in England, we could hear the roar of planes, rising up from airfields all over the land, heading across the Channel. Every once in a while, I would stand behind Ike and massage his shoulders, trying to relax him just a trifle. He liked that. "Um, that's good," he'd always say, but in those tense predawn hours, no matter how much strength

I used, I could not undo the knots at the base of his neck. His eyes were bloodshot, and he was so tired that his hand shook when he lit a cigarette.

It is very hard to watch the man you love going through such a torture, waiting to find out the consequences of one of the gravest decisions that ever faced one man—a decision that, when you really face up to it, was nothing more nor less than a huge gamble, a gamble with hundreds of thousands of lives as the stake. You can't say, "Don't worry." That would be stupid. You can't say, "Everything is going to be all right," because there is a very good chance that everything may not be all right. All you can do is be there—and bite your tongue. It meant a lot to me that I was the person he chose to be with in those crucial hours. If Ike had wished, he could have been surrounded by top brass, by Churchill and De Gaulle, by any of the important personages who were gathered just a few miles away in Portsmouth. But he preferred to wait in solitude. And I was the one he permitted to share his solitude.

"What are your thoughts, Kay?" he asked at one point.

"I can't believe it," I told him. "After living here through the Blitz and everything . . . to be cut off for so long . . . just an island . . . and now to be landing on the Continent! After all these years of waiting and waiting and taking all the defeats from Dunkirk on . . . I just can't believe we've done it.

"I've been thinking of the first time you came to London and I drove you and Mark Clark to Dover. I heard you say something about 'when we get over there,' and I thought that we had a very slim chance of ever doing that. But now we have. You did it."

"We'll see," he said. "We don't know yet whether we did it or not."

It was quiet in the trailer except for the roaring of planes, as wave after wave of bombers streamed across the Channel to provide air support for the men landing on the beaches. The noise seemed to underline how remote and helpless we were at this moment. A couple of times I told him, "Well, you know, I think you ought to go and lie down for a little while." Around four in the morning, he finally agreed and said, "You should do the same." So we went back to quarters. We were all living in tents there at Southwick, and I thought it looked like some American Indian village.

The first reports were telephoned through to him a couple of hours later. Things were going well. The Germans had been caught unaware. June 6 was a beautiful sunny day. It was the beginning of the end of the war.

24

THERE was a terrible letdown after D-Day. Everyone felt it. Ike was tired as if he had run out of steam. And he was very much depressed. Forty-eight hours after the attack had been mounted, he made a quick trip by destroyer to consult with his commanders and see what could be seen from the deck as the destroyer skirted the Normandy coastline, but most of the time we simply sat in the trailer in the woods waiting. Waiting for reports from the front. The Germans were fighting bitterly. We had a lot of casualties. But overall, the reports were encouraging. Ike always wanted to know more, however. We stayed late every night waiting for just one more report to come through. I would call up the mess and have them send over sandwiches for supper, and I would boil water on the little spirit stove for Ike's powdered coffee. He would sit there and smoke and worry. Every time the telephone rang, he would grab it.

When he had to go to London—and there were conferences in London and Bushey Park about every other day—he would insist on getting back to Portsmouth at night, even if it meant leaving London after midnight. Once he was able to set foot in France, some six days after D-Day, and talk to Monty, Bradley and some of the other commanders, he began to feel better. He was able to straighten out a lot of the logistics and communications problems on that visit.

There was something else that helped pull him out of his depression, and that was the knowledge that his son, John, would be in England very soon. Ike had told General Marshall that he was worried that he and his son were becoming almost like strangers. He had seen less of John over the years than most fathers because of the demands of the military life. And during the past three years, he had seen practically nothing of him. Marshall had been extremely sympathetic and suggested that after John graduated from West Point in June, he might spend his leave in England with his father. Ike thought that was a grand idea, and during the spring he had often said things like "When John gets here, we'll do this or that," and "When John gets here, we must be sure to go here or there." He was always making plans for that visit. But then when D-Day was imminent, he told me rather dispiritedly, "I'm afraid John's visit will have to be put off."

"Oh?" said I.

"Yes," he said. "Graduation is on June 6. With any luck, I should be in France then. And I'm not sure that I want the boy up at the front with me."

General Marshall evidently did not share Ike's misgivings, because one of the messages that came into the trailer late on D-Day was to the effect that John would be arriving in Scotland on June 13. Ike sent Tex up to Scotland in *Bayonet* to escort John to London, and late in the afternoon of June 13, a tall, fresh-faced second lieutenant walked into the office at SHAEF, put his arms around the Supreme Commander and kissed him. Ike was just one big grin. After giving John a quick tour of headquarters, we left for Telegraph Cottage. When I left around midnight, Ike and John were still talking a mile a minute trying to catch up with everything.

I was interested to observe that Ike was not a particularly doting father. He loved John very much and he was proud of him, but he was also critical. Sometimes I thought he was supercritical. John was a truly nice young man. He was intelligent, lots of fun, every bit as charming as his father and very simple and unassuming in manner. Not for one moment during his visit did he presume upon the fact that his father was Supreme Commander. He bent over backward to observe protocol and be self-effacing. Nevertheless, his father saw room for improvement.

On that first evening at the cottage, John told us how excited he had been at the idea of coming to England, especially at such an important time. In order to leave West Point as soon as possible after the graduation ceremonies, he had done all his packing and turned in all his equipment, which included the mattress for his cot, the night before graduation. He reported that he had spent an uncomfortable, restless night on the bare springs of the cot.

I watched Ike's face become more and more closed as John was talking. He looked quite stern, although he said nothing. Later I asked him what had been going through his mind that made him look that way.

"What was going through my mind," he said grimly, "was that across the Channel there are thousands of young men sleeping in foxholes—if they're lucky. And my son complains about a restless night on a cot without a mattress."

"He wasn't complaining," I said. "He was just telling a story. What did you expect him to do? Go out and dig a foxhole?"

"I suppose not," Ike grumbled, "but I think he should toughen up."

Then there were times when the brand-new second lieutenant, eager to talk to his father about matters military as one military man to another, would venture some textbook observation only to have Ike snort, "Oh, for God's sake!" Most of the time, however, Ike was the unabashedly proud and beaming father, and he had every reason to be. He enjoyed briefing John on what was going on in the most minute detail, and he took him along on a couple of inspection tours in Normandy.

Ike did his paternal best to teach John everything he knew during those two weeks, and that included bridge as well as military matters. He told John that his game needed sharpening up, so evening after evening we sat around the card table at the cottage while Ike analyzed his son's game and told him what he was doing wrong. This was the only time the house rule about no postmortems was ever broken, and sometimes it got a bit uncomfortable, as Ike was as brusque with John as he was with any other young officer who needed to be pulled up a bit. But John took it all very good-naturedly. No matter how sharply Ike criticized him, it was obvious that he adored this son of his.

But not even John could distract his father's mind from the war. The invasion was still young, and the news was not always good. I remember one day—it was June 19—when Ike heard that the weather over the Channel was so bad that all shipping was at a standstill. That meant that troops and supplies could not be landed. When the bad news was telephoned through to the cottage, Ike said, "I need a drink." This was the first and only time I ever heard him say that. I mixed him a Scotch and water. "More Scotch," he ordered, so I poured in a very healthy slug on top of his usual ounce-and-a-half jigger. "That's good. I needed that," he said as he gulped it down. The reason for his strong reaction was that if the invasion had been postponed earlier, June 19 would have been its next possible date. That storm turned out to be the most violent storm in fifty years, an actual hurricane, and was a real setback for the Allies—but nowhere near the disaster that it would have been if the invasion had been scheduled to take place at that time.

Before John arrived, Ike had worried about exposing him to danger at the front, but as it turned out, life in England had its own hazards. John's visit coincided with the first of the V-1 bombs. We called them buzz bombs. Something like small planes without pilots, they were launched from platforms in France. Usually, the first warning one got was a kind of drone that got louder and louder as the bomb approached. Then the engine would cut out. That was when you started holding your breath, because it meant the bomb was falling. It was impossible to tell where it would land until it exploded. You could see the falling bombs overhead like deadly black wasps. Many people felt these robot bombs were even worse than the Blitz. I never got over the creeps when I heard one, but Ike said their impact was more psychological than physical.

It was the buzz bombs that drove Ike to using the shelter at the cottage. Months earlier, when the P.M. had learned there was no bomb shelter on the grounds, he had peremptorily ordered one built. It was a rather unsightly mound, a quick scamper from the house. Ike had never used it, but now we were grateful for it. The second night of John's visit, we all slept in the shelter. We had been in it four or five times that evening. It must have been quite a sight as we all rushed out of the house and ran down the garden path. Finally Ike said, "Well, we've got to get some sleep tonight. I guess the only place we'll get it is in the shelter." There were plenty of cots, and Ike, John, Butch and I managed to squeeze in along with Moaney and Hunt and Mickey. It was very close quarters, but as the nights went by, we got used to sleeping there.

I was almost as sorry as Ike when John's visit drew to a close. It had really been nice having him around. But then Ike gave me the most glorious surprise. As we were going over the day's appointments in the office one early morning, he asked, right out of the blue, "How would you like to go to Washington with John? Spend a few days there? Maybe go to New York?"

I opened my mouth, but could not get any sound out.

"I'm serious," he said. "I'm going to be in France all next week. There won't be much for you to do here. John is going back in the Fortress, so there will be plenty of room. What do you think?"

"I think it would be smashing," I said. "Thank you."

And on the last day of June, Ike and John and I drove out to the airport together, drawing up next to the Supreme Commander's Flying Fortress, the same B-17 in which I had flown back from Algiers. Tex and Mattie, one of the Powerhouse WACs, and Sergeant Farr, one of the house staff, were there waiting for us. They were also going to Washington.

As we said our good-byes, Ike and I looked at each other. I really did not want to leave him. My face must have reflected this, because "I want you to go," Ike said softly. "John will take care of you." He shook my hand and sort of patted me on the shoulder. He looked over at John, who was talking to Tex, and then back at me. "I'm putting all my eggs in one basket," he said somberly. "Come back safe." He was very serious. I nodded, gave him one of my untidy salutes and ran up the stairs into the plane.

Seconds later it started down the runway, then picked up speed, and we were in the air. As we circled the field, I could see Ike. He was still there standing beside the car. He looked very small. Small and very alone.

"I'm putting all my eggs in one basket," he had said. I turned to John. "Your father's going to miss you very much," I told him. "He's going to miss you too," John said. "Oh well, that's different," I replied.

Flying in those days was no simple jet hop across the Atlantic between lunch and a late dinner. It took a full day and a half—from London to Prestwick to Iceland to Bangor to Washington. No one had prepared me for Washington. No one had warned me about the summer heat, the damp oppressiveness of it. No one had told me how dazzling a city it was. All the colors. All the lights. The women in pretty dresses. And the cars, all gleaming in different candy colors and shiny with chrome. And nobody had warned me that in the United States when you heard a siren, it was a fire engine or an ambulance or twelve o'clock noon. I had been in Washington less than three hours when I heard my first siren—and threw myself flat on the sidewalk. In England this was the automatic response to the wail of a siren when there was no shelter at hand.

My companions stared down at me. "What's the matter? What happened? Are you ill?" their questions came as they helped me up. I brushed myself off and said, "Well, that's one way to try to save your life when the bombs are falling. Aren't you glad you haven't had to learn it?"

Mrs. Eisenhower had been at the airport and greeted me pleasantly before leaving with John. John called me the next morning to invite me to have drinks with his mother and a few friends that afternoon. I really did not want to go. I told John that I thought it was an imposition, but he insisted.

It was not much fun. I felt very stiff and foreign and military among these women in their fluttery light dresses. No other woman was in uniform. And certainly no other woman was being scrutinized as sharply as I was. As I sought out my hostess to say good-bye, John came up and told his mother that we were going to New York together and that he was going to take me to see *Oklahoma!*

She made a face. "Oh, I'm sure Miss Summersby doesn't want to go to New York in all this heat."

"Yes, she does," said John. "We're going to New York and do the town."

I called him the next day and said, "I don't think your mother approves of this trip to New York. And I can understand that. She wants to see as much of you as possible before you leave for Fort Benning. Why don't we cancel it?" I was quite serious.

"No," said John. "We're going." And that was that.

I have always wondered if perhaps Ike had asked John to do this. I know that Ike would never have said much, but perhaps John might have asked him, "Does she mean anything to you?" and his father might have said, "Yes, she does." Or Ike might simply have said, "Kay has worked hard and been very conscientious. I'd appreciate it if you'd see that she has a good time. Take her to a show or something." John would have been scrupulous about doing anything his father requested.

It was in Washington that I became aware of the gossip about Ike and me. Of its virulence. No wonder the women at that little cocktail party had been eyeing me so closely. Wherever I went, I began to feel as if I were on display. I became increasingly sensitive to the whispers. Ike must have been protecting me from a lot of this. Friends told me that there had been several gossip-column mentions of the General's glamorous driver and nastily pointed insinuations about our relationship.

It is a pity that the gossip about the General and me was allowed to persist. One general's wife handled a similar situation very wisely. Her husband, whom Ike and I saw a great deal of, had been living openly with a WAC officer. When the WAC came to Washington, the General's wife gave a party in her honor and went around with her arm in arm, introducing her to everyone and saying, "I want you to meet a marvelous girl. I don't know what the General would do without her. Or what I would do either, since she keeps me informed of what he's up to when he's too busy to write." All during the WAC's stay, Mrs. General saw to it that she was wined and dined and escorted here and there by some of the handsomest officers at the Pentagon. She treated her like a favorite niece, and the gossip died a sudden death.

It was a relief to get on the train for New York with John and get away from the whispers and the side glances. We did a lot of sight-seeing and went to *Oklahoma!* I had never seen a musical like this before, and I loved every minute of it. It was so American. I was completely bedazzled. I had always been mad for the theater, but this was a fantastically exciting experience. I fell in love with New York. I liked everything about it. The skyscrapers, the people, the sense of vitality. I found myself walking faster. And I promised myself that I would come back after the war.

Washington and New York seemed to be bursting with luxury, and at first I reveled in it. If anyone had told me before I

left England that I could have my fill of fresh fruit and chocolate, not to mention delicacies like shrimp and those wonderful
American hamburgers, I would have told him he was crazy. But
I did have my fill in just a few days, and after that the plenty
began to bother me. I was upset at the huge steaks that were
served in restaurants, particularly when I observed that few people managed to finish what was on their plates. I kept thinking
of what it was like at home, and how many soldiers were sitting
at the side of a road or under a hedge in Normandy eating cold
rations.

I was glad when the holiday was over. I had enjoyed most of
it tremendously, and I had fallen in love with the United States,
but now I longed to be back where I belonged. I had stepped
out of that special dimension in which Ike and I had been living
—and I did not like the world I found outside, a world where
war was only incidental. Not a crusade against evil things, not a
way of life that demanded the best one had to give—just an an-
noyance.

I was not the only one who wanted to get back. As the B-17
circled Washington to give us one last view of the city in the
late-afternoon sun before heading north, Tex and Mattie also
agreed that Washington was beautiful, but that they were eager
to get back on the job. Thirty-three hours later I was back at
Bushey Park. Although it was a Saturday, Ike was working, so I
went straight to headquarters, took off my hat, combed my hair
and opened the door to his office.

Ike looked up, rather annoyed, and then he saw it was I.
When that grin flashed, I forgot how tired I was from the trip.
The man who mattered was here. The time that mattered was
now. I closed the door behind me. I had not felt his arms around
me since before D-Day. It had been a long, long time.

"I'm so glad to be back," I sighed.

"I'm so glad you're back," he said. "How was it?"

I told him all about the trip. All the good things. About how much fun John and I had had in New York. I told him about some of the parties I had gone to and the people I had met. But I said nothing, absolutely nothing, about the gossip.

"But I don't have to tell you about Washington," I said finally. "You know what it's like. What has been going on here?"

"The usual," he said. "I wrote everything down in the blue book. Why don't you catch up while I finish my messages, and then we can go home."

I opened the little diary and saw that the General had made entries for every day while I had been away, starting with June 30. That first entry in his neat handwriting had read: *John—Kay—Lee—Pinette—Farr started for U.S. in my Fortress via Prestwick and Iceland. Lee* (that was Tex) *phoned from Prestwick, but neither J or K came to phone.* Other entries of the same day included *In shelter 5 times today on imminent danger,* and *Butch due back from Cherbourg this eve.,* and *Ethel and Mrs. Perry coming to dinner—saw them in dispensary to get throat sprayed.*

I nodded as I read this. Good. He had had a foursome for bridge that night, so he could not have felt too lonely. But he had not said a word to me the day we left about having a sore throat. Typical.

He had left for Normandy on July 1 and stayed for five days. The diary showed he had inspected more than a dozen fighting units and conferred with Generals Gerow, Montgomery, Brooks and others. He had been very much disturbed to learn that Monty felt our Sherman tanks were not capable of taking on the German Panzers. He had inspected the very strong defenses at Cherbourg, had worried that the attack was going very slowly, and he had gone up in a fighter plane to see what the country looked like from the air.

Back in England the afternoon of July 5, he had written, *Buzz bombs chased us to cover about 6 times during afternoon* and 3 or 4 after going home. (I was shocked to discover later on, when we got back to the cottage, that one buzz bomb had exploded so close that it had knocked down the ceiling in one of the bedrooms and broken several windows.) There was a later entry for July 5 that interested me very much: *Received message from Lee that he was still hanging about Wash. awaiting word from me on what to do about K and WACs. I made this plain before he left here, but I am irritated that message was not forwarded to me at Bradley's HQ.*

This was real news. I rushed into his office, diary in hand, and said, "What was Tex doing about me and the WACs?"

"I thought you might be interested in that," he said with a big smile. "Well, you've always said you'd like to join the WACs, and I decided to do something about it."

"Me a WAC!"

"You a WAC," he confirmed. "There'll be no problem. Seems the President put in a good word for you."

"Oh, my goodness" was all I could find to say. "But what about—"

Ike interrupted me. "I'm trying to plan ahead. We're winning this war, although I'm not always sure of it, and I'm not going to be in Europe forever. I told you once that I was never going to let you go. If you're a WAC, I can keep you on my staff later on."

I went back to my office and continued reading, although my mind was darting about, considering all the implications of my becoming a WAC. On July 7, there was a teasing entry that I knew was written with me in mind. *George brought a Countess and an "Honorable" to lunch. Don't know names of either, but both were most attractive.*

Other entries read: *Butch's friends for dinner. Tried to play bridge. Awful!* and *Wish I could get time to see Telek.* Finally there was an entry for that very day: *Party from my office coming home today.*

The next morning I added one more entry for that Saturday. *Had a lovely evening at T* (Telegraph Cottage). *Champagne for dinner. Slept in shelter.* It had been a marvelous evening. Jimmy Gault, a terribly nice Guards officer who had been Ike's military aide for some time, was there with a couple of friends, so we had a festive little supper with champagne, a gift from a British admirer of Ike's. Afterwards, Jimmy went off with his friends and Ike and I sat out in the garden in the last of the light (with double summer time, it was light long into the evening hours), sipping more champagne and talking until the last of the sunset afterglow had disappeared. I was beginning to feel the fatigue from my long plane trip, but I was so happy to be with Ike that I refused to give in to it. He would reach out and squeeze my hand occasionally, and we would smile at each other. We were both very happy. It had been weeks since we had had a chance to really talk to each other.

I think that is what I remember best and miss most. We were always chattering away. We would talk about this and that and everything, leaping from subject to subject. We wanted very much to share all our experiences with each other. There was never any strain between us. That night was one of those nights when we talked, talked, talked. Finally, one of those rotten buzz bombs drove us into the shelter.

A few days later, we celebrated an important event: Telek's release from the kennel. I left the office early to pick him up. Ike had wanted to come, but after our previous experience he decided not to run the risk of more journalists and photographers avid to record the reunion of the Supreme Commander and his dog. Telek hopped into the car without a minute's hesitation, sitting beside me in the front seat, as if there had never been an interruption in his routine. Back at the cottage, he ran straight to Ike and rolled on his back, paws up in the air, a signal that he wanted his stomach scratched. We sat outside and watched

Telek scurrying around, getting acquainted with his first home all over again.

"It's great to have that black scamp back home," Ike said.

I agreed. "It's like having a child come home after he's been away at school for the first time."

We sat there for a while, and then Ike said something that shook me almost as if there had been an earth tremor. "Kay," he asked very quietly, "would you like to have a child?" We had talked about how much we both liked children many times. Ike often said that he wished he had had a big family. Four children, he always said, would be ideal.

I couldn't be coy about this. "Yes," I said. "I'd love to have a baby. Not *a* baby; *your* baby," I corrected myself. Actually, I could think of nothing that I would like better. I had often daydreamed about having a baby, Ike's child. I would love, absolutely love to have his child. I smiled thinking about it. I could see that baby—he was a boy and looked just like his father—toddling about on the grass, grinning a big grin when he fell down. I could see him later perched on the back of a horse, his father teaching him how to ride. And I could see us, when our son was eight or nine, the three of us galloping over the moors and then coming home and laughing and talking as we ate supper. The boy would fall asleep in front of the fire after supper, and Ike would carry him up to bed. We would sit there smiling at each other across his bed as he lay there, rosy cheeked and deep in his child's sleep.

I sighed. "It's impossible, you know."

"I know," said Ike. "But maybe things will be different later. I'd like it, you know. I'd like it very much."

We were quiet for a while. Then Ike asked, "You don't think I'd be too old for the boy?"

He had decided it would be a boy too. "No," I said. "You won't be too old. Not you. Not ever."

We said nothing more about this, but every time our eyes met that evening, it was as if we had advanced into a new level of intimacy. That night after the buzz bombs had chased us to the shelter, Ike reached his hand out to me in the dark and we fell asleep holding hands between our cots.

25

D-DAY plus 335. That little sum added up to VE-Day—victory in Europe. That period from June 6, 1944, to May 7, 1945, was a frantic, topsy-turvy time with a pell-mell succession of advances and unexpected breakthroughs as well as equally unexpected setbacks, defeats and triumphs, culminating in a grimly matter-of-fact ceremony in the predawn in Reims when the Germans signed the surrender papers.

Ike set up his advance headquarters in Normandy early in August, and after that the blessed privacy we had enjoyed at Telegraph Cottage was a thing of the past. Shellburst, which was the code name for all of Ike's advance headquarters in France, was in an apple orchard—all very pretty and bucolic. I lived in a tent pitched in a meadow close to where Ike's big wooden-floored office tent had been set up under the trees. It was so much calmer and more peaceful here just behind the front lines than it had been in England with the buzz bombs that we all slept like babies. The weather was fine, and it was almost like a lovely country vacation, except that we had no time to enjoy it.

We were constantly on the go. One day I would drive Ike up to the front, where he would visit the commanders and talk with the men. The next day we would fly to Portsmouth, and I would drive him to London to confer with the P.M. or to SHAEF at

Bushey Park. Once in a while we would find time to visit the cottage for an hour or two. We would stroll around, and Ike would inspect the vegetable garden. We often returned to Shellburst with an armful of marrows or some beans. Ike had planted corn, but it was very disappointing. The English climate did not seem to agree with it.

We were rarely alone even in the car. An aide always accompanied the General when he visited the command posts at the front, and when we popped over to London, we usually took along a number of staff members. That handful of July days after my return from Washington when we had felt so close and loving now seemed like some long-ago, half-forgotten dream. These days we had to be content with fleeting caresses and glances. Ike would squeeze my hand under the breakfast table, or I would look up into the rearview mirror to find him watching me. Now and again when we were free from observation, he would put his arm around my shoulders and draw me to him, but these little intimate moments were rare, and dangerous. Or so I felt. I had become coldly aware of the virulent gossip about us in Washington and did not want to add any fuel to that fire. If it had not been for Ike's habit of scribbling little messages on scraps of paper that he tucked into my hand almost every day, I might have felt lonely—even though we were always together. I would have loved to do the same thing, but the Supreme Commander could not simply tuck a bit of paper away in his pocket. It would be found by Mickey when he took care of the General's clothes. Nor could he read a message, tear it up and throw it away the way I did. There were always eyes watching the General. I told him once, "If I ever write you a love letter, you'll have to tear it up and swallow it."

"You don't have to write to me, Kay," he said. "Every time you look at me I see a love letter in your eyes." He would say beautiful things like that when I least expected them, and they always meant a lot because he was usually so reticent.

This lack of privacy was not as frustrating as one might think.

There were priorities, and our personal affairs—and those of everyone else involved in this mammoth war—were very far down on the list. We knew that we loved each other, and that was enough for now. Nor did we have time to fret about what might have been. The events of those days—the rapid Allied advance from the Normandy beaches across France and across the Rhine —are all part of history now. What amazes me today is how very routine it seemed at the time. The extraordinary was quite commonplace. We knew nothing else except this high-pressure, high-stakes world of war.

Paris was liberated on the twenty-fifth of August, 1944, and the next day Ike and I left his apple-orchard headquarters early in the morning for the five-or-six-hour drive to Chartres, where General Bradley had established his headquarters in a barnyard almost in the shadow of the great cathedral. As we drove through the French countryside, Ike was struck by the mounds of German equipment littered everywhere. "We certainly caught them with their pants down," he kept saying with great satisfaction.

The mood at Chartres was jubilant. There were almost as many journalists as soldiers there. Many of the correspondents had been in Paris the previous day, and several jeeploads of American and British newsmen were going back that afternoon. I asked Ike if it would be all right if I went along with them, since he would be spending the rest of the day conferring with General Bradley.

"Absolutely not," he said brusquely. "And that's an order. You stay right here, Kay."

I acted a bit like a spoiled child and said something petulant about its not being much fun for me to sit around in Chartres all day with nothing to do. It was inexcusable—the only time I ever presumed on our relationship.

"Listen," Ike said, "it's too dangerous. I don't want you to go anywhere that I can't guarantee your safety. Hold your horses. You'll get to Paris one of these days."

I was already ashamed of myself, and apologized. He patted my cheek and said, "I know. I want to see Paris myself."

It had absolutely nothing to do with my outburst, but the next thing I knew, Ike and General Bradley were making plans to visit Paris the following day to pay their respects to General de Gaulle. Ike invited Monty to accompany them, but Monty, who would never share the limelight with anyone if he could help it, sent back a short, snippy message declining the honor. Ike snorted. Then he laughed. "It's just as well," he said. "The less I see of him, the better it is for my blood pressure."

That night as we were driving over to Bradley's trailer for supper, Ike said, "Well, I told you that you'd get to Paris, didn't I? Wouldn't you rather go with me than with that mob of correspondents?"

"Of course," I said. "Being able to see Paris with you . . . well, I didn't think it would be possible. For the two of us together, I mean." We had a marvelous evening. Bradley and Ike got along very, very well, almost like brothers. We had dinner. Very simple it was. Just rations and a bottle of wine. We played a little bridge, talked a bit. That was all. We had a lot of evenings like this during those 300-some days before the surrender —innocent, high-spirited and very simple good times. Tooey Spaatz would always bring his guitar along when he came to dinner. Georgie Patton would have a store of new anecdotes. This was the kind of relaxation that Ike liked most.

The drive to Paris the next morning took a very long time, since the security people did not want us to go through Versailles, where there was still a lot of sniper activity. But we eventually got there, and as we drove along the Champs-Élysées toward the Arc de Triomphe, it was like a dream coming true. Paris was free. There were happy crowds lining the Avenue, and as Ike and Bradley got out to pay their respects to the Unknown Soldier, they were practically mobbed. A couple of dozen MP's had to throw themselves into the crowd to free Ike and clear a path so that he could get back to the car. He kept his grin, but as I moved slowly away in first gear, he said, "My God, I didn't think I'd get out of that alive." Bradley had fled to a jeep that roared away with its three-star passenger, but not before his face was smeared with lipstick.

On the way back to Chartres, Ike talked about the year he had spent in Paris when John was little. "We lived on the Right Bank near the river, and I often used to walk up to the Arc de Triomphe with John," he said, "but nobody gave me a second look in those days."

After the liberation of Paris, events seemed to race as if they were in some speeded-up newsreel. Ike kept moving Shellburst forward to keep up with the advancing armies. In early September, our advance headquarters was in Granville, a fishing port, where Ike had a house with a picture-postcard view of Mont-Saint-Michel, the ancient Benedictine abbey that, when the tide was high, rose like a magic island in the bay.

The day we set up headquarters there, Ike flew to Chartres to see Bradley. That evening we were starting to worry because he was late. The weather was bad. But when we called Bradley's HQ, we were told that the Supreme Commander had left and was planning to be home for supper. We were about to pull out all stops when a jeep stopped in front of the house. In the front seat was a wet, tired general who could barely walk. Two GI's put their arms around him and lifted him out of the jeep, into the house and up to his bedroom, where Mickey had him stripped, washed and in bed with a hot-water bottle in minutes. We asked no questions, just rushed about to make him as comfortable as possible.

Then we all sat around while he ate his supper from a tray and told us what had happened. His plane had conked out, and the only available replacement was a little L-5, a one-passenger plane with a limited range, designed for liaison work. Visibility was so bad that the pilot could not find the airstrip. And the plane was almost out of gas. They gambled that the local beach had not been mined and set the plane down on the sand. As Ike and the pilot were tugging and hauling to get the plane above the tide line, Ike slipped and twisted his knee. By the time they had walked across the salt marshes to the road, he was in agony. The pilot practically had to carry him the last few yards. What the GI driver of that jeep thought when he was flagged to a stop that rainy night by an Air Force pilot and a four-star general, I'll never know.

Ike was in real pain. His knee was swelling up, and he could not seem to find any position in which he was comfortable. It turned out to be quite a serious injury. A doctor was flown over from London the next day. He ordered Ike to stay in bed until the swelling went down. A few days later, he came back and put Ike's knee in a plaster cast. He told him to stay off his leg for at least a week. Ike stayed off it for about two days. That leg gave him trouble for months. He was often on crutches or used a cane around the house. But never in public. He would rather die than appear handicapped in any way in front of the men. Nevertheless, the pain was so much at times that every once in a while Ike would have to give up and go to bed for three or four days.

This accident turned out to have a silver lining of sorts, because it allowed the two of us quite a bit of time together that we would not have had otherwise. I would go to the office in the morning, take care of things there and then go to the house to have lunch with Ike and go over anything that might have come up. Afterwards we just sat and talked. We might hold hands or kiss, but always very hastily. One never knew who would walk in.

A few weeks later, Shellburst was moved forward again—to Versailles this time. This was more of a formal headquarters than the previous ones. Ike took over the Hôtel Trianon. His office there was so large that he had it partitioned off to make a separate office for me. There was a permanent feeling about the whole setup. Telek and Caacie had joined us—and Caacie was pregnant again. I was living with the WACs again in a flat above what had once been the stables of Louis XV. And Ike was in a handsome mansion that had been hastily vacated by its previous tenant—Nazi Field Marshal Karl Rudolf Gerd von Rundstedt.

Once again we were immersed in the social whirl of VIP's, but I was no longer the star-struck individual I had been in Algiers. I now shared Ike's view that while most of our visitors were charming or brilliant or powerful or all of these things, they were also a nuisance. They took precious time away from the business at hand. And yet, for one reason or another, they were entitled to hospitality and cordiality, so we managed to entertain all of them—from Fred Astaire and Bing Crosby to Madeleine Carroll and Katharine Cornell, from Anna Rosenberg and Bernard Baruch to Prince Bernhard of the Netherlands and a gaggle of Mexican generals.

Ike was always a warm and gracious host, but nevertheless it was a burden. The groups of Congressmen and politicians who kept trooping up to the front were the heaviest burden of all. More than anything else, they wanted to have their pictures taken with General Eisenhower. That really used to irritate him. Once he grumbled, "The fellow who said that politics is too important to be left to the politicians knew what he was talking about." "But who else would want to bother?" I asked. He was always so vehement about not wanting to have anything to do with politics in any way whatsoever that I never dreamed that one day he would be running for office himself.

Ike insisted on visiting as many command posts, talking to as many officers and men as he could and generally leading a nonstop, sixteen-hour-a-day life. We drove to Brussels and Luxembourg, to Nancy, to Aachen. Everyplace. Whenever our armies advanced, he would go to the front to inspect the situation. And when we could not drive, he flew. It was not unusual for him to have meetings in three countries in a single day.

In October, I finally became a WAC. I was commissioned a second lieutenant. Ike pinned on the gold bars himself in a little office ceremony. Now that I was a WAC and an officer, I could no longer drive the General. With winter coming on, I did not mind a bit. As it turned out, I still traveled with Ike almost everywhere he went. And even though I was no longer his driver, I continued to breakfast with him and we still drove to the office together. The only difference was that now I sat in the back with him instead of in front behind the wheel.

Just before Christmas, Ike was told that he was getting a fifth star. Things had suddenly taken a turn for the worse. The Germans had counterattacked in the Ardennes and hit us at our weakest point. Our casualties were high, and we were retreating. This was the action that became known as the Battle of the Bulge. For that reason, there was practically no notice taken of Ike's fifth star around headquarters. But it meant a tremendous amount to him. There was a kind of glow about him for days after it had been made official. To Ike, becoming a General of the Army, the highest rank, was like being made a knight of some immortal round table.

Around the same time, he called me into the office. "Kay," he said, "I've been talking to the P.M. about you." Then he broke into a great grin. "You've got a medal for yourself. The P.M. says you're going to be awarded the British Empire Medal."

I had never imagined that I would get a medal—any kind of medal. The thought had never crossed my mind. Medals were for people who had done something extraordinary, not for a woman who had spent most of the war behind a steering wheel. When I said as much to Ike, he leaned back in his chair and said, "I don't think you realize how valuable your services have been. I do. And so does the P.M. If I were you, I'd just say 'Thank you' and stop arguing." I took his advice and immediately wrote to the P.M. telling him how surprised I was and how humbly appreciative.

Within weeks, the situation in the Ardennes was under control and the tide had turned in our favor once more. This was enough to encourage Ike to move his advance headquarters closer to the front. This time Shellburst was established in Reims, the city of champagne. It was pretty grim, not the kind of place one would associate with champagne. Headquarters was in a dismal red-brick schoolhouse where we could hardly hear ourselves think because it was on the main convoy route and the trucks continually pounded by, but Ike loved it. The proximity of Versailles to Paris had made him nervous.

In Reims, Ike promoted me to first lieutenant and—even more exciting—made me his official aide. I was the first woman five-star aide in history. I glowed over the promotion every bit as much as Ike glowed over his fifth star. There was a special aide insignia—five stars on a blue shield topped with an eagle—that had been newly created. I wore it very proudly. I was no longer a kind of super girl Friday. I was now a first lieutenant and aide to General of the Army Eisenhower, the Supreme Commander. When Ike told me about the promotion, I asked him, "Is this part of your master plan?" and he said, "You bet it is."

The victories were coming thick and fast. Although there was still fierce fighting, it seemed as if we gained new ground every day. Ike was traveling so much that he said he often did not know where he was when he woke up in the morning. His knee flared up and gave him a lot of trouble. He had a series of colds, one of which turned into the flu. A cyst on his back was making him excruciatingly uncomfortable, so one day he had to go to the dispensary to have it cut out. It was a minor operation, but the wound was deep and required a number of stitches. Ike complained that there was not one part of his body that did not pain him. And his temper was truly vile.

If Butch had still been living with him, he might have been able to help Ike relax, but he was now on temporary duty with the Public Relations Division of SHAEF, which badly needed his expertise. And Jimmy Gault, who was now the live-in aide, could not talk as frankly to the General as Butch used to. Butch and Ike, after all, had been friends for many years before the war.

Beetle and I were very much worried. The General's physical and emotional condition was worse than we had ever known it. The two of us were forever having talks about Ike's state of mind and state of health. Beetle was positive that he was on the verge of a nervous breakdown. Finally a solution presented itself. A very rich American let it be known that he would be honored if the Supreme Commander would make use of his villa on the Riviera. The only problem was how to get Ike to agree to use it. It took four days to convince him that he needed a rest. Beetle was very straightforward, told him that he was pushing himself too hard and that he would have a breakdown if he did not take some time off. Ike started to get angry, but Beetle said, "Look at you. You've got bags under your eyes. Your blood pressure is higher than it's ever been, and you can hardly walk across the room."

It was true. When Ike was out in public, he pulled himself together by sheer willpower and looked healthy and vigorous and exuded his usual charm. But the moment he got back to the office or the house, he slumped. And every time he had to take more than twenty or thirty steps, that knee put him in agony. Suddenly Ike gave in. And in the middle of March off we went to the Riviera.

The villa, Sous le Vent, in Cannes was the most luxurious place I had ever seen. We were told that more than three million dollars had been poured into it. Nothing that contributed to comfort was lacking. General Bradley came along with us, and Ruth Briggs and Ethel Westermann and a couple of others. It was a supersecret visit, and Ike did not leave the grounds of the villa at any time. That was no hardship. He was so run down that he could not have left it. For the first couple of days, all he did was sleep. He woke up long enough to eat and move from his bedroom to the terrace. He would eat lunch on the terrace, with two or three glasses of wine, and shuffle back to bed again. After forty-eight hours of this, he began to look somewhat human, but he had had us all very seriously worried.

The others did a bit of sight-seeing, but except for one trip to Monte Carlo, I stayed close to Ike. As he started to feel better, we would sit on the terrace all day long, looking out over the Mediterranean, chatting lazily, drinking white wine and sunbathing. One afternoon, I suggested that we might play bridge that evening, something we had not done during this little vacation. Ike shook his head. "I can't keep my mind on cards," he said. "All I want to do is sit here and not think." He was really blue. "I just can't concentrate," he complained. "My mind is fuzzy."

"Well, you know, you're simply exhausted. You can't push yourself the way you have and not feel it," I told him.

"I suppose," he said, "but the way I feel now, I don't think I'll ever be able to concentrate on anything again."

"Oh, that's silly," I said. "You don't want to think that way."

He sighed. "I've been thinking that way ever since we got here. Why don't you tell me one of your Innis Beg stories? Maybe that will get my mind off myself." He often asked me to tell him about things I had done when I was growing up in Ireland, especially at the end of a day that was more exasperating than usual. The little stories I remembered about my brother and sisters seemed to entertain him. I thought it was a good sign that he suggested this.

"Well," I said, "I'll tell you about once when I felt the way I think you're feeling now. My sister Evie and I used to ride bareback a lot. Once we were racing each other around the house and my horse stumbled. I sailed right over his head and landed on my head in the field. That really hurt, but we were always falling and we never paid any attention unless something was broken. I was a little dizzy when I picked myself up, but I was all right. That night, though, I woke up sick. The governess scolded me. She said I'd made a pig of myself eating green apples."

"Huh," said Ike. "I bet you had a concussion."

"Probably, but we didn't know anything about concussions. I

went around with a headache for a few days, feeling pretty vague and out of it. But then I was as good as new.

"Did *you* ever fall off a horse?" I asked him.

"Oh, sure," he said, "but I never fell on my head."

"I used to fall off a lot when I was first allowed to go hunting. I used to take too many chances. I really wasn't so very fond of hunting, chasing after a poor little fox. But I loved the hunt balls. They were the first dances I ever went to. Everybody would go. All ages. The men would wear their pink coats. I wore the same blue dress three years running. It didn't bother me. In the country we weren't so very fashionable, and I had no call for dancing dresses.

"I don't think I've ever had a dress I liked so much. Not even those beautiful creations from Worth. I used to think that the blue matched my eyes, but what I liked best about it was the ruffles at the bottom. I loved the way the ruffles flounced about when we did the galop."

"The galop?" Ike asked lazily. "What's that?"

"Oh, it's the most enormous fun. Everyone is in a circle holding hands and then you go around and around, then you reverse and go around again. Here, I'll show you."

I got up and pretended I was holding two partners by the hand and started singing "la-la, la-la, la-la, la-la" and prancing around as if I were a fifteen-year-old dancing the galop. Ike started laughing. It was the first time he had really laughed since we had arrived in Cannes.

"You should go on the stage," he said. "That's the funniest thing I've seen in years."

I collapsed, out of breath and very proud of myself that I had got him out of his blue mood. That night after supper he said, "Goddamnit, I'm tired of going off to bed every night while the rest of you do God knows what. How about staying home and playing a little bridge with the old man tonight?" It was a good evening. We won. There was nothing fuzzy whatsoever about his concentration on the cards. By the end of the week, he was so much better that it was hard to believe what a wreck he had been. Just getting some sleep and staying off that bum leg had probably been the very best medicine he could have had.

Back in Reims, everything continued to go well. We had crossed the Rhine. The Germans were on the run. They were demoralized, and many of them were surrendering. There was still scattered hard fighting, but there was no longer any doubt about the outcome.

Then one day there was terrible news. President Roosevelt was dead. This shook us all. Everyone was devastated by the loss. Especially that he had died before victory was completely within our grasp. He had seemed so very vital when I had seen him in Algiers that I could not believe he was dead.

Things were happening so fast now that there was little time to mourn. There was talk of surrender. Yes, they would. No, they would not. Then we heard that Hitler had killed himself, and the atmosphere at headquarters turned into what I once described as "one grand happy mess." Now we knew it was just a matter of days before the Germans surrendered. But how those days dragged on!

The Germans let it be known that they were ready to surrender, but the German generals stalled and dragged their feet, holding out for concessions—none of which were they granted. Finally, after several false starts, General Alfred Jodl, the German Chief of Staff, and Admiral Hans Georg von Friedeburg signed the surrender papers in the War Room that had been set up in our schoolhouse headquarters at Reims. At 2:41 in the morning of May 7, the Germans finally surrendered—unconditionally.

Ike was alone in his office, where he had been since midnight, pacing up and down. I was at my desk in the outside office. And Telek was at my feet. We heard the Germans come marching down the hall, after having signed, at about three o'clock. They marched into my office, straight past me and into the Supreme Commander's office, where they stopped, clicked their heels and saluted. All I could feel was a cold hatred for these men who symbolized for me the evil that we had been fighting, the evil that we had conquered. Butch and I stood in the doorway of Ike's office and watched.

The Supreme Commander's voice was cold. "Do you understand the terms of the document of surrender you have just signed?" I turned to my desk and wrote down his words in the diary. He continued. "You will get details of instructions at a later date. And you will be expected to carry them out faithfully."

That was all. He stared at them. They saluted, turned and left. Telek growled from under my desk.

Suddenly the office was full of people. The photographers rushed in to take pictures. Just as suddenly, it was empty again. Ike sighed, "I suppose this calls for a bottle of champagne," he said. There was no triumph in his voice, none of the elation he had shown when the photographers were there. Now he was alone with his wartime family. We drove back to the château where he lived in Reims—there were about ten or twelve of us—and drank champagne and discussed the events of the last few hours until dawn showed through the window. It was a somber occasion. No one laughed. No one smiled. It was all over. We had won, but victory was not anything like what I had thought it would be. There was a dull bitterness about it. So many deaths. So much destruction. And everyone was very, very tired.

26

"LET's take in a show," the General said a few days after VE-Day. "Something light. A comedy or a musical. I'd like to go to London. Everyone else has celebrated VE-Day. I think we should too."

"Grand," I said. "When do we leave?"

"As soon as possible."

John was in Reims for a few days then, and one Tuesday morning, Ike, John, Jimmy Gault, General Bradley and I took off for London. Jimmy had brought along eighteen bottles of the very best champagne obtainable in Reims. When he declared it at Northolt Airport, the customs officials raised a collective eyebrow—the duty would be sky high. "It's for General Eisenhower's private VE party," Jimmy said. That was all that was needed. The customs officers forgot they had ever seen or heard of those eighteen bottles.

We went straight to Telegraph Cottage. It was a glorious day. Ike and I inspected every corner of the place. His golf clubs were still in the closet. "Goddamnit," he said, "I'd like to try that thirteenth hole again." We walked down the little path to the golf course and played a couple of holes. We were pretty rusty. It had been more than a year since either of us had swung a golf club. On the way back, we passed our favorite rustic bench. Ike took my hand. "Come on, let's just sit here for a few minutes."

That bench held lots of memories for us. Some happy. Some sad. We had done a lot of talking, sitting here hidden from the house by the shrubbery. This was the place where a long time ago Ike had told me about a great tragedy in his life: the death of his firstborn son, Icky, from scarlet fever. Ike still mourned him. We had shared many confidences here.

Now Ike asked, "Do you remember what we talked about the day you brought Telek back from the kennel last summer?"

"About having a baby?"

He nodded. "I want to do something about that. If I can." He turned to me and took me by the shoulders. "Would you like it as much as I would?"

It was my turn to nod.

"Are you sure?"

"Yes, darling. I am very sure."

"Then I'm going to try my damnedest," Ike said. "That's all I can say. But I want you to know I'm going to try."

Actually, I was not too sure what he was talking about. Did he mean—could he have meant that he would try to get a divorce? I don't know. I want to think so. He was not a man to make careless promises. He always weighed his words. He was always discreet. But he was very much elated on this personal, very private VE-Day celebration of his, and I think that a lot of things had been going through his mind in the days since the Germans had surrendered. I think he realized that he had to face up to making decisions about the rest of his life. We had come to the end of the life we had shared for so long. Or almost to the end. The tunnel of war had opened onto the light of a world that would soon be at peace. There were a lot of adjustments to be made.

There was no more time to talk. Lunch was served, and then it was time to leave for London. I didn't want to leave, and I said so. "We'll be back," Ike said. The car was waiting. I took one last look around the house and started down the walk. "Kay," he called, "can you come here a minute?" I went back into the house to see what he wanted. "Come here," he said, stretching out his arms. "You've never given me a victory kiss."

The next item on the celebration agenda was a buffet supper in General Bradley's suite at the Dorchester. Ike had invited my mother to spend the evening with us. John was there, and a friend of mine, a very pretty girl who was in the WRNS (Women's Royal Naval Service), was there as his date. Jimmy Gault and his wife were there. And a couple of other dear, close friends. We had a marvelous time, and the champagne seemed to evaporate. Then we were all off to the theater to see *Strike a New Note*. It was just what Ike had wanted—an amusing revue.

A box had been reserved for the General at the theater. John and his WRN sat on Ike's right and I on his left. General Bradley and my mother sat behind us. I had been dubious about sitting beside the General in such a public place and had suggested that I sit in the second row with my mother, but Ike said, "Come on, Kay. This is where I want you."

We settled ourselves very quietly, but people recognized the General and the word got around in seconds. There were cheers, and everyone clapped and whistled. I don't think Ike had realized how fabulously popular he had become. He was a bit surprised and very, very much pleased. When the audience started shouting, "Speech! Speech!" he spread out his arms to quiet them and then, standing very relaxed with his hand on the rail of the box, he said a few words. He told the audience how pleased and happy he was to be back in England.

"It's nice," he told them, "to be back in a country where I can *almost* speak the language." They loved it and cheered some more. It took a long time for the house to quiet down so that the curtain could go up. It was all tremendously exciting. None of us had had any idea that we would be caught up in this kind of heady welcome.

Afterwards we went to Ciro's for dinner. It was quite a while afterwards actually, because such a crowd had gathered outside the theater that it was ages before we could move. Finally, the police told the driver to release the brake and they simply pushed the car along slowly until it was through the worst of the crowd. Ciro's was marvelous fun. We had a big table against the wall, and as soon as we were seated, the orchestra played "For He's a Jolly Good Fellow," and Ike grinned as if someone had given him the key to the city. Then it was more champagne, and our little party talked excitedly about the welcome the General was receiving. He turned to me. "Kay," he said, "would you like to dance?" Of course I would. No question about it. We got up and walked out onto the floor. And then—I was in his arms. In his arms in public for the first time. I smiled at him and said, "If anyone here tonight could guess how much I love you, they would not believe it." "I would," he said. Then he concentrated on his dancing. A good thing, too. As we circled the floor, a story that Ike had told me long before floated into my mind. I could not help laughing. Ike wanted to know what was so funny. "I'm thinking of how you told me they put you in the awkward squad at West Point because you couldn't march in time with the band."

"You mean I'm not in time with the music?"

"Well, not quite." It was hard to tell what step we were doing or what beat Ike was listening to. We were sort of hopping around the floor. But I didn't care. He had asked me for the first dance. That was my personal victory celebration. After Ike had danced with the other women in our party, we spent most of the rest of the evening talking and dancing together. It was heaven.

Supreme Headquarters was moved to Frankfurt about a week later. No more makeshift advance headquarters for us now. No more camouflaged buildings. No more tents, no more schoolhouses. Now we were in the immense I. G. Farben building, which was a small city in itself. It was very elegant—lots of marble and fountains and indoor flower gardens, great curving staircases and very luxurious offices. Several tennis courts could have been fitted into Ike's office. Bouquets of fresh spring flowers were placed in our offices every day. Mine was like an anteroom to his. We had a little window installed high in the wall between the two offices so that I could stand up and look in and see what was going on. That way if Ike seemed bored or restive, I could go to his rescue with a message just as I had at Bushey Park.

Life in the aftermath of war was very strange. There were dozens of celebrations and scores of honors bestowed on the Supreme Commander. He was always flying off somewhere to be given a medal or a degree or some other token of appreciation. There was one honor that meant more to the General, that stirred him more deeply, than any of the others. More than the Order of Victory bestowed on him by the Russians, an imposing platinum trinket studded with diamonds and rubies that was valued at a hundred thousand dollars. More than the Compagnon de la Libération given him by the French. Even more than the Order of Merit presented by King George VI, one of the most cherished awards of the British Empire and the first to go to an American. The one act of recognition of his services that meant more to him than all of these was the Freedom of the City of London, which was bestowed on him in an extremely moving ceremony in the ancient Guildhall in the City of London, the historic structure that I had shown Ike when I took him and Mark Clark sight-seeing more than three years before.

For three weeks Ike had been working in Frankfurt on the speech he would deliver. And it turned out to be another victory for him. I don't think that he had ever realized until he delivered the Guildhall speech just how directly he could speak to people's hearts. He had worked hard on the text. One night he sat down in his house in Bad Homburg, on the outskirts of Frankfurt, and drafted a first version. I typed it for him. He spent night after night polishing and repolishing until he thought it was right. He asked me to time him while he read it, because he wanted to keep it down to a certain time—ten minutes, I think it was. It was much too long, so he cut a bit here and a bit there; he also added a bit here and a bit there. He would call me into the office time and time again and say, "Let me read you this version," and I would sit with my eye on the clock. "That took so many minutes," I would say. And he would sigh, "That's still too long. I guess I'd better whack away at it some more." He finally got it down to the right length, and then that evening he polished it a bit more and took out a few more words. He handed me the final text in the morning and asked me to type a clean copy.

"You won't have to read this speech," I said. "You know every word of it." When I gave him the final typewritten copy and his original with all the hen-track additions and deletions, he said, "You know, this means a lot to me. It's exactly what I believe. I'd like to give you the manuscript. I know you believe these things too."

I shook my head. "No," I said. "This speech will be part of history. Someday historians will treasure that document. It should stay with all your important papers." I was quite serious; but today, in a selfish way, I regret that I did not accept this generous gift. It would have meant so much to me over the years to be able to look at it now and again and relive that time. But I know I did the right thing. At least, I suppose I did. Now that I am older, it becomes harder and harder to know what the right thing is. Was it right to balk this generous gesture? To deprive Ike of the pleasure of making a gift? As he pointed out very often, he had little to give me. I don't know. Does it mean so much to have those few sheets of paper tucked away in the archives? I don't know. My refusal was a kind of rule-book conditioned response. I had the selfish gratification, at least, of having acted unselfishly.

Everything the General said in the Guildhall speech stirred my emotions. It was a generous tribute to the British and a testimony to how two proud and independent peoples can work together. It was a very human speech. He started off by saying that "Humility must always be the portion of any man who receives acclaim earned in the blood of his followers and the sacrifices of his friends."

And he spoke most movingly of the relationship between the English and the Americans. "Kinship among nations," he told the audience in the Guildhall, "is not determined in such measurements as proximity, size and age. Rather we should turn to those inner things—call them what you will—I mean those intangibles that are the real treasures free men possess. To preserve his freedom of worship, his equality before law, his liberty to speak and act as he sees fit, subject only to provisions that he trespass not upon similar rights of others—a Londoner will fight. So will a citizen of Abilene. When we consider these things, then the valley of the Thames draws closer to the farms of Kansas and the plains of Texas."

I listened intently as he spoke. He was very simple and open. There was an unpretentiousness about him that somehow seemed to lend his words extra weight. It was as if I were hearing the speech for the first time. I looked around at the others gathered in this ancient chamber. There were tears rolling down the cheeks of many of these English who prided themselves on their reserve.

Afterwards the General crossed to the Mansion House, where a luncheon was given in his honor. He and Winston Churchill came out on the balcony looking over the square, which was completely jammed with cheering people. The P.M. waved his arms about for silence and then gestured toward Ike, who leaned over and spoke to the crowd. Just a few words, but enough to provoke them to wild cheers.

"Whether you know it or not," he said, "I've got just as much right to be down there yelling as you do. You see," he told them, "I'm a citizen of London now too."

Such a roar went up that it brought tears to my eyes. Ike and the P.M. stood there for a few minutes before they disappeared inside. The General had a busy day. After the luncheon, he called upon Queen Mother Mary at her particular request. He had tea with the King and Queen and Princess Elizabeth at Buckingham Palace. And he had dinner at 10 Downing Street with the P.M. and some of the most distinguished men in England.

We flew back to Frankfurt for a day, and then it was off to Paris for more honors. Then he left for the United States. He was the Americans' hero, after all, and they wanted to honor him.

We had discussed this trip. After my appearance with the General at our own victory celebration in London, the gossip had become a factor to be reckoned with. The fact that my mother had accompanied us seemed to add fuel to the fire. There was plenty of gossip around headquarters, too. Butch had understood our special relationship for some time now, but he never said a word. And the WACs with whom I lived were discretion personified. But for everyone else, or so it seemed, Ike and I were the number one topic of conversation.

"How about it?" Ike asked. "Would you like to go? There's plenty of room in the plane. I'm going to be busy, but you liked New York. This might be a good time for you to get to know it better."

"No," I said without hesitation. "It would be a mistake." He didn't argue the point.

When Ike went off to the States in his Flying Fortress, I went off to the Riviera in his C-47 to spend a couple of weeks at the Hôtel du Cap d'Antibes. Every morning I rushed out to buy the papers to read all about the General's triumphal tour through the United States. While I was having a marvelous lazy time in the sun, Ike was shuttling back and forth across his native land, charming his fellow citizens with that grin and the truly simple niceness of his personality. He was a national hero. There had been no one like him, one writer stated, since Abraham Lincoln.

When he came back to Frankfurt, he was still very much the

conquering hero. He was feted in Luxembourg, Belfast, Brussels, Amsterdam. In Warsaw, Prague and Moscow. He was showered with gifts, everything from yards of lace to antique swords, but the loveliest of all was an exquisite cigarette case from General de Gaulle. It was fabulous. Platinum and gold with five sapphire stars on it. The clasp was a cluster of more sapphires. Inside the case, *Charles de Gaulle* and the date had been engraved in General de Gaulle's own handwriting. I caught my breath when Ike showed it to me, it was such a fantastic work of art.

All these honors began to depress Ike. "It's hard," he said, "going to city after city and trying to be natural about these things. It makes me feel like an actor. I want to tell them that it's a waste of time, but I know that it isn't. Ceremonies are important. But goddamnit, Kay," he groaned, "I was never a man who liked ceremonies."

Ike was not always the guest of honor. He was host at two marvelous parties in Frankfurt that he gave at my suggestion. It had dawned on me that many people who worked at SHAEF did not know the General at all. A lot of the young officers used to ask me, "What's the General like? What's he really like?"

"You ought to give a party for the lower-ranking officers," I told him. "Half the people at headquarters have never seen you."

He was honestly surprised and exclaimed, "What would they want to see me for?"

"They just want to look at you," I told him.

And they did. The parties went down like hot cakes. He asked all the officers at headquarters with the rank of major and below, and made a point of saying something to every single person. They were simple affairs, just cookies and soft drinks, but everyone had a good time. And Ike made a great hit. He was very unassuming and made it easy for people to feel comfortable with him. He would wander from group to group and smile and say a few words. That grin of his! He had a bit of the actor in him. He knew how to turn on in public.

"That was an excellent idea of yours," he told me afterwards. "I think it was very, very useful."

He was much more relaxed in Frankfurt than I had ever seen him. We were a small colony of conquerors, and we stuck together much as we had done in the early days at Telegraph Cottage. He often came to the WAC house for supper and bridge. This was something he would never have done before. I remember one evening we all sat on the floor and played bridge until four in the morning. He had a really good time. He loved things like that which were a bit childish and very informal. He trusted us completely. None of the WACs ever said a word about the General's being at the house on any of these occasions. If the word had got out, then he would have been expected to accept invitations to all the generals' houses for dinner. And that was the last thing in the world he wanted.

John was stationed nearby, and he used to come to Frankfurt several times a week for dinner. Ike enjoyed sitting around with him and talking. The three of us used to play with the dogs a lot. Telek had sired several litters since Versailles, with the result that there were seven or eight puppies—and none of them trained—tumbling about the house. They were adorable. Every night when we came home from the office, Ike would say, "Well, it's puppy time," and the whole scampering tribe would be let loose in the living room, running here and there, poking their noses into everything, rolling around on the rug and just being puppies. Once Ike scooped them all up into his lap. I was heartbroken that there was no camera to record the scene.

We played bridge and we went riding a lot, almost every afternoon. But Ike was growing restive. His old cronies, the ones who had been so close, were gradually leaving. Tooey Spaatz had gone back to Washington, so there were no more nights of playing bridge and singing old songs to Tooey's guitar accompaniment. Omar Bradley also had gone back to Washington, to

head the Veterans Administration. Ike missed him a lot. He was
an old-shoe kind of friend. The two of them used to replay old
Army football games until everyone else was bored blind. They
would go over a game play by play, man by man, happily analyz-
ing every minute. They seemed to have total recall. Ike was very
lonely. Georgie Patton was still around, but he was in the dog-
house again and Ike had to be fairly discreet about seeing him.
They were still good friends, of course, but it was not politic for
the Supreme Commander to spend much time with him.

Ike's spirits picked up during the Potsdam Conference, when
he flew to and from Berlin almost every day. Toward the end of
the conference, President Truman came to Frankfurt. Among
other things, Ike spoke with him, as I reported earlier in this
book, about my becoming an American citizen. "I think it's
going to work out," Ike told me. "There should be no difficulty.
You've got to write a letter to Byrnes about yourself." He out-
lined the information that my letter to the Secretary of State
should contain and said that he would send a covering letter
along with it.

I wanted very badly to be an American citizen. There was no
other way that I could see for me to stay with Ike. It would be
ridiculous to expect that the American Chief of Staff in that
holy of holies, the Pentagon, could have a personal aide who was
a British subject. And it was definite at this time that Ike's next
post would be Washington and that he would take over from
General Marshall as Chief of Staff. It was only a matter of time.
And Ike kept saying that it would probably happen sooner than
we thought.

Even with the prospect of change* in front of him, Ike was

---

* To be candid, it was a prospect that he did not relish. In my diary for May
17 I had written: *This morning E. got a very secret message from General
Marshall—Relative:* (1) *Bradley being given a job in Washington to do with
returning veterans of this war—* (2) *Marshall is going to try very hard to get
out of his present job. In about 2 months he's going to ask the President to release him and then E. would have to become C/S* (Chief of Staff). *Con-
fidentially, E. would loathe the job.*

restless. "This place is getting on my nerves," he said. Frankfurt *was* utterly depressing. There was rubble everywhere, and the scars of war were much more visible here than anyplace else we had been. Neither of us felt comfortable living the life of conquerors. And after thinking of the Germans as the enemy for so long, we found it difficult to think of them otherwise. Frankfurt was a most unsettling place to live.

"Well, why don't we get away for a while?" I proposed. There really was not such a great deal of work at SHAEF that needed his daily attention. John, who was spending the evening with his father, thought it was a good idea. The upshot was that Ike laid on a trip to the same villa, Sous le Vent, where he had gone to rest when he was near total collapse in Reims. Several of us accompanied him, and Ambassador Harriman and Kathy dropped in for a couple of days. For the first time in all the months I had known him, the Ambassador threw off his cold diplomatic air and joined in all our holiday fun. What he wanted to do more than anything else was play croquet, but the rest of us voted him down and the Ambassador cheerfully accepted the verdict. Ike was able to take advantage of all the vacation activities this time. We went swimming and roared around in a speedboat. We even went out to a couple of nightclubs and restaurants. It was a marvelous few days, when we concentrated on doing just what people do on vacation. Ike and I even managed to have a few hours to ourselves now and again. Our last afternoon there, the two of us were lying on the terrace, sunning ourselves. Ike slept a little and I simply lay there, enjoying doing nothing.

"Where is everybody?" he asked when he woke up. "I think they went down to the beach," I said. "I don't know. Or maybe they're napping, too."

"It's nice here," Ike said. "Whenever we're together like this, it seems so right, the way things should always have been. But perhaps . . ."

He never finished the sentence. But he kept using those two

words, "but perhaps," more and more often in our private conversations. I felt it was his way of saying that if anything could be done so that we could be together, he would try to do it. It was also his way of telling me that he could make no promises, make no proposals—yet.

"It's too bad we didn't meet each other years ago," I said. He nodded. "I never thought anything like this would happen to me," he said. "You know, in the Army, sometimes you don't discover what it's like in the world outside—until it's too late."

Ike worried a lot about his age. "Twenty years is a big difference," he often said. "It's all right now, but what about ten years from now?"

"We can worry about that in ten years. Or twenty," I would say. "Age isn't going to change what we have."

There was nothing said that afternoon that had not been said before, no looks exchanged that had not been exchanged before. But there was a new feeling of peace and oneness, a feeling that we had come through a lot together, that we could face anything together. At least, those were my feelings. I would swear that they were his too.

After that holiday in the sun, Ike started planning more brief vacations. We went on a fishing trip with Beetle. And we visited Mark Clark in Salzburg. Clark took us to see Berchtesgaden, Hitler's mountain retreat. I was very uncomfortable the whole time I was there. Ike had told me about the concentration camps he had inspected in horrible detail, and that was all I could think of while we were looking around this mountaintop hideaway.

There were always a lot of photographs taken when we made these trips. Previously I had always slid into the background out of camera range, but now Ike insisted that I stay with him. "Come here, Kay. Where are you going?" he would say as I started to walk away when the photographers went into action. It was as if he had decided to cast discretion to the winds.

One day Ike started to make a list of all the decorations and other honors and gifts that he had received. "Where's that cigarette case that De Gaulle gave me?" he asked. "It's in the safe," I told him.

"Let me see it."

I unlocked the safe and drew out the fine leather box that held the cigarette case and put it in front of him.

He opened it. "It's very pretty, isn't it?"

"Oh, it's fabulous. Absolutely fabulous!"

"I'd like you to have it, Kay," he said most unexpectedly. "I'll never be able to give you anything like this, and I'd like to think of you having it. The sapphires match your eyes."

He smiled at me, that loving smile, and I just did not know what to say. I would have loved that cigarette case. Really loved it. Not only because it was beautiful and valuable, but because it was a present from the man I loved devotedly. But I just could not accept it. I wanted to. I was dying to say, "Oh, thank you. I'd love it. I'll always treasure it." But I couldn't.

I looked at Ike and my face got red and I said, "Ike, I can't take it. Please. I just can't. It wouldn't be right. I'd love it. But I can't."

He sighed. "I wish you would. It was a personal gift. I can see no reason why I can't give it to you. Kay, darling—please take it."

"I can't," I said. "I just can't."

"Okay." He nodded. And we went on with the list of honors and gifts. I never had second thoughts about refusing this gift. It was too valuable, and if General de Gaulle were ever to learn that Ike had given me the cigarette case, I am sure he would have taken it as a personal insult. And unlike the manuscript of the Guildhall speech, it did not represent a shared experience or emotion.

I did accept another kind of gift a few days later. A gift of a week off. Ambassador Harriman and Kathy stopped off in Frankfurt and asked me to come back to Moscow with them for a visit. I asked Ike if I could go. "Of course," he said. "No problem." And so I had a week in Moscow, a city very few Westerners had seen at that time.

We stopped in Vienna, and I was very much excited at being able to tour the famous Spanish Riding School where the magnificent white Lipizzaner stallions are trained. Even though the school was not in operation at the time, it meant a lot to me just to see the great oval ring where they display their gaits. I would have loved to spend more time in Vienna. Despite some bomb damage, it was still a beautiful and romantic city. I kept thinking, Maybe, someday, Ike and I can come here together.

After Vienna, Moscow seemed drabber than drab. Even the tour of the Kremlin that Mr. Harriman arranged for me was rather depressing. It all seemed very cold and forbidding, and the relics of Russian history that were displayed seemed to hint at a primitive, even barbaric past. But I'm no historian. To tell the truth, what interested me most was the occasional sight of a long black limousine rolling down a street in the Kremlin enclosure. I used to wonder each time I saw one if Stalin was inside. There was no way of knowing. Those Russian limousines were all equipped with curtains, which were always drawn.

It snowed while I was there, and that provided the most beautiful sight of my stay. St. Basil's Cathedral in Red Square, with its gaily painted onion spires, was breathtaking in the snow. Like an illustration in a child's book of fairy tales.

Kathy took me everywhere, from concerts at the Bolshoi to a trip on the famous Moscow subway. It was the handsomest subway I have ever seen. What I liked most of all, though, was just walking around and looking at the people. They were as gray and somber as their city. It was a fascinating experience, but quite oppressive. I told Kathy I didn't see how she had stood it all those months. Although she and her father had been warm and thoughtful hosts, I was glad, for my part, to be going back to Frankfurt.

It was October 14 when I returned. Ike's birthday. It was a very quiet celebration. He came over to our house for dinner.

We had managed to get some steaks, his favorite food next to oysters, and of course, there were a cake and a few bottles of champagne. We all gave him small presents—a handkerchief, a card, a chocolate bar, things like that. And after dinner we played cards. As always when he came to the WAC house, he was the only man present.

The next day we went riding as usual. It was a beautiful golden day. Just crisp enough to make you feel wonderfully alive. Afterwards we went back to Ike's house. We showered and changed—I always changed there, since we so often went riding straight from the office and it would have been a waste of time for me to go back to the WAC house—and then we relaxed with a drink in front of the fire in our favorite room, the library. There was a big leather davenport there that you could just sink down into and feel very, very comfortable. We were sitting there, not saying much, and then Ike got up and closed the door. "Come here," he said and I went right to him. "I've got a surprise for you," he said as he gave me a lot of little kisses.

"Not a cigarette case, I hope."

"No—a trip."

"Where are we going?"

"You're going alone," he said teasingly. He was doing his whole act of building up suspense, and delighting in it.

"Where am I going?"

"You really want to know?"

"Ike," I was practically squeaking in exasperation, "yes, I do want to know."

"You're going to Washington."

"Alone? Why am I going to Washington?"

He laughed. He loved this little game. Then he told me that it had been arranged for me to become an American citizen. I had to go to Washington to take out my first papers. I was terribly pleased. I had been worrying that it might not have worked out, although naturally I had not said anything to Ike about it. It would not have been appropriate. But I had thought a lot about what I would do if I could not go to Washington with Ike. Like very many other people, I would have to make a new life for myself, a peacetime life. It would not be easy. More than anything else, I wanted to stay with Ike, work with Ike—and dream of a time, a place when we would be free to love each other openly.

I should not have worried. Over the months, Ike had gone ahead step by step working toward that very end. He had arranged for me to become a WAC officer, although I was a British subject. And now he had arranged for me to become an American citizen. There would be no bar now, no impediment to my serving on his personal staff as an aide at the Pentagon. It was like a reprieve from heartbreak. I was going to be happy forever after.

"I told you I'd work it out," he said. We were standing, our arms about each other, our faces close.

I kissed him. "I know you did. And I'm very happy."

We sat there on that sofa making daydreamy plans for the future, kissing, holding hands and being quite indiscreet for the rest of the afternoon. Never in all the time I had known him had I had to hold Ike back. He had always been very circumspect, but this afternoon he was an eager lover. The door was closed and I knew that nobody from the household would be walking in. This was quite a formal household in Germany, not like the villa in Algiers or the cottage. People did not burst into rooms here. A closed door would never be opened.

The fire was warm. The sofa was soft. We held each other close, closer. Excitedly. I remember thinking, the way one thinks odd thoughts at significant moments, Wouldn't it be wonderful if this were the day we conceived a baby—our very first time. Ike was tender, careful, loving. But it didn't work.

"Wait," I said. "You're too excited. It will be all right."

"No," he said flatly. "It won't. It's too late. I can't." He was bitter. We dressed slowly. Kissing occasionally. Smiling a bit sadly.

"Comb your hair," he said. "I'm going to ask them to serve supper in here." When I came back from the bathroom, there was a small table in front of the fire, with a bottle of white wine in a cooler, some chicken and a salad. We drank and ate and talked. The door was closed again. It seemed as if Ike had decided that he no longer cared what anyone thought or said. It was strange after all our years of discretion, but there had been a lot of changes in our lives and I liked this change.

There was none of the embarrassment between us that we had felt that night so long ago in fogbound London. We were such a comfortable old couple by now that we were able to talk about what had happened. Or had not happened.

"It's not important," I told him earnestly. "It's not the least bit important. It just takes time. That's all. And I'm very stubborn. You've said so yourself."

"I know you are," he said, "but I'm not sure that you're right." There was no point in arguing with him, I thought. Only time would show him that he was wrong. We dropped the subject.

Two weeks later I left for Washington in Ike's Flying Fortress. Everything went smoothly in Washington, although the days seemed to drag on forever. On the return trip, I sat willing the plane to go faster. I was terribly anxious to get back.

There was a bit of a shock awaiting me when I arrived in Frankfurt. Ike was packing.

"I'm going to Washington tomorrow," he told me. President Truman had asked General Marshall to undertake a special mission in China. That meant that Ike was needed to take over in the Pentagon immediately. "It's just for a few weeks, though," Ike told me. "I'll be back, and we'll both be leaving for Washington around the first of the year."

We had dinner together that night. People were coming and going all evening. The telephone kept ringing. The next morning we were at the office at six to take care of last-minute details. Then it was time for him to leave. We kissed each other good-bye there in the office. "Hurry back," I said, and jokingly added, "I mean hurry back, *sir*"—and I saluted.

"Christ!" Ike said. "If you ever expect to work in the Pentagon, you'd better learn how to salute."

That very afternoon I asked one of the West Pointers at headquarters if he would drill me in saluting just as if I were a cadet. He thought that was grand fun and really had me whipping off a very snappy salute. Every night before I went to bed, I practiced in front of the mirror, eager to surprise Ike when he came back.

27

THE last entry in my office diary for 1945 was on Saturday, November 10. It read: 1:30. *E leaves for Paris en route to U.S.* After that, the pages are blank. Ike never came back. I never showed off my snappy West Point salute. Nothing was ever the same again.

As I wrote earlier, you never know when something important is going to happen, and when it does, you often don't realize that it did until some time later. If I had known that I was saying a final good-bye to Ike that Saturday morning, that we would never talk again in our easy familiar manner, that our hands would never touch again, that our eyes would never meet again in the same meaningful way . . . if I had known . . . Well, I don't believe that it would have made any difference. The tears would have come sooner. That is all.

There was not much to do after the General left. Odds and ends to finish, files to sort out, decisions to be made about what should be sent to Washington and what should stay at SHAEF. Then we heard that he was ill—so ill that the doctors said that he would not be able to fly back to Frankfurt when he got out of the hospital. One of those colds that he was subject to had almost turned into pneumonia, and everyone had had a bad scare. Telexes flashed back and forth between Washington and Frankfurt. We were notified that the General's personal staff should be ready to leave for the States in ten days. Almost immediately after that, a Telex came in from Washington saying that Lieutenant Summersby was dropped from the roster of those scheduled to leave for Washington. There was no explanation. No reason given.

For a moment I thought that Ike must have decided he wanted me to come on ahead of the group. Either that or he wanted me to stay behind for a few days to take care of some of his personal business. But no. There were no substitute orders. There were no messages for me at all.

I was stunned. It took nearly an hour for the truth to sink in. I was not going to Washington with the others. The General did not want me to come earlier—or later. I was here and he was there. I felt like throwing up. And I felt like crying.

With more self-control than I had ever thought I possessed, I left the office very quietly and went home to the WAC house. I went to my room, closed the door, lay down on my bed and stared at the ceiling.

What had happened? What had *happened?* There must be some mistake. I went over and over everything—everything Ike had said, everything I had said, everything we had done since VE-Day, everything we had done since D-Day, everything we had done and said since we first encountered each other— searching for a clue. *What had happened?*

Finally, I cried. And cried. It was midnight when I had cried myself out. I was a wreck. I felt weak. My face was puffed and red. You're a bloody fool, I told myself. Tears won't help.

I could not face the office the next morning. I was sure that everyone would be feeling sorry for me, and pity was the last thing in the world that I wanted. I remembered what Ike had said—"activity helps"—and decided to go riding. It reminded me of the days I had spent at Sailor's Delight after Dick died, galloping recklessly along dusty Algerian tracks. It helped. The next morning I was back at work. I went through all the motions. I smiled a lot. I lunched with friends at the Officers' Club and made plans for a farewell party.

General Lucius Clay, the Deputy Military Governor, told me that he was very eager to have me work for him in Berlin. He had a post, he said, for which I was ideally qualified: running the VIP guesthouse in Berlin. "Ike has told me how good you are with people." I thanked him for asking me and said that of course, I would be delighted to take it on. General Clay said that there would be a promotion involved. I would be made captain after the first of the year. I thanked him for that, too. But truth to tell, nothing meant very much to me, neither the new post nor the promotion.

Any sneaking secret hope I might have had that the whole thing was some ghastly mistake was killed when I received a letter from the General. It had been dictated. It was quite impersonal. He said that it had become impossible for him to keep me as a member of his personal official family. The reasons that he gave were that there would be opposition to anyone who was not a completely naturalized American citizen working in the War Department, and also it appeared that I would be discharged from the WACs promptly upon arriving in the United States, and there could be no question, he wrote, of a civilian's working in the War Department. I could not understand. It seemed to contradict everything that we had been talking about for so long. There was a handwritten postscript saying that he was in bed and taking medicine constantly. The postscript ended, *Take care of yourself and retain your optimism.*

I read and reread that letter. I looked for hidden meanings. I looked for something personal. He had written that he was distressed because he could not come back to give me a detailed account of the reasons I could not come to Washington. I told myself, however, that I should not misinterpret this or read anything into it. The General was always very courteous.

I packed up my things, and Telek and I went to Berlin, where we stayed for almost a year. It was an interesting experience. I met many extraordinary men and women—and many pretentious bores and boors. And I got over the worst of the hurt. I began to think about the future and decided that perhaps my future lay in the United States.

The transfer to the States was easily arranged. I had a lot of leave, and since it seemed as if everyone I had worked with during the past three or four years was now in Washington, that was where I went. I had a marvelous few weeks there, catching up with old friends, making new ones and going to dozens of parties.

There was a rather amusing aspect to those parties in Washington. I was one of the very few people who knew every general—and every general's girl friend. I would be at a cocktail party having a good time, talking to someone's wife—it was interesting meeting the wives of these men I had known so well; I liked most of them very much—about clothes, about my experiences in the war, and I would always try to remember some story about what the woman's husband had done that might interest her. Then I would see the husband hovering about looking nervous. Officers I had known for years would come up, absolutely white, and say to their wives, "Dear, I think we'd better be getting along. It's late." They would be terribly nervous. They shouldn't have been. I never said a word about the things I knew.

I was in and out of the Pentagon a lot seeing old friends. It would have been ridiculous not to say hello to the General. Besides that, I was absolutely dying to see him.

I took Telek along with me. It was a strange experience. The General stood up to greet me as I came into the office. I stooped and let Telek off his leash, and he ran straight to Ike after all those months and rolled over on his back, paws in the air, to have his stomach scratched. I could tell that Ike was very much affected. He got all red, and it was not just from bending over to scratch Telek's tummy. We chatted for a few minutes. Ike seemed concerned about my future plans. I told him that I thought I might stay in the WACs a bit longer to find out if I really liked the United States as much as I thought I did. And then I would probably look for a job in New York.

"Good, good," he said briskly. "That sounds sensible. If there's anything I can do to help you about the job, I hope you will let me know when the time comes."

I thanked him. He had written a recommendation for me months ago that had been forwarded to me in Berlin. Addressed TO WHOM IT MAY CONCERN, it described my work during the war. The General said that my outstanding characteristic was "reliability" and that I had an "engaging personality." I told him that I would not call upon him for help unless it was necessary, but that I appreciated his offer very much. And then I stood up and said, "Good-bye." He asked me to drop in again with Telek. "Anytime," he said. "I can always find a few minutes." And I did bring Telek back once or twice.

I soon got my new orders. I was sent as far from Washington, D.C., as one could get and still be within the limits of the continental United States: California. I was assigned to a small public relations unit. It was terribly dull. I could never feel that anything we were doing had the least importance. Who needs this? I said to myself, and applied for my discharge.

I headed straight for New York. And the first thing I did was go shopping. I think I wore a rut in the sidewalk as I trotted back and forth on Fifth Avenue from Saks to Bonwit's to Bergdorf's. After seven years in uniform, I found the idea of wearing clothes that made me look feminine very exciting. There was an exhilarating feeling of freedom in waking up in the morning and realizing that I had a choice of what to wear. I had saved quite a bit of money while I was a WAC and really indulged myself. I bought a couple of tweed suits and some sweaters—practical things. Some long dresses. Pairs and pairs of shoes. What I remember best was a smashing black satin suit and a hat from Sophie with a drooping feather on the side.

For the first time since I had been a very young woman in

London, I spent my days sleeping late, having my hair done, lunching with friends, going to cocktail and dinner parties and dancing all night. Weekends, I would visit friends in the country and play bridge and golf. In my spare time, I worked on my book *Eisenhower Was My Boss*. I was happy.

Then one day I picked up the paper and saw that General Eisenhower had been appointed president of Columbia University and would be moving to New York. I had thought I was completely over the affair. I was having a very good time and had two quite attentive men friends, one of whom I was to marry a couple of years later. But that newspaper story—well, my hands were shaking when I finished reading it. I started thinking and dreaming about Ike all over again, lovesick as a young girl. There was nothing I wanted more than to see him and talk with him. I was obsessed with the idea. I missed him bitterly.

I started haunting Columbia University. I would take the subway up to 116th Street, go through the iron gates and walk around the University. I soon learned where his office was in the Low Library and where his house was. Finally one spring morning, only a few weeks after he had been installed at Columbia, I ran into the General as he walked through one of the gates leading onto the campus. He was very much surprised to see me. And I acted surprised too. I had a story ready. I told him I was there to look up the sister of an English friend of mine who was in the graduate school. I am afraid that he did not believe me. He looked very much bothered, and after a few minutes, he said, "Kay, it's impossible. There's nothing I can do." He sounded terribly distressed.

I looked at him. There were tears in my eyes, but I tried to smile. "I understand," I told him. And I did. We had had a fabulous relationship, but it was over. Completely over.

After that, I thought, What's the good of forcing an issue and upsetting him when nothing can be done? So I made a determined effort to put him out of my mind. And I more or less succeeded. One gets over everything. Time really does heal the wounds.

A few months after that encounter, I learned that the General was going to speak to the Fellowship of United States–British Comrades. I made up my mind to attend the meeting. It was at the Seventh Regiment Armory on Park Avenue, probably the most chic armory in the world. I sat far back in the audience, since I did not want to call attention to myself. The General looked fine. It was the first time in my life I had seen him in formal civilian clothes. White tie. He wore them well, but to my mind he never looked as marvelous in anything as he did in his uniform. As soon as he had finished speaking, I slipped out. There was a reception afterwards, but I still did not trust myself to go up, shake his hand and say the conventional empty words. I had the feeling that if I were to touch him, I would cry. The few times we had met in the Pentagon I had carefully avoided shaking hands with him by bending down to unsnap Telek's leash. I just did not think I could bear it.

I discovered after that evening that the gossip about us was still as virulent and wildfire contagious as ever. Even the very proper *New York Times* in its report on the General's speech made a point of noting that I had been in the armory and had left without speaking to the General. When I read it, I wondered what Ike would think when he read it in his copy of *The Times*.

My book was published that fall and was quite a success—so much so that a lecture tour was set up that took me to forty states. This was when I really got to know the United States. At first I had a marvelous time, but it was a lonely and exhausting way of life—going from hotel to hotel and living out of suitcases for weeks at a time. After several months, I decided that enough was enough. I wanted to go home. And I did—home to New York.

Thanks to the book and the lecture tour, I had no pressing financial worries. I resumed my giddy social life. Telek and I went out almost every night. He was checked in all the best cloakrooms in town: the Stork, "21," El Morocco, the Copacabana—everywhere that people went to have a good time. The hatcheck girl would say, "Are you sure he'll be all right?" And I'd assure her, "He won't move." And he never did. I would say, "Telek, sit down and stay." And he would. Sometimes he would stretch out and sleep. Other times he would just sit there, very alert, cocking his head and observing life in the cloakroom.

I went to England to spend the summer with my mother, and we read in the papers that General and Mrs. Eisenhower were in London for a visit. Mummy was quite excited and said, "We should ask them for tea or drinks. The General was always so very hospitable." So I wrote a note to the Dorchester, where they were staying, saying that my mother and I would be very pleased if the General and Mrs. Eisenhower could come by for drinks one afternoon.

There was no reply.

A few days later, a very charming young major appeared at Mummy's. He introduced himself and said, "Well, I came around because General Eisenhower asked me to take you out for a drink." I said, "Oh, that would be lovely." We talked, and it turned out that we had several mutual friends. Finally, he said, "Kay, it's impossible. The General is really on a tight leash. He is not his own master." He was a terribly understanding man and told me a bit about how the General was always surrounded by political people who practically dictated his every move. The General had obviously sent him to tell me that there was nothing he could do.

I was not particularly upset by this. If anything, I felt rather comforted that the General had cared enough to send this major around to see me. To me it was his way of letting me know that I still did mean something to him, although there was nothing he could do about it. And I had realized long ago that nothing could ever come of it. Nothing. Nothing. Nothing.

I wrote the General when I got married to Reginald Morgan,

and he sent me a very sweet note wishing us happiness. From that time on, there was no contact whatsoever between us. I did write him when my mother died, but he never responded to that letter. I followed his activities on television and in the newspapers. When he was elected President, I was so proud of him! That man, who had always described himself as a simple country boy, was President.

I tried to watch all his press conferences on television. He really did not handle them very well, although he had been highly skilled with the press when he was Supreme Commander. I think the difference was that during the war he could tell the journalists what he thought they should know; he did not have to tell them what they *wanted* to know. Sometimes when I was watching him I would think, Oh my goodness, he's absolutely livid. I could see that temper flaring up. After all, he had spent his whole life in the Army, where his word was a command. This was something different.

When I heard about his illnesses I worried, and I felt very sorry for him at times. I remembered how he had told me once, "All my life I've just worked. That's all I've done. That's all I do." He was a man who had never had much fun in his life, but there were times when he was President that I thought he was probably having a bit more fun than he used to. When I would read about his going shooting quail with his rich friends or playing golf, I'd say to myself, He must be enjoying that. I truly think he was.

But somehow, there were always memories coming back to haunt me. I'd hear that old favorite song of mine, "I'll See You Again," and think of the time he had played the phonograph record to surprise me. It was a rather sweet sadness. But there was one time that was very bad. That was when Telek died.

That Scottie was seventeen years old when death finally caught up with him. One morning he staggered as he got up, and fell down. He tried to get up again, but just could not manage. I knew what this meant. He had been treated for various old-age ailments for a couple of years now. The vet had told me I must expect this.

I picked Telek up, put him in my lap and talked to him. I told him how much he had always meant to me, how much I had loved him. I told him that he was an important part of my life, that when I was sitting at home and he was curled up at my feet, I never felt alone. I talked to him about Ike. I told that poor tired Scottie how much Ike had liked him. I reminded him of how he used to ride in the car with us, of how he had visited Buckingham Palace, of how President Roosevelt had held him, of all the adorable scampering puppies he had sired. I suppose it was a bit silly, but Telek knew that I was loving him. I let my voice and my memories surround him. I wanted him to feel comfortable, loved and secure. Then I put him on my bed, buckled his little tartan coat around him and carried him out to a taxi and to the veterinarian.

"Please put him to sleep," I said, and burst out crying.

Such a gallant little dog. Such a faithful, loving friend. It hit me very hard. It was not just Telek's death I was mourning. He had been my last link to Ike, the man I had loved more than anyone else in my life. And I was grieving for my own loss. From now on there would always be something missing in my life: the spirit, the gaiety, the devotion of a small dog named Telek.

I could never get used to the idea that the General was getting old. I always saw him as he had been in 1945. Then I would see a picture of him in the paper and think, Oh God, I can't believe it! With each of his illnesses, he seemed to shrink a little. During his final illness, my heart ached for him. It was so cruel. I felt relieved when he died. He had suffered too long. Far too long. And I had had the feeling that he had craved the peace of death.

And that is the story of the Eisenhower affair.

Do I regret anything? No, truly not. I cried a lot of foolish tears. I was hurt. But I have no regrets for what was. It was all perfect. A few regrets, perhaps, for what might have been. But it could not have been.

The General was a very ambitious man, and while I think he might have been happy if somehow we could have found a way to spend the rest of our lives together, I do not think that he would have been able to respect himself if he felt that he had gained a measure of personal happiness by giving up the privilege of serving his country.

That is why when I read about the letter that the General was supposed to have written to General Marshall saying that he wanted to marry me, everything seemed to fall into place and make sense. It may have been all right for King Edward VIII to turn his back on his empire for the woman he loved, but with the General, duty would always come first. He told me once that if there are two paths a man can take, both of them honorable, then all things being equal, he should take the path along which he will do the most good, inflict the least hurt. And that, I believe, is what he did.

So let there be no more whispers. No more speculation. This is what happened. All that happened. We were two people caught up in a cataclysm. Two people who shared one of the most tremendous experiences of our time. Two people who gave each other comfort, laughter, love.

Now that I am very close to the end of my life, I have a strong sense of being close to Ike again. It is almost as if he were looking over my shoulder as I write. Laughing now and then. Saying, "Christ, I'd completely forgotten about that." Or "Oh, that was a great day. Didn't we have a good time that day!" Right now, he's saying, "Goddamnit, don't cry."

In my heart will ever lie
Just the echo of a sigh,
Good-bye.

—from *Bittersweet*
by Noël Coward